Strictly Liable

by

Tony Bayliss

WARNING: This book contains strong language and adult themes

www.tonybaylissbooks.com

England, 1998

3

In 1998, it was a criminal offence to take 'indecent' photographs of a girl who was under the age of sixteen, or to have sex with her.

The Prostitute

Doreen reached down between her legs and realised she'd come on. She lifted the duvet and looked at the large red stain on the sheet.

"Fuck it!" she groaned, and turned over, wanting to go back to sleep. But having stirred, her morning cough started, and she had to sit up. She reached for a cigarette, lit it, and inhaled deeply. Her coughing became more acute, her bony shoulders turning inwards, and her face growing redder with each cough as her lungs convulsed in an effort to rid themselves of yesterday's filth. Eventually, feeling the phlegm rising to the back of her throat, she leaned over the side of the bed, spitting the green slime two inches to the right of its intended target, a half-full coffee cup.

She looked at the clock. One fifteen. What day was it? Tuesday? No, Wednesday. Or Tuesday. Whatever. She listened for sounds in the house. Nothing.

"Mandy?" she shouted. "Mandy? You there?"

There was no reply.

"Mandy!" she shrieked, causing her to cough again.

Still, there was silence.

"Mandy! I knows you ain't gone to school. Mandy!"

From another room a young, sleepy voice answered.

"There ain't none. It's a teachers' training day."

"You fuckin' liar! Get your arse out of that fuckin' bed and get to that fuckin' school."

"But it's dinner time, mam. It ain't worth goin' for the afternoon."

"You'll have the fuckin' kid-catcher 'round 'ere again. You get up an' go to that school, you lazy bitch."

"There ain't no lessons this afternoon anyway. It's PE."

"You still go. Get up, you lazy slag, an' make me a cup o' tea."

"Why don't you get up and make it yourself?"

"Don't you give me none o' your fuckin' lip or you'll feel the back o me 'and. Now get fuckin' up!"

Doreen settled back on the pillow and lit another cigarette. Little bitch, she thought to herself. If I'd spoken to my mother like that when I was fourteen, I'd o' been thrashed. Kids these days . . . well, they ain't kids once they're up big school. They just do what they fuckin' want. And them bloody teachers don't do noffin'. They can't keep control these days, not like when I was at school.

She heard Mandy moving around. Fifteen minutes later she walked in with a mug of tea. Mandy wrinkled her nose.

"What's that 'orrible smell in 'ere?" said Mandy.

"What smell? What you on about? I can't smell no smell."

"Well, you wouldn't. It's 'orrible. It smells like, like . . . you got the reds, 'ave yuh?"

"I leaked a bit, that's all," said Doreen.

"What, in the bed? Well, why don't you do something about it?"

"I will when I've 'ad me tea. Anyway, don't you go givin' me none of your fuckin' cheek. Just remember I'm your mother."

Mandy put down the tea and turned to go out. Doreen noticed what she was wearing.

"What the fuck are you all dressed up for then, in that little skirt, with yer arse 'angin' out."

Mandy spun around. "That's me school uniform, Mam."

"You ain't goin' down no school dressed in that."

"Why not? It's what all the girls wear."

You walk down the street in that my girl, and you'll have so many drivers lookin' at you there'll be a fuckin' major road accident."

Mandy smiled. "Wass wrong with a few blokes looking then? The teachers like it. The PE teacher couldn't take 'is eyes off me yesterday. I think 'e even 'ad an 'ard-on. I could see it under 'is tracksuit."

"Dirty sod. I'll fuckin' report 'im. You wear that skirt and you deserve what you get. Now fuckin' take it off."

Mandy decided to try a different tack. "Aw, come on mam. Look, It ain't worth goin' to school now. It'll be finished by the time I get there. I'm going down Debbie's."

Doreen put her tea down and looked hard at her daughter. "You fuckin' ain't. I don't want no fourteen year-old daughter o' mine goin' down there. You ain't goin' on the game, and that's final!"

"Course a ain't goin" on the fuckin' game. What d'you take me for?"

"An' don't use any o' that fuckin' language wi' me, you fuckin' little slag. You ain't goin' down Debbie's, and that's that!"

"I fuckin' am, an' you ain't gonna stop me. Anyway, I don't do nothin'. I just answer the phone."

Doreen sipped her tea again, and looked thoughtful. "You sure?"

"Course!"

"Well, what does Debbie give you for it then?"

"This an' that."

"How much?"

"Not a lot. I do all right."

Doreen drank the remainder of her tea and handed Mandy the mug. "Well, just so long as you're only answerin' the phone . . ."

"I am. Like I said."

"They got any speed down there?" asked Doreen.

"Reckon."

"Can you get me an 'enery then?"

"Mam! You want me to get you drugs?"

"Oh come on, pet. Just a little 'enery for your old mam. I'll let you go if you bring back an 'enery. Or a bag o' brown."

"She ain't got no brown. I could get a draw, maybe."

"All right. But get me a wrap, if you can."

"If I can. I'm off. You'd better get up, mam. It's Friday. You got a regular comin' at two."

"It ain't fuckin' Friday, it's fuckin' Wednesday."

"It fuckin' ain't."

"Oh, fuck me, you're fuckin' right. Shit."

Mandy turned on her six-inch heels and clumped down the stairs. Doreen heard the front door bang. She swung her legs over the side of the bed and stood up, steadying herself as slight dizziness passed, and then turned to pull the bedclothes over the offending red stain. She put in her teeth, and then kneeled down, scrabbling around under the bed for her make-up bag. She'd have a bit of a wash later, she decided.

Ten minutes later she stood back from the mirror to inspect the transformation. In the poor light of the dingy room, she failed to notice that grey roots showed clearly as the blondness of her hair parted company with her scalp, or that the thick foundation make-up ended abruptly like the edge of a mask just under her chin and behind her ears. She had already put on a grubby white basque which lifted and squeezed her flaccid breasts into a crumpled cleavage, and now she was searching from drawer to drawer for a clean skirt. She looked at the clock, and rushed into Mandy's room, throwing open the wardrobe.

"Fuck me! Where did the little cow get all this gear? She ain't paid for this from answerin' the fuckin' phone, the lying little bitch," she muttered to herself.

She grabbed a tiny skirt with a deep split in the side, and eased it up over her hips. Seconds later, the doorbell rang and, after a final check in the mirror, she went downstairs to answer the door.

"Come in, bab" she said to the middle-aged man standing awkwardly on the doorstep. "Go straight up and get yourself ready. I'll be up in shake."

"All right, Doll," said the man, and he trudged heavily up the narrow staircase and went straight into Doreen's room.

When Doreen entered the room five minutes later, he was sitting, naked, on the side of the bed, his knees together and his arms folded across a large, white stomach.

"Usual is it, bab? asked Doreen, getting a bottle of baby oil out of the bedside cupboard, "or do you want something special today? I'm in a good mood, so you can 'ave what you like, only anal's extra, of course."

The man smiled, nervously. "No, I"ll just have the massage and the straight, if that's all right with you, Doll."

"All right, bab. Let's 'ave the money up front then. You knows the rules."

The man handed Doreen the thirty pounds he was clutching in his hand, and then turned onto his stomach.

"You want a full strip then?"

"Oh no, Doll. That's all right. Just as you are."

Doreen sat astride his hips and prodded his shoulders absent-mindedly.

"Busy week for you, then?" she asked, out of habit.

"Fair to middlin'," he replied

"Family all right?"

"Fine."

"D'you wanna turn over now, bab?"

Doreen climbed to one side so that the man could turn over onto his back. She grabbed hold of his soft penis, and began massaging it roughly. "Don't seem in the mood, do 'e?" she said, swapping hands.

"Oh, he'll wake up soon," said the man, anxiously. "Maybe it's because I'm a bit tired. Been working too hard, I expect."

The truth was that Doreen could no longer arouse him. He had been seeing her for nearly a year, and what had seemed exciting and adventurous at first, had now become dull and mechanical. He wasn't sure why he still came. Doreen looked years older than the twenty-nine she claimed to be, and she always seemed to be in such a rush.

"Well, 'e still ain't interested, is 'e? I'll go down on him and see if that wakes 'im up."

The man looked down at the crown of her head as it bobbed up and down. "It's no good, Doll," he said, "You'd better leave it. P'raps we'd better call it a day."

"But I don't like to send me customers away not satisfied bab, and you knows I can't give yuh money back."

"I know, Doll. It's not the money, it's just, well, don't take this personally, but with you it's getting a bit like the wife. I've known you too long. So it isn't exciting anymore."

"But you will come back and see me again, won't you bab?"

Doreen couldn't afford to lose another regular. She was already down to five. Once, she'd had fifty.

"Well, I might. For old time's sake. Maybe I ought to give it a rest for a while, or try to find some new blood."

"I can get you a new girl," said Doreen, desperately. She couldn't let this man go without trying to get a commission from introducing someone else. "What d'you want? Blonde?

Brunette? D'you like black girls? I could get you a black girl. Or an Asian. They're nice, Asian girls are."

The man sat looking at his feet, and did not respond. Doreen scratched her head.

"All right then, what about a young girl then? A new one? You'd like a little school girl, wouldn't yuh, bab? All the fellas like schoolgirls. She'd make your old man sit up."

He looked up, showing interest. "You know some young girls do you, Doll? But, trouble is, they're all shy and don't know what to do."

"No, no, bab. I'd find a girl what's really got it, if you know what I mean. Looks like a little virgin, but shags like a rabbit."

The man smiled. "OK then. Sounds good," he said. "When can you get one?"

"You come round on Monday. Same time. Can you come then?"

"Yes, OK."

"All right then, bab. And I'll have something special for yuh. But it cost you a bit more, of course."

"How much?"

"How much can you afford?"

"Depends."

"You want top quality, don't yuh? Little pretty thing like a virgin school girl. There ain't many around. I 'ave to pay other people commission to find a girl like that, understand, bab?"

"How much then?"

"Well, you wanna nice fresh girl what's never worked, don't yuh? Just maybe done it once or twice with a boyfriend like, so she's clean and you can do it without, and not 'ave any risks of catching anything, know what I mean?"

"How much?" repeated the man.

"Eighty."

"No, that's too much."

"Not for this girl, it ain't. I could get two 'undred for 'er in London, I could. An' if you like 'er, you could see 'er regular like afterwards, and it'll be seventy each time."

"Sixty each time."

"Done!"

* * * * * *

Amanda was eight when it happened the first time. Her eldest brother Wayne had just started an eight year sentence for armed robbery, and so seventeen-year-old Kevin now had the bedroom to himself. Free from the tyranny of his brother, Kevin could put up his own pictures, and spread his things out around the room.

Little Amanda sensed that things were easier too. The shouting had stopped. Her mother seemed happier and, now that she wasn't giving all her money to Wayne, she started buying sweets, and even new clothes for Amanda.

When her mother was locked in her bedroom with one of her gentlemen visitors, Amanda often wandered into Kevin's room for company. Sometimes, if he was in a good mood, he would let her stay, while he watched his videos.

One evening, she was lying on his bedroom floor, colouring a large picture in a magazine. From time to time she looked up at Kevin's television screen, stared for a while, and then looked back at her colouring.

"What they doin' Kev?" she asked.

"What you think they're fuckin' doin'?" he replied.

"It's rude."

"Shuddup."

Amanda picked up a red crayon and began to fill in Michael Jackson's nose.

"Well, I think it's rude," she muttered. "You can see everything."

"Why don't you fuck off to bed?" grumbled Kevin.

"I'm not tired. Anyway, Mam said she'd get some chips later."

"Crap! She'll be in there all night now. She's got that Roger bloke in there."

"But she said I could 'ave some chips. I ain't 'ad no tea."

Kevin ignored her.

"Aint "ad no dinner neither 'cos I dropped me plate, and the dinner lady sent me out."

Kevin began panting.

Amanda turned on one side, and looked up at him. "What you doin" Kev? Oo, you got your willy out. What you doin' that for?"

" What d'you think I'm doin"? Wanking, innit?"

"What does it do?"

Amanda stood up, and moved to the side of the bed, looking down at Kevin, who was rubbing himself frantically.

"It's big ain't it?" said Amanda. I never saw your willy so big. It's just like that geezer on the telly. What you rubbin' it for?"

"You'll see," said Kevin, in a breathless, strangulated voice. "Me arm's tired. You do it for me."

"I ain't touchin' it. It's 'orrible."

"Aw, come on, Mand. Just for a bit. I"ll get you some chips if you do."

"Will yuh? Promise?"

"Yeah."

"All right then. What do I do?"

"Just what I was doin"."

Mandy kneeled on the bed and leaned across. "It's really 'ot! Is it all right?"

"Yeah, yeah," panted Kevin. "Keep goin'. A bit faster. That's it. That's it."

Kevin arched his back and groaned. Amanda jumped back.

"Errr! Wass that? You peed! It's gone all over the place. It's on me arm. It's all sticky. Wass that?"

"That's better", Kevin murmured. "That's better."

Amanda wiped her wrist on the bedclothes. "Is that the baby stuff?"

"The what?" replied Kevin.

"The stuff what makes babies?"

"Yeah."

"It's 'orrible. It's all sticky. Is that what goes in the woman then?"

"Yeah."

"I wouldn't like it in me. It's 'orrible. What about me chips then?"

"Only if you do it again later on. I'll get you a fish an' all."

"Don't like fish. I"ll 'ave jumbo sausage though."

* * * * * *

Several hours later Amanda was asleep in bed when she felt Kevin climbing in beside her. "What you want, Kev? What you doin'?"

"You said you'd wank me again, Mand, remember?"

"Oh, not now, Kev. I'm asleep."

Kevin rolled her over onto her tummy, climbed on top and moved his hand between her legs.

"Oh come on, Mand. Open your legs a bit more. Let me put it in."

"No, Kev! Don't. Ow, that's 'urting, Kev. That's really 'urting."

"Oh come on, Mandy. Be a good girl. No one'll know."

"It's too big, Kev. It won't go in!"

"Come on, Mand. Just open your legs a bit more. That's it, Mand. I'll get you some new trainers tomorrow, if you let me do it."

"You ain't got no money."

"Yes I 'ave. That's it, Mand. Nearly in now. Good girl. That's it. That's nice, Mand. That's nice."

* * * * * *

When Amanda was eleven Kevin was arrested for stabbing a man outside a night club. He never came home. She now spent most of her time alone, while her mother was busy with clients. She was lonely, but she was glad that she no longer had Kevin coming to her bed.

Increasingly, she learnt to take care of herself, seeing her mother only between clients, or between fixes.

When she started secondary school she was teased mercilessly because her uniform was second-hand and ill-fitting, and she had none of the fashion accessories that all her eleven-year-old friends considered essential to their existence. She struggled in lessons, and rarely completed her homework. But by the time she moved into the second year, and was approaching thirteen, she found allies in some of the older boys, who began to pay her attention in playground.

"All right, Mand?"

"Y'all right?" she replied, surprised and pleased to be noticed by three fourteen-year-old boys, as she stood by the corner of the science block one lunchtime. The boys grinned at one another, as if sharing a private joke.

"You live down Bankside, don't yuh, Mand?"

"Yeah," she said.

"Yeah, seen yuh there."

"Yeah?"

"Yeah. Your Mam's that Doll, ain't she?"

"Yeah. Doreen."

The boys nudged one another, grinning more, as they moved in closer to Amanda, completely surrounding her, with her back pressed against the wall.

"Your Mam, that Doll, Doreen or whatever, she's on the game, ain't she?"

"What?"

"On the game. You know."

"No she ain't."

"Come on, Mandy. Everyone knows she is."

"She ain't."

"You do it, do yuh, Mand?"

"What?"

"You on the game too are yuh?"

"Course not. What d'you mean?"

" 'ow old're you, Mand?"

"Twelve. Thirteen next month."

The boys moved closer, checking over their shoulders to see that they couldn't be observed. One boy reached forwards and slipped his hand inside Mandy's blazer. The other boys grinned. Mandy smiled, nervously.

" 'ow come you got such nice tits then if you're still only twelve?"

"Dunno," she said, looking down at his hand as it squeezed and fondled her breasts.

"You like me doin' that, Mand?"

" 's all right." She felt confused. She knew she should move away but, like a moth to a flame, she was transfixed, knowing what she was doing was wrong, yet wanting the attention, enjoying the new power her body was giving her.

One of the boys saw a teacher enter the other side of the yard, and they all quickly pulled back, releasing Amanda. The school bell rang.

"You goin' down the youth club tonight, Mand?"

"Dunno."

"We'll see you there, OK?"

"Dunno," replied Amanda as she walked away towards a classroom block.

* * * * * *

Later that evening Amanda walked slowly to the youth club, but was nervous about going in alone. The boys were nowhere to be seen, so she stood outside for several minutes, enduring the stares of others who were arriving.

Lacking confidence, she decided to go back home, and set off, returning across the path that passed behind the allotments, and through wasteland. Just as she reached a derelict concrete building, the three boys she had met earlier came around the corner, accompanied by several others. She stopped, and smiled, uncertainly.

" 'ullo, 'ere she is lads! Little randy Mandy. What you doin' out so late, Mand?"

"I was just goin' 'ome, she said."

"Don't go 'ome yet. We was comin' to see yuh."

"Was yuh?"

"Yeah, we was, wasn't we, lads?"

The boys sniggered, and looked at one another. "Come an' 'ave a fag with us!"

Mandy hesitated. "Oh, all right then. Got some 'ave yuh?"

"Course we 'ave."

Mandy followed the boys across a field and onto a grassy slope, where they all sat down, and started passing around cigarettes. Mandy sat slightly to one side. For a while, they chatted among themselves, seeming to ignore her. The boy who had put his hand inside her blazer kept looking at her, and whispered to another boy next to him. After a while, he called over to her.

"Wanna fag then, Mand?"

"Yeah, OK."

"Come over 'ere then an' sit next to me."

Mandy stood up, and picked her way over the prone bodies. One boy tilted his head and looked up her skirt as she stepped over him.

"Hey, lads, Mandy's got pink ones on!"

They all laughed. Mandy sat down next to the boy offering her a cigarette. He turned to the boy next to him.

"She's got nice tits, ain't she?"

The boy nodded.

"And she don't mind yuh 'avin' a feel, do yuh, Mand?"

"Dunno."

"Well, yuh let me 'ave a feel this mornin'", didn't yuh?"

"S'pose."

"So, if I give you a fag, can I put me 'and inside yuh bra then?"

"Dunno."

"Not for long. Go on, Mand."

" 'ow long?"

"Til you've smoked the fag. Just a few minutes."

"Well . . ."

"Go on, Mand. I won't 'urt yuh. You got such nice tits, ain't she, lads?"

The boys were all looking at Mandy, expectantly. "Yeah!" they chorused.

"All right then. But give us the fag first," she said.

The boy passed her a lit cigarette and then sat closer, reaching across to unbutton her blouse. The other boys jostled for a better view, as he pushed his hand inside and cupped her breast.

"Wass it like?" asked a boy on the edge of the group.

"Nice. She got lovely tits, ain't yuh, Mand? Lovely."

A warmth spread slowly through Mandy's body as the boys pressed against her from all sides. She looked at the thier eager faces as the hand massaged each breast in turn, and then withdrew, leaving her blouse open for all to see. Mandy smiled as the boys drew even closer.

"Can I 'ave a go?" asked another boy.

"An' me."

"What about me?"

Mandy's brow furrowed slightly, and then she grinned. The boys grinned back. Now they were nervously excited, anticipating a new experience, an initiation. Would she? Would she? For the first time in her life, she felt in control.

"Maybe," she said, quietly, "but it'll cost yuh."

"What about downstairs?" asked the first boy.

"What, outside me knickers or inside?"

"Inside. Inside", said the boy with growing excitement.

"Dunno. All right then. One fag for upstairs and two for downstairs."

"Yeah, OK", they all called out excitedly.

"I ain't got no fags!" cried one boy, with disappointment.

"Me neither," said another, "Can I owe yuh, Mand?"

Mandy paused. "No way! OK, ten pence instead then, only I wan' it before you do it."

The boys urgently turned out their pockets, amassing a small pile of cigarettes and coins. Mandy leaned forwards, her blouse still hanging open, and put the offerings into her shoulder bag. She lay back on the soft grass and looked up at the faces surrounding her. "OK then," she said.

Immediately, numerous probing, reaching, sticky hands were on her body, undoing and untucking her clothes. She felt fingers running up and down her thighs, across her stomach, and between her legs. Her bra was completely removed pushed to one side. She closed her eyes.

"Is that all right, Mand?" asked the boy whose fingers were now penetrating her.

"Yeah, OK," she whispered, "but go careful.

"OK, like that, Mand?"

"Yeah."

"You got your finger in?" asked another boy.

"Yeah."

"Let's 'ave a go!"

" 'ang on, I ain't finished yet."

One boy was sucking her nipples. "Lovely tits, Mand! Very tasty!"

"You ain't supposed to eat 'em!" laughed a boy whose hand was inside his trousers.

"You'll get all milky!" said another.

Mandy laughed. "No 'e won"t. I ain"t got no milk in 'em yet." Mandy propped herself up on her elbows. "That's enough now, you lot. Time up!"

The boys removed their hands without protest, and sat or kneeled to watch as Mandy dress herself.

"You're cool, Mand!"

"Yeah, cool," they all agreed.

"Come on down the club with us."

They stood and walked back across the field, this time with Mandy in the middle of the crowd, and they entered the club together. Throughout the evening, the boys packed around her, none wishing to relinquish his claim on her. Mandy loved the attention, and enjoyed noticing other girls whisper and point.

The next day at school almost every older boy she saw greeted her by name, laughing and winking. Many asked her what she was doing after school. Enjoying her new-found celebrity status, she was unaware of the boys conspiratorial sniggers, and thought that the girls' ignoring of her was borne of jealousy.

Now that boys seemed to find her attractive, she started taking more care of her appearance, stealing items from her mother's make-up bag, and spending more time on her hair. Wherever she walked, she now noticed when people looked at her, and smiled inwardly when she heard whistles. She turned up the hem on her school skirt and found the money to buy shoes with heels and a semi-transparent cotton blouse. As well as the older boys, she found that some of the male teachers were taking an interest in her, and some seemed to spend longer than necessary hovering behind her chair in class. Although school regulations required the wearing of a tie, most girls flouted this as far as possible by cutting the ends off the tie, reducing it to little more than a choker. Mandy went further, putting the tie on her bare neck and ensuring that the only one or two of the buttons on her blouse were ever done up so that the loose ends of the shortened tie dangled into her deep cleavage.

The young geography teacher was particularly attentive. He always made a point of leaning over her when checking her work, and she could feel his eyes feasting on the view. On one occasion he called her to sit next to him at the front of the classroom so that he could mark her exercise book. Unabashed, she sat close, and could feel his leg pressing against hers. Instead of moving slightly away, she kept very still to see what would happen. Sure enough, he was emboldened by his success, and next put his free hand on his own leg, rubbing it up and down, each time allowing the tips of his fingers to brush against the outside of Mandy's naked thigh. Mandy looked sideways at him and noticed that his face was very red. None of the other pupils seemed to be aware of what was going on, so she reached down, grasped his hand, and drew it to the inside of her thigh. Immediately, the teacher pulled back, startled. Mandy was surprised. She picked up a pen lying on the teacher's desk in front of her, and wrote the margin of the book he was reading: "That was nice, sir. Do you want a shag, or what?"

The teacher gasped, pulled clear of Mandy, and asked her to return to her desk. As she went she looked back at him. He was still very red in the face, but was now trying to turn his attention to another pupil.

Thereafter in her geography lessons, she did little or no work but always received good marks. If she saw the teacher looking at her, she would make secret suggestive gestures to him, rub her breasts or slide forwards in her seat, opening her legs slightly so that he had a glimpse of her knickers. She could always make him look at her, and enjoyed the embarrassment it caused him.

But as time went by the enthusiasm the boys had shown her was turning to name-calling, and the girls still kept their distance from her. One day she was told that there was graffiti about her in the toilet next to her tutor base. She went in to look.

'Mandy Kinch is a slag' and 'Mandy does it for fags' had been written in felt pen across two walls.

She began missing half days at school to avoid the taunts, going instead, into the town centre, where she wandered from shop to shop. There, she sometimes met up with girls truanting from other schools. They would sit for hours on the edge of the water fountain in the precinct, smoking and talking, taking care to move on each time the security guards appeared. For dares, they went on shop-lifting sprees, one looking out for the other in a team operation. Mandy went to school less and less, preferring instead to spend time with her new-found friends, who seemed to have more in common with her.

One day she noticed a man sitting in the outdoor café opposite the fountain. He was looking at her, and when she looked at him, he didn't look quickly away, as most men seemed to do. He was in his twenties, she thought, black, very tall, and good-looking. He wore an expensive leather jacket, and gold earring. After a while he got up and sauntered over towards her, smiling as he sat down on the edge of the fountain next to her.

"Y'all right?" he said, in a deep voice.

Mandy looked down at her knees and said nothing.

"Y'all right?" he asked again.

"Yeah," she replied, without looking up.

"Seen yuh around."

" 'ave yuh?"

"Yeah. Wass yuh name?"

"Mandy."

" 'ullo, Mandy. I"m Jerome."

"Oh."

"So 'ow old're you then, Mandy?"

"Sixteen."

"Like fuck! Come, gel, 'ow old?"

Mandy turned and looked at his face.

"How old you think then?"

"Well, you got great looks, no doubt. You could be sixteen with that figure, but I bet you ain't."

Mandy smiled. "Thirteen."

"I thought so. So what's a pretty little gel like you doin' 'ere all on yer own then?"

"I ain't on me own. Me friend's in the shop."

"Yuh girlfriend?"

"Yeah."

"Gotta a boyfriend, 'ave yuh?"

"No."

"Why not?"

"Dunno."

"They should be queuin' up for yuh, babe. Wass wrong with the blokes 'round 'ere?"

Mandy smiled broadly.

"Ged off!"

"Straight up. You're the best lookin' tart I seen in weeks, and thass no lie."

"I ain't."

"Y'are. Wanna coffee then?"

"Nah, don't like coffee."

"Milkshake then?"

"Go on, then."

Jerome stood up and started walking towards McDonalds. Mandy followed, uncertainly, a few paces behind. "Come on!" called Jerome. "I won't bite yuh."

He bought her a drink and a cheeseburger, and made a point of displaying a thick wad of banknotes as he paid the bill. They sat down at a corner table and Mandy sucked shyly on her straw.

"So what yuh doin' 'angin' 'round down 'ere every day then?" he said.

"Not much."

"Why ain't you at school?"

"School's shit."

"I know, gel, I know. I couldn't stand it neither. All them teachers tellin' yuh what to do."

"Yeah."

"So you come down 'ere?"

"Yeah."

"What about your dad then? Do 'e know you ain't at school?"

"Ain't got no dad. Never knew 'im."

"Me neither, gel. Mine is in fuckin' Jamaica."

"Oh."

"What about yuh mam then?"

"She thinks I'm at school, silly bitch."

Jerome laughed. "So you got any sisters as good-lookin' as you?"

"Nah, just brothers, but they left now. Anyway, who says I'm good lookin'?"

"Oh, come on, gel, you're a bit o' class, you is," said Jerome, leaning forwards.

"Whadya mean?" she replied, her eyes flashing with pride.

"Well, look at yuh. Nice 'air, all long and curly like, pretty face, nice long legs, sort o' skinny but sexy, and great tits. Yeah, you got great tits."

"I ain't."

"Yes you 'ave. You could be a fuckin' model, you could."

"Gedd away. I ain't tall enough."

"Nah, not fuckin' catwalk. I mean like glamour model what you sees in the magazines and papers."

"What, nude an' that?"

"Course! Most gels'd give a lot to 'ave a figure like that. You could make a lot o' shit."

"Could I?"

"Course. I knows a photographer what takes great pics. I"ll get 'im to do yuh if you like."

"I dunno . . ."

"Well, think about it, babe. Anyways, I could do with a bird like you."

"Whadya mean?"

"To be my bird. I could do with it."

"Could yuh?"

"Yeah. Me mates'd be dead jealous, they would. An' I knows how to treat a class bird like you. I'd look after yuh."

"Would yuh? Like what?"

"Like buyin' yuh the right gear and stuff. Trash that fuckin' school uniform and get some proper gear. Make yuh look like a real woman. I ain't short of a few bob, yuh know."

Jerome grinned broadly, and Mandy found herself captivated by his shining white teeth and pink tongue. He reached forwards and gently squeezed her cheek between his big thumb and finger. "I could get you some stuff now, if yuh like," he said

"What?"

"Decent dress. Some nice 'igh 'eels. A coat. And you could do with some jewellery. What about some gold earrings? That'd make yuh look like a real lady."

Mandy felt dizzy. "Gold earrings? I ain't never 'ad no jewellery. Would yuh really?"

"Course. Like I said, when I 'ave a tart, I look after 'er."

Jerome stood up, grabbed Mandy's hand, and led her through the door.

"There yuh go. You're my woman now, right?"

Mandy said nothing, but followed Jerome with growing excitement.

In Miss Selfridge she tried on several outfits and Jerome insisted that she parade each one in front of him.

"Nah, that's no good," he said each time she chose something herself.

"But I like it."

"Nah. It's too baggy. 'ere, try this one on," he said, thrusting a transparent top at her.

"I can't wear that. You'll be able to see everything through it."

"Thass the idea, gel. I want all the blokes to see what they can't 'ave."

They left the shop, Mandy clutching several bags with one arm, and holding on to Jerome with the other. She felt ecstatic. She had never owned so many clothes before.

"Where're we goin'?" she asked, as they descended the stairs.

"Back to my place. I got a little flat in Jessop Street."

"What, your own place?"

"Course. An' I've got a little surprise for yuh."

"What?"

"You"ll see."

* * * * * *

"It's a bit dark, ain't it?" said Mandy, as Jerome led her into his sitting room.

All the curtains were closed, and she could vaguely make out Bob Marley posters on the walls. Two old settees faced one another in the centre of the room, and a large ashtray spilled its contents onto the carpet. Around the edges of the room were piles of clothes and magazines.

"It needs bit of a tidy up," he said noticing her looking at the mess, "but that's women's work, ain't it?"

"Yeah, I could tidy up a bit for yuh, if yuh like."

"Nuh, you just sit down and make yourself comfortable. You ain't doin' no cleanin' today."

Jerome left the room and came back with a small bag. He sat down next to her, opened the bag, and spread its contents on the floor in front of them.

"There! I said I'd got somethin" for yuh, didn't I? Take yuh pick."

"Wass them then? Drugs is it?"

"Yeah. Jus' for a bit o' fun like."

"I don"t want no drugs. Me Mam's on brown an' it's doin' 'er 'ead in."

"Nah, nah, it's all right. You 'ave to know 'ow to use 'em. Me, I'm an expert like."

"Are yuh?"

"Yeah. Brown's shit. I got a bit o' speed 'ere. That'll pep yuh up. An' we can 'ave a draw. I got hash. No problem. No 'arm neither."

Mandy picked up a small container. "So what's these others then?"

"That's what I sell 'round the clubs. E's."

"E's?"

"Ecstasy. There's different sorts. I got Christmas trees, White Doves, and Bart Simpsons. But Mitsubishis are the best. I get 'em for two quid and sell 'em for a tenner. Some nights I unload an 'undred. That's eight 'undred quid profit."

"Eight 'undred in one night?"

"Yeah."

"You're rich!"

"I do all right, gel. So, you fancy bein' a rich bloke's tart then, do yuh?"

Mandy smiled. "Yeah, I do."

"So yuh like me then do yuh, gel."

"Yeah, Jerome. I do. You're cool."

"Come 'ere an' give us a kiss then."

Jerome pulled Mandy towards him with both hands on her shoulders and pushed his large tongue into her mouth.

"Tasty!" he said pushing her back again. "Wanna smoke then?"

"Go on then," she said, trying to control her excitement.

She sat back on the settee while Jerome prepared the smoke. She felt comfortable and relaxed. This beat going to school. If only those silly little bitches in her class could see her now! If only her mother could see her. But no, she could never tell her mother.

"So you like your clothes then?" said Jerome, blowing dark smoke into the air and handing her the draw.

"Yeah. A lot. But I don't know when I'm goin' to be able to wear 'em. They show too much."

"Thass the point, babe. You got it, you flaunt it." He turned towards her. " 'ere, show us yuh tits then."

"What, now?"

"Course. There ain't no one else 'ere. Come on, gedd 'em out!"

Mandy smiled and unbuttoned her blouse.

"Nah, take it right off. And yuh bra. That's it. Less see 'em proper like. Yeah, them's great tits."

He reached forward and kneaded one breast.

"Yeah, nice an' firm. You like me doin' that do yuh?"

"Yeah. Not too 'ard though."

Jerome ignored her and moved his hand to the other breast.

"Yeah. Very good. An' you got nice little pink nipples. Very young like."

"Well, I am young, ain't I?"

"Yeah course, but some gels, they got 'ard nipples like old prunes. Yours is nice an' soft. That's good."

He let her go and sat back, drawing the smoke deeply into his lungs. Mandy reached for her bra.

"Nah, don't put that on. I like the view. Anyways, we ain't finished yet. Stand up and less 'ave a look at yuh proper like."

Mandy stood up.

"Come on, be like a model."

" 'ow?"

"Just walk up the end, and twirl around."

Mandy did as she was told.

"Thass it, babe. Shit, you is a fuckin' model, you is!"

"Am I, Jerome? Am I really? You really think I"m a model, do yuh?"

"I do, babe. Take the rest off. Less 'ave a look."

"What, me knickers an' all?"

"You ain't shy, are yuh? I can't have a bird what's shy."

"Nah, I ain't shy."

"Well come, gedd 'em off then! That's it. Beautiful!"

"You really think so?"

"Course. 'ere, come close. What a nice pussy. That's lovely. Ain't a pussy at all. Like a fuckin' kitten that is."

He pushed two fat fingers between the top of her thighs and probed around.

"Hey, you ever been fucked?"

"Yeah."

"Have yuh? What many blokes?"

"Only one."

"D'you like it then?"

"Not much."

"Bet you'd like to fuck me. Would yuh?"

"Dunno."

"Course you would. 'ere, take a look at this."

Jerome unzipped his trousers and took out his penis.

"Fuck me, Jerome, it's so big!"

"Fuck you? That's just what I intend to do. I'm gonna ram it up that little kitten of yours, I am. 'ere, kneel down and get yuh mouth 'round that."

"What, suck it?"

"Yeah."

"I ain't never done that. I seen on the video though."

"Well, just get as much down yuh throat as you can. Thass it. Thass it. Deeper. Deeper."

Mandy wretched.

" 'ere, don't you spew on me, yuh bitch. You'll 'ave to practise more. "Ere lay back and open yuh legs."

"What, on the floor?"

"Yeah, come on. Don't mess about. I'm gonna show you what a good shag is. You ready for it, are yuh?"

Mandy lay back.

"Yeah, OK. Be careful, Jerome. You won' 'urt me, will yuh?"

"Course I won't. Nice little soft pussy like that, it'll just slide in sweet. I'm gonna shoot my load right in yuh, Mand."

* * * * * *

Later, they lay together on the settee smoking new joints.

"Was that all right, Jerome? You do like me, don't yuh?" asked Mandy, anxiously. "Did I do it OK for yuh?"

"Yeah, fine."

"You sure?"

"Yeah, yeah. Just fine. Don't go on, gel."

"How old're you, Jerome?"

"Twenny-nine."

"Oo, thass nice. I never been with a real man before. My friends would be dead jealous. So you don't mind me bein' thirteen then."

"Nuh. Younger the better. I like fresh cunt."

"But I do look older though, don't I?"

"In that new gear, you looks eighteen, like."

Mandy sat up and looked down at him.

"Do I really?

"Fuckin' do. So, you wanna be my woman then, do yuh?"

Mandy threw her arms around him.

"Yeah, Jerome. I do. I do."

"But you'll do as yuh told and be a good girl then, will yuh?"

"I"ll do anythin' for yuh, Jerome. I won't let yuh down."

"You better not, or you'll be out, like the last bitch. So you'll do anything then?"

"Yeah."

"What, like shag another geezer if I tell yuh?"

Mandy sat up.

"What? But I thought I was your woman, Jerome. Why'd you want me to shag another geezer?"

"Never mind why. You don't ask questions. You just do as I tell yuh, right? An' if you don't you're out. You behave yourself, an' I"ll look after yuh, an' give yuh a good time, right? So, would yuh shag another geezer if I said?"

"S'pose so," answered Mandy, in a quiet voice. "Whatever you say, Jerome. I just wanna make you 'appy."

"Thass more like it. Thass a good girl. 'ere, give my cock another suck. will yuh? E's wakin' up again. An' make sure you swallow it all. I can't stand tarts who make a mess."

Later, Mandy was getting dressed. "I gotta go, Jerome. Me mam'll be goin' spare. Can I come tomorrow?"

"Course you can, babe. But listen, I got this little job I want you to do for me."

"What?"

"Well, I got a little cash flow problem at the moment."

"But I thought you was loaded. You got tons in yuh pocket, ain't yuh?"

"Mind yer own fuckin' business, bitch!"

"Sorry, Jerome, I only meant . . ."

Jerome softened. "Thass all right, Mand. But listen up. There's this guy what supplies me, an' 'e wants payin' tomorrow an' I ain't got enough readies."

"So 'ow can I 'elp Jerome? I ain't got no money."

"Nah, nah, but you can get it. I know this place where you can do a few tricks. Get thirty or forty a time with your looks."

"What? I ain't working on no street."

"Mand, Mand, it's safe. I wouldn't send yuh to no crap place. It's the other end of town. No one'll know yuh down there. You put on that sexy gear I got yuh, and I'll be nearby, watching out for yuh."

"But why you gotta pay this geezer?"

"Cos I owes 'im for two months' supply, an' 'e gets nasty if 'e don't get 'is money. You wouldn't wanna see me all cut up, would yuh?"

"No, but . . ."

"Thass all right then."

"So when I gotta do it?"

"Tonight."

"I can't tonight, me mam, she'll . . ."

"Just a couple o' hours, babe. It's not much."

"So what do I 'ave to do then?"

You just stand there in yuh short skirt and smile at the drivers, an' when they stop you just get in. I'll show yuh a good place to take 'em. Then you just do the business in the car. It's all very quick. Make 'em pay first though."

Jerome stood up and went into the bathroom. He returned with a handful of small packets. " 'ere, make 'em wear these. Stick 'em in yuh boots. Don't let 'em do it without a condom. Don't want you catchin' nothing."

Mandy looked unsure. "Dunno, Jerome. What if I don't like 'em?"

"You don't 'ave to like 'em, you silly bitch. You just sucks their cocks and opens your legs. It's all about money. When they're doin' it, just think about all the money you're earnin'. You know 'ow to put on a condom do yuh? 'ere, let me show yuh . . ."

* * * * * *

Later that evening Jerome cruised around the streets in his BMW until he found Mandy standing by a phone box. He pulled up beside her.

" 'ow yuh doin', babe?

"Oh, Jerome, can I go 'ome now? Me feet're bleedin' freezin' and me mam'll go spare."

" 'ow much you got then?"

"Loads. Take me 'ome now, Jerome. Please."

"All right. Jump in then. Less see what you got."

Mandy emptied the contents of her bag onto Jerome"s lap.

"Fuck me! You done well, babe. Very well. I knew you would. You got class, you 'ave."

He counted out the money. "Two 'undred and seventy quid in two hours. Thass fuckin' great, babe."

"Four hours."

"All right, so I was a bit late. But you done great. You're my best girl, you know that, don't yuh?"

"What d'yuh mean, best girl?"

"Like I said, you're my woman."

"Am I, Jerome? Am I really? Did I do good?"

"Too right. 'ere, 'ave twenny for yuhself. You earnt it."

"Oh, thanks, Jerome. Can you take me 'ome now?

* * * * * *

Four months later Mandy was still Jerome's 'best girl' but, by then, she had met some of his other 'best girls'. When she found out that she was just one of many, and asked to stop working, she went home with a black eye, which was difficult to explain to her mother.

One evening a car containing two men pulled up beside her. She backed away. She had been told never to get into a car with more than one man inside.

" 'ullo, love," said the man in the front passenger seat as he wound down his window. "What're you doing?"

She looked long and hard at the man, and hesitated. Something in his manner unsettled her. The Vice! The other girls had warned her about plain clothes policemen touring the beat, but this was the first time she had seen them.

"Oh, um, I'm just waitin' fuh me mam."

"Funny place to wait, love. Does she know you're here?"

"Oh yeah. She's phonin' this phone box any minute now."

"What's your name, love?"

"Um, Kelly."

"Umkelley? You sure about that, are you?"

"Yeah."

"Umkelly what?"

"Kelly Smith."

"And how old are you, Kelly Smith?"

"Sixteen."

"Sixteen?"

The man smiled and muttered something to the driver. Mandy glanced sideways down the street, wondering whether she could run. The car door opened and the man got out. Mandy backed further away.

"Don't be scared, love. We're police officers. Get in the back of the car, will you?"

He opened the rear door and beckoned Mandy in. Mandy froze.

"But I ain't done nothin' wrong. I'm waiting for me mam."

The policeman was insistent.

"Get in, love."

Mandy got in and the man shut her door before climbing back into the front.

"Just take it round behind the skips, Dave", he said to the driver.

The car moved up the road, took a sharp right between some trees, and pulled up behind a row of bottle banks out of sight of the road. Mandy reached for the door handle, but the child locks were on.

The man saw the movement and turned around to look at her. Mandy felt uncomfortable as his eyes travelled up and down her body. He was staring at her white thighs as he spoke.

"It's no good trying to run away, love. You've been a naughty girl, haven't you?"

"No I ain't."

"Oh, but we think you have, don't we, Dave? Pretty little thing isn't she, Dave? Very pretty indeed. Now then, Kelly Smith, or whatever your real name is, have you got any knickers on?"

Mandy clamped her knees tightly together.

"What?"

"You heard."

Mandy blushed, and squirmed awkwardly.

"Come on! Answer my question." he said, leaning over the seat back, and leering at her.

"You can't . . ." Mandy protested.

"I can't what?" he said, cutting her short. "Listen, young lady. Do you want to spend the night in the cells?"

"No, but . . ."

"But nothing. Now you just answer my question. Are you wearing knickers?"

"Yes."

"But we don't believe you, do we, Dave?"

Dave remained silent, looking straight ahead, with his hands on the steering wheel.

"So pull up your skirt. Pull it up!" he barked.

Mandy's eyes filled with tears as she wriggled forwards on the seat until her skirt had risen to her hips.

"There you go, Dave! I was right. What did I tell you? Now, there's only one reason why a little girl like this would be standing on a corner wearing no knickers, isn't there, Dave?"

Dave nodded.

" 'cos she wants a fuck, doesn't she, Dave? She's ready and begging for it, the little slut, isn't she, Dave?"

"No I'm not. I ain't no slut. I'm waiting for me mam. An' you can't touch me. I'm only thirteen."

"Oh, no, you can't have it both ways, love. You said you were sixteen. Take off your boots."

Mandy hesitated.

"Take 'em off! Now!" he shouted.

Mandy unzipped her boots and lifted up each leg to pull them off.

"Take a look at this, Dave."

Dave turned around and watched Mandy as she lifted her knees, struggling to pull off her boots. Both men stared between her legs.

"Sweet little cunt, isn't it! Very cute. Fresh and young!"

Mandy tried vainly to cover herself while still struggling with the boots. As the second boot came loose, condom packets fell out around her.

"So what would a thirteen-year old be wanting with all these then?"

Mandy quickly retrieved all the packets and put them back in a boot.

"They gives 'em out at school."

"The fuck they do! Not to thirteen-year-olds, they don't. Hey, Dave, take a walk. Give me ten minutes."

Dave got out, lit a cigarette, and walked away from the car. The man in passenger seat climbed over into the back and sat next to Mandy.

"Move over!"

Mandy shuffled across the seat.

"Right, my name's Phil Watson. PC Watson. Remember that, right? And my partner in PC Dave Wright. How long have you been working?"

"What? I . . . I . . ."

"Come on! Don't bullshit me. How long?"

"Just a few weeks."

"Right. Now we're getting somewhere. OK, so this is how it works. You listening to me?"

"Yeah."

"Right. You want to work without any trouble, then you do exactly what me and Dave tell you to do, right? If not, we'll have you in court before you can blink. Understand?"

"Yeah."

"Good. I think you do. So if I tell to you watch out for certain customer you do it. If I tell you to write down a car registration, you do it. If I wire you up with a microphone, you do it. Understand?"

"Um, yeah."

"Yes Phil, OK?"

"Yes, Phil."

Phil reached across and pushed his hand up between Mandy's thighs. She jerked back against the door of the car.

"And if me or Dave want a freebie, you do it, yes?"

Mandy looked at him.

"Yes?" he repeated.

Mandy nodded.

"And you enjoy it, right? "Cos we're not your usual seedy punter. We're police officers, and it's an honour for you, right? And if you don't look after us properly, then we forget about the little deal we have, and you end up down the cells, with your name in the papers, right?"

"Yeah."

"So what are you going to show me then?"

"What? What d'yuh mean?"

"Come on, Kelly, open your legs nice and wide. I want to see what you've got. Yes. That's it. Use your fingers. Pull it right open. Good. Show me how you play with yourself. Do it! That's right, you dirty little girl. Now you're just dying for me to stick it in, aren't you?"

Mandy looked down at herself.

"Aren't you?"

"Yeah," she whispered.

"I didn't hear you properly, Kelly. What did you say?"

"I said yeah."

"Yes please, Phil, I want you to fuck me – say it."

"Yes please, Phil, I want you to fuck me."

"Beg me, go on, beg me."

Tears rolled down Mandy's cheeks.

"Please fuck me, Phil. Please. Please.

Mandy burst into heavy sobs.

"Well, stop that bloody crying then and I might consider it. All right, undo my trousers then."

Mandy reached forwards and began to undo his trouser belt. Ten minutes later, Dave returned, and Phil took a walk.

* * * * * *

The next day Mandy went to Jerome's flat to tell him what had happened, but she found his front door off its hinges, and some of his belongings strewn in the street. She walked into the flat and saw that it had been smashed up. Jerome had gone.

So she went home and, after a few days, returned to her previous existence, spending most of her time, when not going to school, in the shopping precinct. Every day she looked across at the coffee bar where she had first seen Jerome, and every day she was disappointed not to see him there.

Some weeks later she bumped into one of Jerome's other girls.

"All right, Mand?"

"All right, Stace?"

"What yuh doin" then? Ain't seen yuh out."

"Nah. Don't go out no more. Jerome's gone. Know where 'e is then?"

"Down London, they say. Got some dealers with shooters after 'im."

" 'as 'e? Well I never."

"Yeah. We're well rid of 'im. Bastard."

"Yeah. S'pose."

"Aw come on, Mand! What yuh mean, you s'pose? The bastard tried to cut me."

"Did 'e? "E 'it me once."

"Once? Bastard 'it me all the fuckin' time. So what you doin' then?"

"Not a lot."

"So you're not workin' then?"

"Nah."

"So you got cash 'ave yuh?"

"Nah, I'm skint."

"So why ain't yuh workin' then?"

"Got fed up with it. 'ad trouble with the Vice."

"What, that cunt Watson?"

"Yeah. And 'is mate. Dave somethin'."

"Them're worse'n the pimps them are."

"Yeah. They 'ad me in the back of their car. I told 'em I was thirteen, but they still made me do 'em.

"Bastards."

"Yeah."

"That's the problem with the streets. It's not the fuckin" punters you 'ave to worry about, it's the fuckin' pimps and the fuckin' filth. They all say they're looking after you but they fuckin' ain't. They just looking after their fuckin' selves."

"Yeah."

"I'd cut their fuckin' balls off."

Mandy laughed. "And bite their cocks off," she said. They both laughed.

"You ought to work in an 'ouse, Mand."

"I don't know nowhere."

"But don't your mam work?"

"Yeah, but she don't know I work, and I wouldn't work with 'er, anyway."

"What about Debbie's?"

"Who's Debbie?"

"You know. Round Craddock Street. The big white 'ouse."

"Oh, yeah, I know it. Can yuh work there then? I'm too young, ain't I? I'm fourteen next week"

"Nah, Debbie's all right. She'd like a new young girl like you. She tell the punter's you was sixteen. Any road, some of 'em specially asks for young girls. You could pretend to be twelve if you want for some of 'em."

"But I dont look twelve. Most people think I'm about seventeen."

"Yeah, but what you do is you shave down below and put yer 'air in pigtails. You gets more money if they thinks you're young, like."

Mandy laughed. "What, an' pretend I ain't done it before?"

"You're getting" the idea, Mand. Look, I'll take yuh 'round to see Debbie tonight, if you like"

"All right. Thanks, Stace."

* * * * * *

Debbie was delighted. She hadn't had a girl with Mandy's looks and youthfulness for years.

"You can do all me schoolgirl work, Mand," said Debbie. "I got a nice little uniform you can wear - white see-through blouse, short pleated skirt, long white socks an' that. What I do is I say you're just visiting, and you don't work, and then they starts begging me and I says, well maybe, and so on like that. They ends up payin' twice the normal rate, and most of 'em won't even want sex with you – they just wants yuh to roll around on the floor and show yuh knickers, or undo yuh blouse and that, an' you can even make 'em pay again when they begs yuh to put yer 'and in their trousers an' that. An' some of 'em wants yuh to call 'em daddy or sir an' that, an' to start pantin' when they touches yuh knee, so they think yer dyin' for it"

Mandy smiled. "Sounds easy. An' they won't want sex then?

"Oh, some of em will. Is that all right, Mand? You done it, 'ave yuh?"

"Course. It ain't no problem."

"An' some want oral. You done that, 'ave yuh?"

"Yeah. I done a lot o' that."

"An' swallowed?"

"Yeah. I done that. It's all right."

"Well make sure they think you ain't done it before. Tell 'em how big their cock is an' that, and 'ow you'll never get it in yer little mouth. They love that!"

Mandy held up her little finger and put it to her mouth. "Oh, it's so big sir! I"ll never get it in! Be gentle, daddy!"

Debbie laughed, raucously. "You're a caution, Mand. You'll do well. What about anal? You done that?"

"Only once. Didn't like it. It 'urt too much."

"Well, you ain't gotta do it. Anyway, they'll be more than 'appy if they thinks they're the first one's what got into yer knickers, so they won't be wanting anal."

"But if I'm a schoolgirl, they won't wanna use condoms, will they?"

"No, most won't. Is that all right? It's up to you, Mand. It's what we call specialisin'. If yuh specialise yuh does it without. Make 'em wash first. Charge 'em even more. Yuh just 'ave to make up yuh own mind dependin' on whether 'e looks clean or not."

"OK. So, do I give the money to you then?"

"Course yuh don't, love. They pays me twenny when they comes in, an' some of 'em tips me when they goes out, but whatever they give you, you keep."

"What, all of it?"

"Course. I ain't no pimp. Your mam works, don't she? She worked 'ere for a while. Long time ago though. Do she know you're down 'ere, then?"

"No, she don't. You won't tell 'er, will yuh?"

"Course not, bab. But listen up. If any one asks, you ain't workin 'ere, right? You're just visitin' or answering the telephone. I'm only s'posed to 'ave one girl 'ere at a time. If I 'as two or more, then it's a brothel, and I can get busted. So bite yer tongue, right?"

"Course."

"An' if we gets a visit from the filth, you gives a different name and says yer sixteen, right?"

"Course. No problem. I dun it already with the Vice."

"Thass OK then. So when you wanna start?

* * * * * *

Mandy continued to put in the occasional appearance at school, but spent most of her time at Debbie's, where she enjoyed the companionship of the other girls, the attentions of all the best customers, and the continuing warm praise from Debbie for the sudden increase in trade.

* * * * * *

Several months later, Mandy arrived home one evening, just after midnight.

" 'ere's yuh wrap," she said, throwing a small package in Doreen's direction.

"Oh, thanks, bab, you're good to yer old mam. D'you want some?"

"I got some."

"Come on then, come and sit next to me an' we can 'ave a smoke together. I know I shouldn't let yuh, but you're growing into quite a big girl now, and you seems to do what you want most of the time anyway."

"I ain't a baby, mam."

"No, no, and you're a good girl really, I knows that. But I know you ain't just answerin' the phone down Debbie's."

"Yes I am."

I know you ain"t. I seen all them fuckin' clothes in your wardrobe. You don't get all them from answering the fuckin' phone. I knows what's goin' on, my gel."

"You been in my fuckin' wardrobe?" screamed Mandy.

" 'old on, 'old on. I just needed to borrow me a skirt. An' I put it back."

"You better 'ave."

"I 'ave. So 'ow come you got all them clothes then?"

"Debbie give 'em me."

"She fuckin' didn"t."

"She fuckin' did."

"I don"t fuckin' believe you. Some of them's designer stuff, and it's in your size, not fuckin' Debbie's. She twice your size."

"Well, I don't care what you fuckin' believe, thems my things, so you keep yer fuckin' 'ands off."

"All right, all right. Keep yer 'air on. Anyway, 'ow many girls Debbie got down there then?"

"Two or three each day. Different ones different days."

"Any young ones, then?"

"A couple. Depends what you mean, young. There's Sammy, she's seventeen."

"Seventeen? I know 'er. She ain't no seventeen. She looks about fuckin' thirty. Got two kids, ain't she?"

"I dunno."

"No, I mean, any what looks young."

"Chantelle looks young."

"Who?"

"Chantelle. Well, that's 'er workin' name. Real name"s Claire. Claire Skitt."

"What, little black girl, is she?"

"Yeah."

"She's not fuckin' young, neither. She's at least twenny-one, an' she's 'ad a kid too."

"Well, I'm the only young one then."

"But you don't work."

"No."

"You sure you don't work?"

"Course I fuckin' don't. What d'you take me for?"

"You don't fool me, young lady. I knows you're fuckin' workin'."

"You fuckin' don't."

"Well, it's a pity they don't 'ave any young girls down Debbie's 'cos I've got this regular what wants a young girl. Good payer 'e is. Quite a nice geezer."

" 'ow much do 'e pay then?"

"Fifty."

"Fuck off. You won't get a young girl for fifty."

" 'ow much then?"

"More like an eighty."

" 'ow do you know, if you don't work?"

" 'cos I answers the phone, don't I? I knows what they pays."

"Well, 'e might pay more for a special girl, a virgin like, what's gagging for it. Know what I mean?"

"And 'ow much you takin' out o' this then?"

"Nothin'."

"Bollocks!"

"Well, if I could find the right young girl, maybe she'd slip me tenner for introducin' 'im, like."

"Who're you kiddin"? There's no way you'd only take a tenner for that. So 'ow much is 'e really payin'?"

"Depends."

"On what?"

" 'ow good the girl is. An' 'ow young she looks. Need to tease 'im a bit, make 'im think 'e can't 'ave 'er unless 'e pays big bucks. You know 'ow it goes, don't yuh?"

"Yeah, I know. So, who're you gonna ask, then?"

"Dunno. I thought you might know someone."

"Well, I don't."

"Right, OK. Shame really, 'cos 'e's such a good punter. It'd be a shame to lose 'im."

"Yeah."

"So . . . Um . . ."

"Yeah?"

"Look, I don't want you to work. You're only fourteen. Mind you, I started when I was thirteen like, and it ain't done me no 'arm."

"Ain't it?"

"Whadya mean by that, Mand? Nothin' wrong me, my girl."

"If you say so, mam."

Doreen paused, and looked at Mandy. "All right Mand, I'll level with yuh. I don't want you to work. But maybe just this once. Just this one punter. It'd be good money. 'e's a good payer, like I said. So what about it, bab? Just this once?"

"I might."

"You might?"

"When's 'e comin'?"

"Monday."

"But I'll be at school."

"Wouldn't 'urt you to take the afternoon off, would it? Just this one time?"

"But you said I gotta go to school."

"I know, I know. But, then again, wass the fuckin' good o' that school? They don't learn yuh nothin'."

"They don"t."

"Waste o' fuckin' time."

"True, it is."

"You're better off earnin' some cash. So, you'll do it, will yuh?"

"I might. But I want eighty, no matter what commission you're takin'."

"Eighty? Fuck me! That won't be easy."

"Course it will. Like you said, you just play 'im along. I comes in wearing me school uniform and I sits on the floor showin' me knickers an' that, and sits on 'is knee and just plays around. He gets an 'ard-on a begs you to let him take me upstairs, and you keeps sayin' no till 'e empties 'is pockets."

"You sound like you done it before. I dunno. Fuckin' eighty! I was lucky to get ten bob when I was your age. An' then I kept gettin' fuckin' pregnant. I 'ad Wayne when I was fifteen, and Kevin when I was seventeen."

"Did your Mam know you was workin' then?"

"No, I was in the children"s 'ome then. An' they didn"t even tell me about the pill. Least, I don't think they did. You wanna be careful you don't get pregnant too."

"I'm on the pill."

"Oh, are you then, and you don"t work do yuh? But you're on the fuckin' pill, then!"

"Just in case."

"In case o' what? In case you sit on somethin' you shouldn"t is it? You don't get fuckin' pregnant off the toilet seat, my girl."

Mandy looked at Doreen and laughed. Doreen laughed back.

"So you gonna do it then, are yuh, Mand?"

"Yeah. But I definitely want eighty 'cos I knows I'm worth it. Everyone says."

"Who?"

"The girls. An' there was this geezer a few months back. 'e said I could be a model."

"Well, yuh could. So who was this geezer then? What, a photographer, was 'e?"

"Nah. Just a geezer. 'e's gone to London now. I wouldn't mind bein' a model though. I could do it you know."

"Course you could, Mand. Course you could."

* * * * * *

It was Monday, and Doreen was perched on a high stool in the kitchen, painting her toe nails. "You ready yet, Mand? 'e'll be 'ere in a minute."

Mandy shouted back from upstairs. "All right, all right! Yuh want me to look good for the punter, don't yuh?"

"They don't fuckin' notice most the time."

"They'll fuckin' notice me," said Mandy, as she walked into the kitchen.

"Jesus F Christ!" exclaimed Doreen. "You can't fuckin" wear that!"

"Why not? You said you wanted me to look young."

"Not that fuckin' young! You look about twelve – except for them tits bustin' out o' that little blouse."

"But they like school uniform, don't they? Anyway, 'e's gotta think that I'm your little niece, ain't 'e, not a workin' girl. Thass the plan, ain't it?"

"Yeah, well, you just be nice to him an' pretend you don't know wass goin' on, OK? Can you speak a bit posh, like?"

"Of course I can, mother dear."

"Oo, thass good! When d'you learn to speak like that, Mand? Thass real posh, that is. Hey, listen, thass a car door slammin'. Nip upstairs till I call yuh, right?"

The doorbell rang and Doreen checked herself in the mirror before opening the door.

"Oh 'ullo, bab, come in," she said to Len.

He brushed past her in the narrow hallway and went into the sitting room, looking around as he went.

"You got her then, Doll?" he said. "Where is she?"

Doreen followed him in.

"Well, Len, I've 'ad a few problems. I 'ad a girl all lined up, no, two, but they let me down. You know what it is, these young girls. Not reliable. I'm just waiting for a phone call now from a friend what's got a girl. Says she'll phone any time now, and the girl can be 'ere in ten minutes, if yuh don't mind waitin', bab."

"I don't mind waiting if the girl's good. What's she like then?"

"Oh, I'm not sure. They just said she was young, like, and not very experienced."

"Sounds OK."

"So, would yuh like a cup o' tea while yuh waitin' then?"

"OK, thanks."

"Right, I'll just go an' put the kettle on then. I got me little niece staying 'ere at the moment, but she's off to school in a minute, so she'll be out the way."

Doreen opened the door and called up the stairs.

"Mandy! Are you ready for school yet, love? Come on down. You'll be late."

Mandy walked down the stairs and stood in the hall, out of Len's view.

"No I won't, Auntie. It's a teachers' training day. I just phoned my friend. Oh, have you got a visitor, Auntie?"

"Yes, come and say 'ullo to Uncle Len while I make some tea."

Doreen winked at Mandy, and went into the kitchen. Mandy walked into the sitting room where Len stood with his back to the fireplace. She smiled at him and walked straight towards him.

"Hello, Uncle Len!" she said, cheerily.

Len's mouth dropped open, and his eyes raced around her body, trying to take in the short skirt and long legs, the bulging blouse, the hair in bunches, and the sheer prettiness of her. He involuntarily stuck out his hand.

"How d'you do," he muttered, still devouring her with his gaze.

Mandy ignored his outstretched hand and reached up for his shoulders, pulling herself up on tip toe to kiss his cheek. Her bust crashed against his hand, and he breathed in the clean freshness of her. Her kiss left a wet patch on his cheek. He leaned back against the mantelpiece, confused and overcome, as she stood before him, smiling innocently.

"Why don't you sit down in this big chair," she said, leading him, stupefied, by the hand. "Auntie Doreen will bring the tea in a minute."

Len slumped into the chair and gazed up, speechless. Mandy smiled again and looked down at her white socks.

"Oh look at that! They just won't stay up!" she said, pointing to one sock rolled around her ankle. She lifted her foot high onto the arm of his chair, and proceeded to pull the sock up. Len stared at the triangle of white knickers now exposed three feet from his nose, and Mandy smiled coyly, as she slowly adjusted the sock.

"There we are!" she said. "Not that it matters now 'cos there's no school today, so I might as well take of my blazer. It's very warm in here, isn't it? You're sweating, Uncle Len, did you know?"

Len quickly wiped his brow with the back of his hand, and watched Mandy ease herself out of her blazer. Her blouse underneath was made of very thin, see-through white cotton, and he could see Mandy's bra quite clearly. At the front, only two buttons held the blouse together, and even they seemed on the point of bursting open.

"So I'd better go back upstairs, and do my homework, I suppose. Or maybe I should go 'round to my friend's house and do it there 'cos I expect you and Auntie Doll want a bit of peace and quiet."

Mandy slung her blazer over her shoulder and walked towards the door. As she opened the door, the blazer fell to the ground in front of her, and she bent over very slowly to pick it up. Again, Len was transfixed by the view of thin white knickers stretched across her tight rounded bottom.

As Mandy climbed the stairs, and Doreen walked in with two mugs of tea.

Len was struggling to regain his composure.

"It's bad news, bab," said Doreen. "Just 'ad a phone call. The little bitch 'as let me down. I'm sorry you've 'ad a wasted journey – unless you wanna see me, of course."

Len appeared not to be hearing her. "Who was that?" he stammered.

"Who?"

"That girl!"

"What? Mandy, you mean? Me niece?"

"Yes. Mandy. She's . . . she's . . ."

"Me niece. Like I said. What d'yuh mean?"

"Is she . . . Is she . . .?"

"What?"

"Doll, do you think . . . would she . . . would she . . .?"

"What? Oh no, you can't mean . . . not Mandy. She's me niece. Come off it, Len, she's only a kid. I couldn't let yuh . . . it'd be more 'n me life's worth. No way."

"But I'd pay very well, Doll."

"No way, Len. Not little Mand. She ain't never been with a man. She's too young. Me sister'd kill me if she found out."

"But, Doll, she isn't going to find out, is she? I mean, you wouldn't tell her, would you, and maybe if we looked after Mandy, she wouldn't tell either. D'you think she'd be willing? I mean, she seems very flirty. Showed me her knickers – twice! She knows what she's got, Doll."

"No, I just couldn't, Len. Not with me own niece. I just couldn't."

"Oh, come on, Doll, you know I'm a straight-up guy. I'd pay really well, and we could make it regular. I'm not short of a few bob."

"Well, I dunno. How much then?"

"Well, maybe I could run to eighty-five."

"Eighty-five? Don't make me laugh, Len! What, for a real virgin schoolgirl what's never been near a bloke? Would I risk me own neck for eighty-five?"

"OK, Doll, just name your price. I really want this girl."

" 'undred and fifty!" said Doreen. "And I don't guarantee noffin'. You can 'ave her on yer own for an hour, an' if she says no, thass no. But you pays me up front, and takes yer chances."

Len frowned. "Tell you what, Doll. I'll make it a hundred and twenty, and then a hundred every time afterwards. How's that sound?"

"Done! But like I said, no guarantees. An' I"ll need to speak to 'er first like. Tell 'er you're all right and that so she don't get scared to be on 'er own with yuh. But I'm tellin' yuh this, Len, don't you 'urt 'er or upset 'er. Right? I don't want no trouble from this. Come on then, Len, let's see the colour of yer money first, you knows the rules."

Len counted out a hundred and twenty pounds and handed it to Doreen. She pushed it down inside her blouse and went into the hall to call Mandy down. Mandy walked into the sitting room and smiled broadly at Len. This time, Len returned the smile.

"Listen, Mand. I gotta pop out for a while to do a bit o" shoppin'. I want you to stay an' look after Uncle Len for me. Now you be a good girl and do as you're told, all right? Don't you go annoying Uncle Len, 'cos 'e's a very nice man an' I don't want no bad reports when I get back. You'll be all right with Uncle Len. You understand me do yuh, Mand?"

"Yes, Auntie," smiled Mandy, walking across to sit on the arm of Len's chair. Len moved his hand onto the back of Mandy's waist.

"She'll be all right, Doll," he said. "I can see she a nice, bright girl. I'm sure we'll get on very well."

Doreen turned to go out, and the front door slammed. Mandy twisted around on the arm of the chair, putting her legs across Len's lap.

"So what're we going to do, Uncle Len? Shall we watch a video or something?"

Len hesitantly moved his free hand across and placed it on Mandy's thighs, patting her gently. She allowed the hand to remain there, and continued smiling at him.

"I know," she said, "you can help me with me homework!"

Len frowned and withdrew his hand. Mandy continued.

"D'you know any biology, Uncle Len? Only we're doing pulse an' that, and we have to find the pulse on someone who's drowned. D'you know how to do that? The teacher said you can find it in four places."

Len's frown deepened. "On the wrist?" he suggested.

"Yes, that's one. Here, put your hand on my wrist and see if you can find my pulse then. No, not like that. You have to hold the wrist in one hand and put your fingers on the top. That's it. Can you feel anything?"

"Yes. Bump, bump, bump. You're still alive, Mandy!"

Mandy laughed. "OK then. And the next place is on the temple, here." She took his hand and placed his fingers on the side of her head. "Can you feel that?"

"Um, no, I don't think so."

"Oh, so I'm dead after all. OK, and the next place is on the heart. Here, put your hand on my heart, Uncle Len."

Len slowly took his hand from Mandy's head, and very gently placed it on the opening of her blouse, above her breasts.

"Can you feel anything?"

"No."

"I don't suppose you will through all the clothes. If I was drowned I s'pose you have to undo the clothes a bit."

"I s'pose I would."

"Well, you can then. "Cos you have to pretend it's for real."

"Can I? You sure? But maybe I shouldn't do that."

"Oh, come on, Uncle Len, don't be shy. It's all right."

Mandy slid from the arm of the chair down onto Len"s lap and quickly undid the remaining two buttons of her blouse. She took Len's hand, and thrust it between her breasts.

"Can you feel anything?"

Len's breathing quickened and he felt himself becoming aroused. Unknown to him, Mandy felt it too, and began very slight gyrations with her hips, pushing her bottom down onto the growing hardness.

"I think you are feeling in the wrong place, Uncle Len. You have to move your hand around till you feel the heartbeat."

Len moved his fingers down her cleavage, up the side of one breast, down again and up the other.

"You got beautiful br . . . you're , um, very grown-up, Mandy."

Mandy smiled and looked down at herself. "Thanks, Uncle Len. That's what the boys at school say. They're almost falling out, aren't they. But I don't like the boys at school much though."

"Why not?"

" 'cos they stupid and spotty. I like the teachers best. Older men are more fun. Anyway, have you found it yet?"

Len's hand was now inside one cup of her bra. He quickly pulled it out.

"What? Oh, um, no, I can't find it, Mandy."

"OK, just one place left. The groin."

"The groin?"

"Yes. That's the easy one. Here, lets see."

Mandy lay back across the arm of the chair and lifted one leg across Len's chest and over his shoulder so that her crotch was exposed fully to him. Len looked down at the flawless pink thighs, the flat tummy and the thin white knickers, and noticed a slight dark shadow under the small mound between her legs.

"You just put your fingers there and feel," she said, taking his hand again and leading it to the edge of her knicker elastic on the inside of her hip. Slowly, he ran the tips of his fingers down the edge of the elastic and then stopped at the point where he felt the pulse.

"Yes! I can feel it there!" he exclaimed. "Quite strong. So you're alive after all."

Mandy smiled at him but kept very still. Len allowed his fingers to wander back along the edge of the elastic, caressing her very gently.

"That's nice, Uncle Len. Don't stop! It tickles a bit, but it's really nice."

Len continued to stroke her and, gradually, let the tips of his fingers dip under the elastic into the edge of her fine pubic hair. Mandy remained quite still. After a few minutes, she sat up, pressing her hand deep into his lap as she did so.

"OK, my turn."

"Your turn for what?"

"To find your pulse, of course. You have to take it in turn with your partner. That's how we do it at school."

Len allowed her to feel his wrist, his temple, and to thread her small cool fingers between the buttons of his shirt and onto his chest.

"Now the groin," she announced. "Come on, it's easier if you lie on the floor. You'd better undo your belt."

Len did as he was told and lay back, ready for the examination. Mandy sat astride him and immediately pulled his trousers down onto his thighs."

"Oi!" he shouted, in mock surprise.

"Don't be shy, Uncle Len, I wasn't."

Mandy very gently trickled her fingertips around in the hair on both sides of his groin, watching as the erection inside his pants throbbed with anticipation. She sat back.

"It's big, isn't it, Uncle Len?

"What?"

"Your thing?"

"You cheeky little girl! You're not supposed to be looking at that."

"Can I get it out? Would you mind? Only I've never seen a real man's before. Just my little brother's that's all."

Len sat up on his elbows.

"OK." He whispered.

Mandy pulled down his pants and his penis sprang out, fully erect.

"Oo, it so big!" She leaned very close until he could feel her breath on him.

"Oh look, that's the hole where the baby stuff comes out, isn't it? I saw video of it coming out into a lady's mouth. She was sucking it."

"Would you like to suck mine, Mandy?"

"Oh, no, I couldn"t, Uncle Len. Anyway, it's too big."

"What if I give you something."

"What?"

"Some money."

"How much."

"What about twenty pounds?"

Mandy reached forward and put her fingers around his penis, rubbing her hand very gently up and down its length.

"No, I couldn't do that, Uncle Len. Thanks all the same."

Len became more breathless from the actions of her hand.

"All right then, Mandy. What if I give you forty pounds? Would you do it then?"

"Well, maybe . . . oh all right, Uncle, but don't tell Auntie Doll, will you? I don't want to get into trouble . . ."

* * * * * *

Mandy was in the kitchen when Doreen came back.

"Where is 'e?", she whispered.

"Upstairs. In the bathroom", replied Mandy, releasing the bunches in her hair.

"Everything all right?"

"Course."

"Did 'e, did 'e do it then?"

"What?"

"You know."

"Nah. Didn't need to."

"What d'yuh mean?"

" 'e just wanted a blow job, but 'e cum before I even got me mouth near 'im."

"Did 'e? God, 'e must've been excited then."

" 'e was."

"Good girl, Mand. So 'e got an 'ard-on then?"

"Course. He was bustin' 'imself as soon as 'e saw me, wasn't 'e?"

"Yeah. S'pose 'e was. 'e don't get much of an 'ard-on with me no more."

They heard Len coming down the stairs. Doreen went into the hall to show him out of the front door. Mandy listened from the kitchen.

"Everythin' all right, Len?" she heard Doreen saying.

"Fine. Just great. She's bloody gorgeous, Doll."

"So, you wanna see 'er again, do yuh?"

"You bet, Doll. Hundred next time though. That's tops. All right? I"ll call you."

"All right, bab. Bye." Doreen shut the front door and went back into the kitchen.

"What did 'e mean an 'undred next time then? 'ow much did 'e give you?" asked Mandy.

"Oh, just an 'undred. Thass what I screwed out o' 'im. Twenty for me and' eighty for you, like we agreed. Same every time like. Good, ain't it?"

"You sure 'e didn't give you no more?"

"Course not, Mand. I wouldn't cheat you, would I? "Ere's yuh eighty, Mand."

Doreen handed Mandy four folded twenty pound notes.

"Come off it, Mam! You're keepin' more back than you're tellin". Gi' me another tenner!"

"Fuck off, Mand! 'e was my punter. I found 'im for yuh. Any roads, I bet 'e give you a good tip an' all."

"No 'e didn't!"

"I bet 'e fuckin' did. Oh come on, Mand, 'e'll be back for more, you knows that. 'e'll be your regular now. All you gotta do is tip me a bit now an' then for usin' the 'ouse. Listen, Mand, I reckons we're onto a good thing 'ere. I mean, I got lots of old regulars an' that what'd like to meet yuh. Their eyes'd be popping out o' their fuckin' 'eads if they saw yuh in that schoolgirl uniform. Len's was, wasn't they?"

"Yeah. An' 'is old man was popping out of 'is trousers, too!"

Doreen exploded into a loud cackle. "Yeah, it fuckin was, wan' it!"

Gradually her laughing subsided, and she drew deeply on her cigarette. "But listen, Mand, I know I said I didn't want you to work an' that, but now, well, to tell the truth, Mand, we could earn a fuckin' fortune at this schoolgirl game."

"We?"

"Well, I'll be lookin' after yuh, gel. I'll find the punters. It's my fuckin' 'ouse.'

"It's the fuckin' Council's 'ouse, and you don't pay no rent cos you get 'ousing benefit."

"Well, it's in my fuckin' name."

"But it's me what'd be doin' the fuckin' work!"

"Yeah, but you needs a good maid, don't yuh? Someone to answer the phone an' that. An' to keep away the 'ead bangers and perverts. Thass gotta be worth twenny pound a throw. So, what about starting tonight then? I got these two geezers comin' . . ."

"I dunno. I gotta go down Debbie's later on."

"You don't wanna go down there, Mand. Keep it in the family. Anyway, there's other girls down there. Up 'ere you don't 'ave no competition."

"I don't 'ave no competition down there neither. The punters always choose me first."

"Yeah, but you don't get eighty a trick down there, I"ll be bound."

"No, but they looks after me. Debbie's all right, she is."

"I know, I know, bab, but I'll look after you too. Honest I will. Oh, come on, Mand. What about it?"

"Well, all right. I'll do some up 'ere and some down there. See 'ow it goes like."

"All right. Good girl, Mand. 'ere, less 'ave a little drink to celebrate, shall we?"

* * * * * *

" 'ullo? Is that Doll? Is Mandy there? It's Stacey."

Over a year had gone by and trade was brisk at Doreen's house. Mandy had grown a further three inches in height, and had the figure and looks to grace any catwalk.

Doreen made sure that she never had less than six visitors a day, and her list of newcomers was climbing all the time. To cope with the demand, Doreen had taken in another girl, a plumpish nineteen-year-old with a young face, called Avril. When Mandy was fully booked, customers were fobbed off with Avril at a reduced price. Most stayed, and Avril didn't seem to mind being second best.

Doreen put her coffee on the draining board. "She's busy right now, Stace. What d'you want?"

I've got a punter for 'er. Is she still workin'?"

"Course she is."

"Oh, only Debbie was telling me she 'adn't been down there for ages, so I thought maybe she'd gone to London."

"Nah, she's still workin' 'ere. So who's this punter then?"

"Oh, special guy. I met 'im when I was working for Gentlemen Prefer Blondes."

"What, that escort agency?"

"Yeah. Seen 'im a couple o' times, I did. Really nice bloke. Would make a really good regular."

"So why ain't you still seein' 'im then?"

"I blowed it. 'e caught me with me 'and in 'is trouser pocket when 'e was in the shower, so 'e won't see me no more."

"Not surpised. That was a bit stupid, wan' it, Stace?"

"Yeah, but you know 'ow it is, don't yuh, Doll? So I was thinkin' that maybe Mand would be interested, 'cos Gentlemen Prefer Blondes ain't got no more nice girls at the moment. They've 'ad a few, an' 'e seen them, but they wus students an' they ain't with the agency no more. Them students don't stay long. The ones what's left are crap. You know what most of them escorts are like – all in their thirties an' worn-out like, so I thought Mand might like to meet this guy. I got 'is mobile number. 'e's a very good payer. Really nice bloke, treats yuh like a lady. Just up Mandy's street, I reckon. Drives a Bentley, 'e does, an' lives over Westley. Very posh."

"So will 'e come 'ere then?"

"Nah, 'e likes girls to go back to 'is place. Got a lovely 'ouse. 'e'll collect 'er an' drive 'er back after. 'e likes a proper date, like. You know, 'oldin'' 'ands, an' kissin' an' that. His wife fucked off a couple o' years back, an' he just likes the company."

"What no sex then?"

"Oh, yeah, 'e likes sex too. A lot. But 'e's not ugly. Ain't got bad breath nor noffin'. Quite fancy 'im, I do. 'e'd look after a girl 'e would. 'an 'e likes 'em slim an' pretty like Mand. She'd do all right. Be up there every week. Even do some all-nighters, I reckon."

"Yeah, Mand'd like that. So 'e wants 'er in 'er schoolgirl stuff do 'e?

"Shit, no, Dor. He wouldn't touch a girl under eighteen."

"But Mand can pass for eighteen or nineteen if she wants. An' she can speak all posh an' act real mature like."

"I know she can. She always could."

"So 'ow much for his phone number then, Stace? You ain't gonna give it for free are yuh?"

"What about eighty?"

"What about ten?"

"Fuck off, Dor!"

"Ain't no use to you no more is it, Stace? Any road, 'e might not wanna see Mand."

"Aw, come on, Dor, I knows 'e'll go for Mand. It's worth more'n ten. How about fifty then?"

"Twenny."

"Twenny-five."

"All right, Stace. Yer on. By the way. Wass 'is name?"

"David."

As Doreen was finishing the call Avril shuffled into the kitchen, and picked up the kettle.

"It's already boiled, bab," said Doreen.

"Oh, 'as it?" said Avril. "You wanna a cup then?"

"I got one somewhere. Where'd I put it?"

Avril walked to the sink. "Is this it, on the draining board?"

Suddenly, there were loud bangs on the back door. Doreen jumped. "What the fuck's that? Watch out, Av. Sounds like trouble. Some shit punter, or a drunk or somethin'."

She went to the door and peered through the spyhole.

"Fuck me, it's Wayne and Kevin. Quick, Avril, run upstairs an' tell Mand to get rid o' her punter. Get 'im out the front door. Quick!"

"Oi! Open the fuckin' door, you slag! We knows you're in there!" called a male voice from outside.

Doreen cowered behind the door waiting for Avril to bring the man downstairs.

"Open the fuckin' door or we'll kick it in!" shouted the man.

Doreen heard Avril on the stairs.

"All right, bab. I'm comin'! Didn't 'ear yuh. Sorry, I was on the bog. 'ang on a minute while I find the key."

She heard the front door close, and Avril came in, red-faced and sweating. Doreen opened the door, and Wayne pushed past her, followed by Kevin.

" 'ullo Wayne. 'ullo Kev. You boys out then?"

Wayne ignored her and stood glaring at Avril. "Who's this tart, then?" he growled.

"Just a friend. That's Avril. Say 'ullo, Avril."

Avril trembled and said nothing.

"You runnin' a fuckin' brothel 'ere, or what??" shouted Wayne.

"Where's Mandy?" joined in Kevin.

"She's at school, bab." answered Doreen.

Wayne turned to Kevin. "Go an' check, Kev."

Kevin ran to the stairs.

Wayne turned back to Doreen. "If you're working that girl, I"ll fuckin' kill yuh, understand?"

"She ain't workin', Wayne. What d'yuh take me for? She just a little girl."

"Thass not what I 'eard."

"What you 'eard? All fuckin' lies!"

Kevin thundered back down the stairs. " Ain't 'ere, Wayne," he said.

"Like I said," protested Doreen, "she's at school."

Wayne opened the 'fridge. "Wheres the beer then?" he barked.

"I ain't got none, bab. You wan' a beer, do yuh? 'ere, Av, take this tenner an' go down the offy an' get some beer for my boys."

Avril grasped the note and scuttled out, pleased to be away.

Wayne and Kevin sat down at the table.

" 'ow long you two been out then?" asked Doreen.

"If you'd come to visit us, you'd know," said Wayne.

"I know, I know. It was difficult, what with one of yuh bein' at Featherstone, and the other at The Green. The buses. They's terrible."

"But you never come once even," moaned Kevin.

"I know, bab, I know. I kept meanin' to."

"An' you never wrote nor nothin'," said Wayne, glowering at her.

"It's just so difficult, what with lookin' after Mandy an' that. She's not an easy girl, yuh know. An' what with all the shoppin' and the cleanin' an' that . . ."

"Bollocks!" snorted Wayne. "Since when did you look after Mandy? When you aren't upstairs with some dirty old sod dribblin' between yuh legs, you're as 'igh as a fuckin' kite."

Doreen tried to change the subject. "Well, I must say, you're both lookin' well. Are yuh all right, boys? Where you livin' then?"

" 'ere," spat Wayne.

Doreen gasped. " 'ere? But you can't live 'ere. I ain't got the room. I . . .I . . ."

Kevin grinned. " 'e's 'avin' yuh on."

"We wouldn't live in this piss'ole if you fuckin' paid us!" snapped Wayne. "An' payin' is what we come about."

"What d'yuh mean?" whimpered Doreen.

" 'and it over!" ordered Wayne.

" 'and what over?"

"We didn't come to check yer 'ealth, you old bitch. We come for some cash. So 'and it over."

"I ain't got none. That the truth. Honest. I'm stoney. That was me last tenner what I just give to Avril."

Wayne looked at Kevin and grinned.

"Kev, floorboard under 'er bedroom window. Check it."

Kevin dashed upstairs again. Doreen turned white.

"No, no, Wayne. Bab. Please. I gotta pay the rent. An' the bills. An' Mandy needs new school clothes an' that. Oh, come on, Wayne, don't do this to me!"

Kevin returned with an Aldi carrier bag.

"Look at this, Wayne. The old cunt is fuckin' loaded!"

Doreen screamed and lunged for the bag. Kevin pulled it quickly beyond her reach, and threw it to Wayne. Wayne peered inside.

"No, Wayne, don't, thass me life savin's. Don't take that, Wayne," pleaded Doreen. "Thass every penny I got in the world, that is. Please, Wayne. Tell 'im, Kev."

Wayne walked up to Doreen and looked down at her.

"It's all right, mam. We'll look after it, won't we, Kev? You wouldn't want your little boys to go 'ungry, now, would yuh?" He laughed loudly. "Well, we'll be off now," he said. "Cheerio, mam. Nice seein' yuh after all this time. Don't worry, we'll be back. But just one little word of warnin'. If we find out you're workin' our Mand, we won't be so friendly next time. Got it?"

They pushed past her and went out of the back door, meeting Avril on the garden path. She staggered backwards, her high heels becoming impaled in the flowerbed.

" 'ere bitch, 'and over that beer!" snapped Wayne.

He grabbed the beer and pushed Avril backwards. She fell heavily into the earth, and sat there, motionless as they walked up the path towards the gate. She waited until they were out of sight before picking up her shoes, and hopping into the kitchen.

Doreen was slumped over the table, sobbing. She lifted her head when Avril shut the door. "They took all me money, Av. Every last fuckin' penny. I was keepin' it to pay for the brown I got last week. That Gus'll fuckin' kill me if I don't pay 'im. What am I gonna do?"

Avril stood by the cooker clutching her muddy shoes, and said nothing.

"Where's Mand?" asked Doreen. "Where did she 'ide?"

"In the airin' cupboard. I'll go an' let 'er out."

Avril went upstairs and helped Mandy out of the tight space in the airing cupboard.

"It's all right, Mand. They've gone."

"You sure?" said Mandy. "Why you got mud all over yer arse?"

"They pushed me in the flower bed. You'd better come down. They took all yuh mam's cash an' all."

"Bastards."

"Your mam's a bit upset. The money was for Gus."

" 'e'll cut 'er up."

"I know."

They went down into the kitchen where Doreen was still wailing at the table.

"Come on, mam!" said Mandy. "It's not that bad. We've still got plenny of regulars comin' in. You'll soon get that cash together."

"I won't get enough in time," wailed Doreen.

"When's "e comin' then?"

"Tonight. Oh shit, Mand. What am I gonna do? Mand, can yuh borrow it me? I'll pay yuh back, honest I will."

"No way. You'd never pay me back."

"But I will this time. Honest I will. On me mother's grave."

"She was cremated, mam. There ain't no grave. No. I sorted you out too many times. It's down to you this time."

Doreen sat up, wiped her face with the back of her hand, and lit a cigarette.

"All right then, madam," she said. "You won't help me? Then I won't tell you about this stinkin' rich new punter I got for yuh."

"What rich punter?"

"Ah, that perked you up, didn't it? He's a bloke what drives a Bentley. Rollin' in it, 'e is. An' 'e wants a new young girl."

"You're fuckin' lyin'."

"I fuckin' ain't."

"So 'ow'd you meet this punter then? Don't remember you goin' to any royal garden parties an' that lately."

"I've got contacts."

"Fuck you 'ave! Who?"

"I'm not tellin' you that. You bail me out an' then I might get you 'is phone number."

Mandy hesitated. She knew when her mother was lying, and this was not one of those occasions.

"All right then, but before I say yes, tell me a bit more about this geezer then."

"Lives over Westley. Very posh over there, it is."

"I know."

"Gotta big 'ouse an' drives a Bentley. Treats girls real nice. Pays well. Soft touch an' that. Lives on 'is own. 'is wife left 'im. You could get yuh feet under the table there, Mand."

"Likes young girls then, do 'e?" asked Mandy. "Like a sugar daddy is 'e?"

"Nah. "E don't want the daddy routine. You gonna have to dress older for 'im. Pretend you're eighteen. Can you do that then?"

"Course I can. Make a change to wear some decent gear instead of all this schoolgirl stuff all the time. Anyway, 'ow d'you know all this?"

"Me contact. I'm gettin' 'is mobile number tonight."

"Are yuh?"

"Yeah, but you ain't gettin' it till you borrow me some cash."

Mandy hesitated. "All right then, if I do, when do I get it back?"

"Tuesday, I promise. I can do it by Tuesday."

"All right then. But if you're lying about this geezer, or if I don't get it back, I'm goin' back to work at Debbie's, understand?"

"No, no, straight up. This is yer chance to move into the big time, Mand. Be an escort!"

"An escort!" Mandy liked the word. "What, a bit like a model? A girl what goes to 'otels and posh clubs an' that, you mean?"

"Thass it. This ain't gonna be a five minute open-yuh-legs job. You gets paid by the hour fuh yuh company."

"Me company?" Mandy smiled.

"Yeah. 'e picks you up in 'is car."

"In 'is Bentley?"

"Yeah."

"Oo!"

"Yeah, 'e picks yuh up, and 'e takes yuh to 'is 'ouse, an' yuh 'ave to chat 'im up, all posh like. I 'eard you talk posh before. You're good at that. But 'e must think you're about eighteen 'cos normally 'e 'as girls a bit older. Me contact told me 'e wouldn't wanna know if 'e thought you was younger. But, like I said, you looks older anyway."

"I do."

"An when 'e gets yuh in bed, 'e'll think you're older 'cos you knows yuh way around, don't yuh?"

"You been peeping through key'oles?" laughed Mandy.

"No, bab. I wouldn't do that. I knows you're good 'cos the punters keep tellin' me, an' they keep comin' back for more, dont 'em?"

* * * * * *

Doreen was glad that Mandy was in the bath when Stacey came around that evening with the telephone number. She felt that Mandy would have been less willing to give her money if she knew that Doreen had simply intercepted information from one of Mandy's own friends. From her reserve stash of money behind the fridge, Doreen took the twenty-five pounds to pay Stacey, and kept her on the doorstep on the pretext of being busy with a customer. As soon as Stacey had gone, she went upstairs and banged on the bathroom door.

"I got the number, Mand" she called.

"What number?"

"The number of the rich punter. You comin' out? We can phone 'im now if you like?"

The bathroom door opened and Mandy came out, tying her dressing gown around her.

"Come into my bedroom, bab," said Doreen. "Thass it. Sit on the bed. "Ere's the number."

"No, you do it, mam."

"What? You shy all of a sudden?"

"No, it ain"t that. Just that 'e'll think it odd if some girl calls 'im what's never met 'im before. You have to call 'im and pretend you're an agency or something."

70

"Oh, yeah. Thass a good idea, Mand. All right. 'ere goes."

Doreen cleared her throat and dialled the number. Mandy leaned close to the phone, listening in. They both heard the ringing tone, and waited, apprehensively. The phone clicked.

"Oh, um 'ello. His that David?" said Doreen putting on her best possible voice.

Mandy smiled and signalled a thumbs-up to her.

Doreen felt more confident. "Oh, well you don't know me, David, my name is Delores, and um, I 'ope you don't mind me ringin', I thought you might be hinterested in meetin' a new hescort."

There was a long pause.

"Um, well, I got your number from a friend. Someone you 'ave met before. She told me that you 'ave used Gentlemen Prefer Blondes and . . .um, well, yes, we're a new agency just starting out and we're tryin' to find top class clients, like your good self, for our top class girls. We only cater for the very best. We can get you whatever sort of girl you want, models, students, only the best.... Yes, we do really 'ave models. In fact, I 'ave one sitting right next to me as we speak... OK, well she's about five foot six . . ."

Mandy nudged her and mouthed "seven!"

"Oh, she says she's five foot seven. She's very slim, definitely only a size eight, and hextremely pretty. Long dark 'air, clear skin, an' big green eyes . . ."

"Blue!" interrupted Mandy.

"And a very firm figure, rounded in all the right places. Never 'ad no babies. No stretch marks. In fact, she his very new to this. Not like your haverage hescort. Very refined, she is. From a very good family. She is perfect, she really is. So, would you like to meet 'er? ... She's just turned eighteen... Oh,

no, that wouldn't be a problem at all. She loves older
men...Yes, definitely... Of course, and she's a very hintelligent
girl too, hinterested in all sorts of things. She reads a lot. I'm
sure conversation won't be a problem... Well, of course, if you
decide you don't like 'er, then you're hunder no obligation at
all. In fact, I could bring another, older girl along so you'd 'ave
a choice. But I'm sure you'll take to Mandy...Yes, seven
tomorrow is fine. Mandy his nodding 'er 'ead... Well, if you
give me your haddress, we can bring 'er to you... Oh, yes, if
you prefer, that would be OK. Lets see, do you know a pub
called The Cock and Bull on Crabtree Avenue, just off the ring
road?...A green Bentley? Oh, that"s nice. Right, we'll meet you
at seven then . . . Bye, David."

Mandy was frowning.

"Why did you tell 'im you'd take two girls? Who else
you gonna take? I thought you said 'e was for me?"

"Calm down, calm down! 'e is for you. We'll take Avril
along. There's no contest between you and 'er an' 'e's bound
to pick you. Just wanna make 'im think we're a proper agency,
like."

"Oh, I get it. Very clever! So what shall I wear, d'you
think?"

"That little white vest thing what you bought last week.
The one with thin straps what's cut away at the sides of yuh
tits and comes down low, and just about covers yuh nipples.
'e'll think yuh tits 're great!"

"They are great!"

"Course, so we gotta show 'em off, ain't we? An' no bra,
of course."

"An' shall I wear me new trousers?"

"No, you got great legs too, so you gotta show 'em. Wear
that pencil skirt what's split up the side to the waist, with the
gold rings 'olding the split together. Thass real class that is."

"But it don't show much o' me legs, 'cept what you see through the slit."

"Thass the general idea, bab You don' wanna be too obvious, and he'll be strainin' 'is bloody eyes to look through the slit, won' 'e? 'specially if a couple o' them gold rings come undone accidental on purpose, like!"

"Oh, I get yuh drift. So I don't wear no knickers then, right?"

"No, thass a bit too obvious. 'e might think you're a tart. Which you ain't. No, nice little plain white ones – you can't beat that. Nothin' too frilly. 'e'll be able to see 'em through the slit, won' 'e? An' wear yer 'igh 'eels. That makes yer legs look longer 'n the M1! An' not too much make up, neither. You don't need it anyway. Just a bit on your eyes, and a bit o' lip gloss."

"OK."

"An' I'll tell Avril to wear them pink 'ot pants of 'ers."

"What? She looks fuckin' awful in them! 'er arse hangs out each side!"

"Exactly. Thass why. But I'll tell 'er they really suit 'er. She won't understand wass goin' on anyway. She never knows what day o' the week it is!"

Mandy laughed.

"So there you are, Mand. It's up to you now. So what about me cash then? Guss'll be 'ere later."

"You sure you gonna pay me back Tuesday?"

"Oh, Mand, when did I ever let you down? Would I cheat on me own daughter?"

* * * * * *

The Punter

"So who is he then?" said Maggie as she waited for the pint glass to fill. "He's always sitting over there in the corner. Looks so lonely."

"Hang on a mo," replied Dawn pushing the key from her waistband into the till. The drawer sprung open and she put in the twenty pound note, counted out the change and placed it in the customer's outstretched hand. She turned back to Maggie, and lowered her voice.

"They say he used to be high up in the Council. I saw his picture in the paper a few times. Always posing in front of some new building, or with the mayor and a silver spade."

"Silver spade?"

"Or trowel. You know, planting a special tree or laying the first stone of a building. Think he used to be quite important."

"Used to be?"

"Well, I think he got made redundant or something like that, and they say his wife left him. I saw her a couple of times. He brought her in here. Pretty thing she was. Younger than him."

"It's sad, isn't it? You never know what's gone on in people's lives, do you? They come in and just sit there. They've all got stories to tell, I suppose."

"So what d'you think his story is then? Reckon he beat her up then? Killed her? Maybe she was sleeping around."

"No, he'd be in prison if that was the case. I reckon he's the victim."

"How can you tell that?"

"Well, he's always so nice and polite. Often buys a drink for the person serving him."

"Yes, he does that."

"And he's very well spoken. Educated an' that."

"That doesn't mean nothing. He could be a mass murderer for all we know."

"Not him! Listen, you take my word for it. I"m usually right about people. He's a straight-up decent guy and he'd make some woman happy, he would."

"Well, she'd certainly make him happy, that's for sure."

* * * * * *

David stood by the bedroom window watching the robin as it unearthed grubs beneath the beech hedge. The day before it had followed him all morning while he raked leaves, flashes of silent brown movement to keep him company as he worked alone. Once, it had even perched on the end of his rake, only to fly off quickly when he dared to bend too closely.

Behind his shoulders, the empty rooms of the big house yawned their silence. Morning had always been a busy, noisy time, but now the children had grown up and gone. No longer did the vast kitchen echo with the clatter of plates and cups, and eager high-pitched voices.

The robin flew out of sight and David waited several minutes to see if it would return. A squirrel ran across the lawn. Kezzie had liked watching the squirrels, David remembered.

He poured himself another cup of tea and opened his diary. He'd got a meeting at eleven with Tom, the builder, a dental check-up at two, and squash with John at six. Another fairly empty day. There had been too many empty days since he'd taken early retirement from the Planning Department, and his new business wasn't keeping him busy enough, now that there was no family to care for. Time was when he would get the family breakfast, do a ten-hour day at work, do the shopping on the way home, read the bedtime stories, and still be lively enough to take Rachael out for the evening. The hardest thing for him was having no one to care for. Looking after people had been his raison d'etre ever since he had been ten, and found himself caring for his younger brother after his mother had left. He loved being needed and being appreciated. Life without that was purposeless and selfish.

Perhaps, he thought, it had been a mistake to take early retirement so soon Rachael had left him to move in with her young lover. She had fluttered into David's life like a hesitant butterfly, spread her wings and paused a while, just long enough to have Freddy, only then to drift off on the first warm wind that came along. He had pleaded with her not to go, and had offered her as much freedom as she needed if only she would stay, but she had made up her mind and wouldn't listen. So then he asked her not to take Freddy, because he remembered only too well, after Sue had left, that keeping the children had been his salvation. Without Freddy to look after, he dreaded being engulfed by loneliness during the five days each week between Freddy's weekend visits. But Rachael wanted Freddy too, and David wasn't prepared to get into a tug of love. Freddy's needs came first, as had the needs of all his children. So it was agreed that Freddy would go with Rachael and spend as many weekends as possible with David.

His new business was going well, even if it was not yet big enough to demand his full-time attention. Some years earlier he had used a modest inheritance to buy a field on the edge of town, and obtained permission to turn it into a site for mobile homes. He had spent many weekends and summer evenings there developing the site and, as funds allowed, engaging contractors to install the services. The site accommodated thirty-six mobile homes, each of which paid David a site rent. After his retirement, he used his lump sum pay-off to buy an adjacent field and to develop that to take a further twenty homes, and his income from the site was now nearly three times the size of his pension. He had already identified another site on the other side of the town and was now awaiting final planning approval for development. He had done a deal with the local authority to house asylum seekers: the Council would supply the mobile homes and he would supply the site, with the funding for asylum seekers' rent coming directly from the government.

People could be forgiven for thinking that David was wealthier than he really was. While still married to Sue, he had moved to London to work for the Greater London Council and, during the six years they were there, house prices had risen dramatically so that when he returned to the cheaper Midlands with his second wife, he was able to buy an enormous Georgian house with extensive grounds. His do-it-yourself skills ensured that the house was always in pristine condition and furnished well with quality pieces he had bought cheaply from auctions, and restored himself. He had also managed to buy an old Bentley at a knock-down price and had spent a lot of time bringing it back to its former glories. It was expensive to run, but he loved driving it, even if it meant that he had sometimes to endure abuse and aggravation from young male drivers who shouted obscenities, or hustled him at traffic lights.

But success, in itself, meant little to him anymore. He had finished one successful career, and had a business which was growing well, but now there was no one to share that success, or to stoke his ambitions. He missed being able to talk each day about his problems, his dreams or his hopes. He hated shopping for one, and had stopped bothering to cook properly.

When Rachael left, so had many of his friends, who found it difficult to cope with him as a single man instead of half of a couple. But once or twice a week he looked forwards to his game of squash with John, a local teacher. His relationship with John wasn't deep, but it was regular, and had lasted ten years. There were whole areas of one another's lives which the other knew nothing about, and each conformed to the unwritten rule that conversation was to be restricted to sport and women. Unknown to his wife, John was an amateur glamour photographer, and he sometimes hired local studios and booked hourly sessions with models. Every few weeks he would bring along his latest set of photographs to show David as they sat drinking beer. David was a keen photographer himself even though he knew nothing about processing. He enjoyed photographing street scenes when he went on lone trips to third world countries, and he had also been on nature tours and developed an interest in photographing wildlife.

John enjoyed boasting about his numerous extra-marital affairs, none of which David believed. Indeed, John was dominated by a strong and over-powering wife, to whom he was devoted, and David knew and understood that John's sexual adventures were the stuff of fantasy.

* * * * * *

John picked up David at six that evening. After the game they went to the bar overlooking the swimming pool. Even though he'd showered, sweat still glistened on David's forehead.

"I told you that you wouldn't even see the ball!" laughed John.

"You were just lucky, that's all," replied David.

"Lucky! What'ya mean lucky? I don't call nine-four, nine-two, nine-seven lucky. That's a comprehensive annihilation, that is. Lucky, my arse!"

"It's that new racquet of yours. I'm sure it's not legal!" laughed David.

"Excuses, excuses! Your round, I think."

"But I bought the first round!"

"But you lost!"

"Yeah, yeah, all right."

David returned from the bar with two pints, to find John looking at some photos. "Are these the latest then?" he asked, as he sat down. "Who is she this time?"

"Some hot chick. She was begging for it."

"In your dreams! Why would a gorgeous young thing like that fancy a bald old git like you?"

"Not so much of the old, if you don"t mind. Bald, I'll grant you!"

David thumbed through the pictures and whistled. "Are you seriously trying to tell me that you and this girl. . .?"

John smiled and winked, conspiratorially. "Don't tell 'er at 'ome."

David laughed. "She wouldn't believe you either!"

"So, are you still enjoying life as a single man then David? Who're you shagging?"

"No one, I'm afraid."

"Afraid? What's holding you back, man? If I was free like you, I'd be at it every night!"

"Well, by all accounts you're at it pretty often anyway, so what's the difference?"

"The difference is that I have to be home by ten o'clock!"

David laughed. "I'll tell you what, John, I'd gladly swap with you. Any day."

"What, you fancy my missus? You must be mad!"

"No I don't fancy your missus, but I'd much rather have someone to go home to than be 'free' as you call it. Then again, I'm scared stiff of getting into any sort of relationship again because I've tried it twice and failed."

"You just need to lighten up, and enjoy yourself. You're not getting any younger. Why don't you join one of these dating agencies? There are a lot of single women out there, you know. And bored housewives who want a bit on the side. No commitment there, just fun."

"Oh, I don't know . . . Maybe you're right."

"Course I'm right. And if they all turn out to be crap, there's always the escort agencies. Hire yourself a dream girl for the evening." He picked up the photos again. "Like this one. She's a part-time escort, you know."

David look at the picture more carefully. "Are you serious?"

"Course. I can get her for you tomorrow if you want. Just takes a phone call. You can afford it!"

"I'm not sure."

"Come on, man! Life's for living! Go for it! A young thing like that would put a smile on your face!"

"Um, maybe . . . no, I think I'll try the dating agency. I think I'd rather have a proper date than just sex."

"Suit yourself, but I'll expect a progress report next week! You never know, it might even improve your squash. Can't get any worse, can it? Your round again, I think . . ."

* * * * * *

David stood outside the wine bar feeling very conspicuous. Under his arm he carried a rolled-up newspaper, as agreed, so that Judith would recognise him. She'd sounded very pleasant on the phone, and he'd been out with a Judith in his teens. This Judith said she was in her early thirties, just divorced, and had two young children.

A tall blonde got out of a taxi and walked towards him. He felt his heart rate quicken as she approached. She was very glamorous, beautiful even. He smiled and raised his hand in a half wave. She saw him looking at her and quickly looked away, walking straight past, and on into the wine bar, where another man at a table stood to greet her. Wrong woman. David felt foolish.

"Hello, are you David?" said a voice from behind him.

He turned and looked down at a round, plump, smiling face.

"I"m Judith. Hope you haven't been waiting too long."

This wasn't the Judith he'd imagined. Nothing like the Judith from his youth. She'd said on the phone that friends told her she was very attractive. Well, friends would, wouldn't they? Maybe he should have asked more questions before agreeing to meet. But perhaps she was disappointed too. He wanted to run, but a lifetime of being polite, being professional, being courteous, prevented him from giving in to his basic instincts.

They went into the wine bar and found a table.

* * * * * *

"And the judge ordered him to pay me one penny a year maintenance! I mean, it's just a joke isn't it? What's the point of that?"

David sat with a vacant half smile, nodding appropriately at intervals, as Judith unburdened herself of her childhood history, her messy divorce, her hysterectomy, and her mother dying of cancer. At the end of the evening he was glad he'd taken his father's advice and not gone into social work.

"Come on then, tell all!" said John, as they sat down for a drink the following week. "How many have you met then?"

"Three."

"Three? You randy old sod. There you go, I told you there were loads of women out there begging for it! So, you're feeling shag-happy now, aren't you? Didn't do much for your squash though, did it?"

"That's because I didn't shag anyone."

"What? You must be joking! You have three dates with women who are desperate for it, and you don't get laid? What's wrong with you, man?"

"They weren't desperate. And neither was I. In fact, once I'd met them, sex was the last thing on my mind."

"Oh my god, they must've been complete dogs then. Poor old chap. Were they?"

"The first one was short and fat, when she said on the phone that she was tall and slim. She spent the whole evening telling me what a shit life she'd had, and wanted to show me her operation scars."

"Oh yuk. What a turn-off."

"And the second was a dull librarian who buggered off without saying anything when I went to the bar to get the second round of drinks."

"The bitch!"

"And the third arrived forty minutes late, and turned out to be a journalist researching an article on lonely hearts."

"Crap!"

"You could say that again."

"So did you give her one?"

"What? The journalist?"

"Yeah. You should've taken her back to look at your etchings. Purely in the interests of research, of course."

"Of course. No, I didn't fancy her either. The trouble is, I really don't know what I'm looking for. I certainly don't want a woman with loads of emotional baggage. It's not that I can't sympathise or listen to them but I just don't want the burden. Then again, much younger women who've still got a lot of living to do are unlikely to find me attractive. I really would like some good sex, of course, but what I really want is what I can't have."

"What's that?"

"Being able to spend time with someone who's been to the same places as me, done the same things, brought up the same children. I miss having a wife, and that's it. It's as though my whole life has been wiped clean because I can't share memories with anyone."

"You got to stop looking back and start looking forward. You can't live in the past. Like I said, live a little. Just go out and get yourself laid by a young, sexy girl. Take it from me, it'll make you feel a whole lot better."

"But I just told you, they won't find me attractive, and anyway, I'm certainly not going to start hanging around in noisy nightclubs like a sad old wanker."

"No, no, of course not. Look, just phone an escort agency. It's as easy as that. No more hit and miss. You just tell them what you want. No problem."

* * * * * *

The next evening David sat in the pub reading the local paper. He flicked through the classified ads section. *Hoovers, concrete slabs, personal services. Leggy Tracey, discreet side entrance. Two girl special.* He turned the page. *Gentlemen Prefer Blondes – high class escorts.* He took out his pen and ringed the advertisement.

* * * * * *

"Hello? Can I help you?" said a female voice.

David had returned home. The alcohol had made him relax, and gave him the courage to make the phone call. But now he hesitated, unsure what to say. He put the phone down. Damn! What should he ask? What did he really want? Did he really want to pay for sex? Would it be too expensive? He thought about the girl in John's photographs. Would it really be possible to spend an evening with someone like that, someone who wouldn't say no? The idea of certainty was very appealing. He picked up the phone again.

"Hello? Can I help you?" said the same voice in exactly the same way. She had obviously said it a thousand times that day.

"Um, hello, is that the escort agency?"

"Yes. Can I help you?" she whined.

This sounded like customer services at a call centre, thought David, except they're selling sex not insurance. He half expected to be offered four options.

"I, I was wondering if I could meet one of your options, um, escorts."

"Are you in a home or a hotel sir?"

A home? Did she think he'd been committed? Or geriatric? Perhaps he should be in a home.

"A home."

"Where are you?"

"Westley."

"Oh, that's a little far out sir. Was it for tonight?"

Why was she talking in the past tense? It IS for tonight, you idiot.

"Um yes, if that's possible."

"I'll see what we can do, sir. Can I have your full address and phone number?"

David gave her the details.

"Right, sir, I'll call you back in five minutes."

The phone went dead. David sat back. He was sweating. He suddenly realised that he hadn't asked any questions. She knew everything about him, and he knew nothing. How much would it cost? What sort of girl would they send? Shouldn't he have told them what he wanted? Would someone just turn up at the door?

The phone went and he jumped.

"Hello?" he said, tentatively.

"Dad? What's the matter?"

It was Kezzie.

"Oh, Kezzie! Hello, sweetie. Sorry, I was just watching a film, and you made me jump."

"What're you watching?"

"Oh, um, Gentlemen Prefer Blondes."

"Do they, Dad? So there's no hope for me then!" Kezzie laughed.

"Oh, I think you do all right, Kezzie."

"This is just a quick call, Dad. I'm coming up to Westley this weekend, but the only train I can get is in peak hour . . ."

"And you want me to pay your fare?"

"Oh will you, Dad? I'll pay you back!"

"You know full well you won"t, Kezzie. All right, but just so long as I see something of you this time. You hardly ever come to see me when you're up here. You spend all your time looking up your old school friends."

"I'm staying Friday night with Erica, and I'll be with Sophie all day Saturday. We're going shopping together, and then I'm seeing Jeremy later."

"Oh, that's nice."

"So why don't we all come to you for Sunday lunch?"

"Can't you come to stay on Saturday night? Freddy will be here, and he'd love to see you too."

"Can't this time, Dad, but I promise to next time, OK?"

"OK, I'll see you Sunday then, about midday."

"OK. And can you run me back to the station afterwards? My train goes at four twenty-six."

"So I get to see you for four-and-a-half hours then. Just enough time to feed you and give you your train fare. Par for the course, I guess. OK, see you Sunday then, lovey."

"Bye, Dad!"

"Bye."

Typical Kezzie. In and out like a tornado. Feet never touch the ground. The phone rang again.

"What, changed your mind already?" asked David, expecting it to be Kezzie again.

"Hello, is that David?" said the mechanical voice.

"Um, yes."

"This is the agency."

It sounded like the voice of doom.

"Yes. Right."

"We have a young lady who is willing to come over to Westley this evening. Her name is Geraldine. She gives a full personal service."

Just like the garage, thought David. Change the oil, new spark plugs, top up the battery.

"Would you like me to describe her to you, David?"

"Oh, um yes. Yes please."

"Right. She's twenty-three, five foot five, with a lovely figure of thirty-six, twenty-two, thirty-six. And an all-over tan."

"All over what?"

"Just all-over," she replied, clinically.

"Oh."

The voice went on with the list.

"She has short auburn hair, big brown eyes, and she is very attractive. She's one of our most popular girls."

"Right. OK. Um, and how much do I . . ."

"The agency fee is twenty-five pounds for the first hour."

"Is that all? Well, that's very reasonable."

"And you discuss the rest with the young lady."

"The rest?"

"Any extra services. And the young lady's fee."

"Oh, I see. So that's twenty-five for the agency, and another fee for the lady."

"That's correct."

"I see."

"Is that OK then? Do you want me to ring the young lady to confirm the booking?"

"Oh, um, yes. Well, OK."

"Right, David. She'll be with you by nine-thirty. Was it just the hour you wanted?"

"Um, yes, I think so."

"Right, so Geraldine will be with you shortly then."

For the next hour David paced the house wondering what he had let himself in for. He washed up and tidied around, and then went for a shower and shave. Should he change the sheets? He was more nervous than excited. What would she be like? At what point in the hour should he suggest sex, or would she take control? He kept going onto the landing and staring down into the street. By ten he had just decided that she wasn"t going to arrive, when the doorbell went. He opened the front door.

"'ullo, are you David?"

"Yes."

"I'm Geraldine. Can I come in?"

"Um, yes."

David moved to one side and Geraldine stepped into the hall. David looked at her, and tried to hide his disappointment as she took off her coat. By no stretch of the imagination was she anything other than very plain. She was little more than five feet tall, but wore very high heels. Her bust was non-existent, and her bottom enormous. She had a large nose, and he guessed her age at about thirty-five.

"Very nice place you've got 'ere. Where shall I put me coat?"

"Oh, I'll take it."

He hung her coat over the banister and went into the sitting room. Geraldine followed him in.

"Yes, very nice place," she said, sitting down on the edge of the settee, her plump knees pressed together. "Shall we get the business out of the way first? Then we can relax and enjoy ourselves."

"The business?"

"The money."

"Oh, right, yes, so that's twenty-five for the agency, and, and . . ."

"Seventy-five for me."

David looked surprised.

"Didn't she tell you? I charge seventy-five for the full personal. For the first hour, that is. Fifty for every other hour."

"Right. Um, do you take cheques?"

Geraldine's mouth tightened and her voice dropped an octave.

"Strictly cash, dear."

"Right, no problem. I'll just pop upstairs and get it."

He came back and handed her the money. She counted it slowly and then put it into her bag. David felt queasy.

"Is that a drinks cabinet you've got over there, dear?" she said.

No, it's an ocean-going liner, he thought to himself.

"Oh, yes, would you like a drink?"

"Don't mind if I do."

"What would you like?" he asked, springing to his feet.

"Vodka and orange. A double."

This isn't a bloody pub you cretin, he thought. A double! Does she think I use optics?

"OK, well, here's a large one."

"Oo, that is a big one. Anyone would think you're trying to get me tipsy!" she cackled.

No chance, he thought, smiling politely.

She gulped down the drink in two swallows and held the glass out towards him.

"Any chance of another? Just a small one. Not too small!"

Perhaps you'd like me to get you a bucket, he thought.

"OK, here you are."

He gave her the re-filled glass and sat down on the settee next to her. She swallowed the second drink even more quickly and then stood up and started to remove her clothes. David sat in silence, watching her peel off the layers. When she was completely naked, she turned to him.

"Are we staying in here then, or going upstairs?"

David looked at her, horrified. Her breasts were little more than flaps of empty skin with large dark brown, gnarled nipples. Her buttocks and thighs were dimpled deeply with cellulite, and her stomach was corrugated with stretch-marks.

Her pubic hair ran up to her navel and down the inside of each thigh. If she had been the last woman on earth David could not have brought himself to have sex with Geraldine.

"Upstairs then, or here?" she repeated.

He had to put an end to this. It couldn't go on. "Look, Geraldine. I'm sorry, but this is the first time I've done this, and, um, I don't think it's going to work for me . . ."

"No problem, love," she said, cheerily, "can I use your phone?"

David was surprised and relieved by her reaction. He had expected her to be insulted and angry. He guessed it had happened before. Geraldine quickly dressed and dialled a number.

"Where are you, Errol?" she said. "Right, I've finished 'ere. Come 'n pick me up. Yeah. We can fit that other one in now. Yeah. Two minutes. OK."

She put down the phone and turned to David.

"Right then, love, I'll be on me way. Sorry you didn"t like me."

"No, no," lied David, "It's not you. It's just that I . . . I . . ."

"I know, dear. It's all right. But you know I can't give you your money back, don't you?"

"I see," said David quietly, realising that it was no good protesting because Geraldine and Errol now knew where he lived.

After she had gone, he took her glass into the kitchen and washed it thoroughly, taking care to remove the dark red lipstick smudge. He stood at the sink cursing his stupidity, and feeling seedy. He'd been had. His depression flooded back. What now? How pathetic he was.

Later, he was just going to bed when the phone went.

"Hello?"

"Is that David?"

"Yes."

"I hope you don't mind me phoning. It's Victoria from the agency."

"Oh, but you're not the girl I spoke to earlier."

"No, she just answers the phone. I own the agency."

"So what do you want? I'm surprised you're phoning me after what happened tonight."

"Yes, that's why I'm phoning. I'm really, really sorry. I understand things didn't go too well."

"That's an understatement. I was told that the woman was twenty-three, when she was clearly in her mid-thirties, and that she had a model figure, and so on. How can anyone honestly call that woman young and very attractive? It's just nonsense. I really can't imagine any circumstance where she would merit being looked twice at in the street."

"I know. I'm really sorry, David. The thing is, none of our regular girls were available tonight, and we got her from another agency. I hadn't met her before and we were just going on what we'd been told. But when she came in tonight to pay us the agency fee, I couldn't believe what I saw. She told me you had cancelled and, frankly, I'm not surprised."

"Well, I appreciate the apology and your honesty, sorry, what did you say your name was?"

"Victoria."

"Well, I appreciate you phoning me, Victoria, but I'm afraid this has rather put me off. This was the first time I had done this, and maybe I was expecting too much but . . ."

"If you'll give us another chance, I'm sure we can find someone more to your liking."

"So, they don't all look as bad as Geraldine, then?"

"My mother doesn't look as bad as Geraldine!"

David laughed. "Well, I'm not sure, Victoria. I need to think about it. It's too late tonight, anyway."

"Look, David, I'll be honest with you, and put my cards on the table. You're just the sort of regular customer I need. We get a lot of passing trade from businessmen and tourists staying in hotels, and often they don't treat the girls well. But I can tell that you're an educated and refined man, and since you live locally, it's in my interest to keep you happy so that you keep coming back for more. We need regular customers like you."

"More money than sense, you mean?"

Victoria laughed. "No, of course not. And as to money, well, if you'll give us another chance, we won't charge an agency fee next time, and if you don't like the girl, you just send her packing without paying a penny. In fact, don't pay until afterwards."

"Well, that's very fair. But the problem is that once they know where I live, I might a get brick through the window if I upset someone."

"In that case, we'll arrange it for you to pick the girl up, if that suits you. Then, if you want to cancel, they won't have been to your home first. If you're happy after meeting them, you can take them back to your place and return them afterwards. Would that be better for you?"

"Yes, I'd have no problem with that."

"So just tell me exactly what you're looking for, and I'll do my best to find someone."

"OK, well, I suppose I'm looking for someone who is slim. . ."

"How slim? Do you mean skinny? Thin? Like a catwalk model?"

"Well, that would be nice. But do you really get girls like that?"

"Not that tall, I must say, but we certainly get very slim girls. Size eight."

"Is that slim?"

"That's slim."

"OK. And, er, pretty, of course."

"Obviously. The prettier, the better, yes? And what about age? How old?"

"Well, not as old as Geraldine, that's for sure! Having said that, it's not the actual age that bothers me, it's more about youthfulness, vitality, freshness."

"I'm getting the picture. To be honest, you'd be better sticking to the eighteen to twenty-five age-range because girls older than that have usually had babies, and these girls don't always look after themselves very well, and childbirth takes its toll. The younger girls are usually more enthusiastic and genuine anyway. Not as hardened as girls like Geraldine. We get quite a few students. That might suit you. The conversation would be a bit more up-market too. Look, leave it to me David. Would you like me to call you when I've found someone?"

"No, I'll call you. Thanks, Victoria. You've cheered me up a lot."

* * * * * *

All through the next day David agonised about what he was doing. He was excited about the prospect of a brief physical encounter with a beautiful young woman – he'd lost track of when he'd last had sex – but he was also uncomfortable, and needed to rehearse the issues in his mind. Should he really be paying for female company? What were the alternatives? The dating agency hadn't worked. Most of the women there seemed to have more problems than him.

The prospect of going to singles discos and the like horrified him. How did men of his age meet new people? He no longer went into a working environment every day and his social life was non-existent, apart from his squash, so the chances of meeting someone were extremely slim. Of course, he knew that the best way was through a chance encounter in the supermarket or at the bus stop, but maybe that only ever happened in films and, in any case, he couldn't wait for that. How many more lonely evenings would he have to endure before that might happen?   Paying for sex was not a moral dilemma for him. Even though he had endured a typical religious schooling in which sin and guilt were drummed into him as the consequences of enjoyment, he had long since rid himself of that burden, and was able to rationalise that some women provided a service which some men needed to buy. Nevertheless, the social acceptability of such a transaction was another matter, and he knew full well that this was not something he would be able to share with his daughters, or even his neighbours. Sometimes he despaired at the hypocrisy of British society.

But what he was thinking of doing was legal, he could afford it within reason, and he felt it would provide him company, without the complications of a relationship, which in his present state of mind, was the last thing he wanted or needed.

He resolved to call Victoria after the weekend.

* * * * * *

On Sunday morning the kitchen was filled with the smell of roasting meat and potatoes, and David busied himself with the vegetables, while Freddy painted models at the kitchen table. The phone went. It was Sophie.

"Hi, Dad. Just to say we're running about twenty minutes late 'cos Kezzie's still doing her hair."

"Surprise, surprise!"

"Well, you know what she's like, Dad. Will the meal still be OK?"

"Of course. Nothing will spoil. I was timing it for half one anyway."

"OK. See you in a bit then. Bye."

"Bye, sweetheart."

Half an hour later the old house came to life when they all arrived. Freddy jumped up and dragged Jeremy, and Sophie's boyfriend, into the sitting room to watch cartoons, Kezzie disappeared upstairs to 'do something in the bathroom', and Sophie started pouring everyone drinks.

David smiled. "Why don't you all just make yourself at home?" he said.

"Oh come on, Dad, you wouldn't want it any other way," laughed Sophie, "and anyway, this place is still home to us."

"No, no, I love it actually. It's a bloody miserable place when I'm here all by myself. This is just like it was when you were teenagers."

"Except now we ask if we can use the phone!"

* * * * * *

Later they all sat around the table helping one another to food from serving dishes.

"Typical Dad!" laughed Kezzie. "You've cooked enough for about twenty!"

"I know. It's difficult to gauge it."

The girls grinned at one another and David sensed the conspiracy. "All right, all right, you two. Anyway, the leftovers will do me very well next week. I won't need to cook again, will I?"

"So what're you doing next week?" asked Jeremy.

"Oh, I've got a few site meetings. Some rent to collect. The environmental health officer is in on Wednesday. That'll take most of the morning. And I've got an architect coming to look at the bottom of the garden."

"What, the wood? What for?" asked Jeremy.

"Well, I was thinking of getting outline planning permission to build a couple of bungalows on it, and then sell it off with permission. It should fetch about forty grand."

"No way!" screamed Freddy. "That's where the foxes live. You can't sell that!"

"No, Dad, you can't," joined in Kezzie. "That's our childhood down there. Remember all the tree-houses you built us?"

"But you've all left home now. Life moves on. I could do with the money to invest elsewhere. There's a really good site coming up for sale in Endersleigh."

"Sounds a good idea to me," said Jeremy. You've got to move on, haven't you? You've got to keep busy."

"Well, yes," replied David. "Not quite busy enough, really."

"So what d'you do with yourself in the evenings, Dad?" asked Sophie.

"Oh, um, this and that, you know."

"No, we don't know. Tell us!" she laughed.

"Well, I play squash with John once or twice a week, go to the cinema occasionally, you know."

"Dad," said Sophie, more seriously, "you really ought to get out more, meet new people."

"Yes!" echoed Kezzie. "We were talking about it this morning. You can't just sit around moping."

"I don't sit around moping!" protested David.

"You do!" insisted Kezzie. "That's just what you do. Why don't you go and join an opera group and do some singing, like you used to do. You loved doing that."

"I know, but that was all a long time ago. I've really grown out of all that – prancing around in silly costumes and so on. But, in any case, what with Rachael moving to Leeds next month, I'm going to be spending a lot of time travelling at weekends to see Freddy." He turned to Freddy, who had impaled a large roast potato on his knife and was licking off the gravy. "Isn't that right, matey? And cut that potato!"

"Yes, matey!" giggled Freddy. "Dad's going to get a little cottage just for me an' him to live in at weekends!" he spluttered.

"Sounds cool, Fred!" laughed Sophie. "But that still doesn't fill up your weekdays, Dad, does it? You could still join an opera group, and when it came to production time, it wouldn't hurt Freddy if you missed the odd weekend. And he'd love to come to see you on stage, just like we did when we were little. You're good at it, Dad! Freddy would love it!"

"I don't know . . ."

"Oh come on, Dad, just do it!"

"Oh, stop bullying me, you lot. The thing is, what's nice about going to an opera group is going with someone. And you can help each other with lines and things when you're at home. It's not the same going on your own."

"Well, in that case," said Sophie, it's time you met someone. Time you got yourself another woman."

"I don't want to get married again, thank you very much."

"Who said anything about marriage?" said Sophie. "Just a girlfriend."

"Oh no, don't get married again," joined in Kezzie. "Don't get serious with anyone. We want you to stay here just as you are for us to come to see you."

"That's really selfish, Kezzie," joined in Jeremy.

"No it's not!"

"Yes it is!"

"Shut up, you two!" cut in Sophie. "Look, Dad, ignore Kezzie. Just go out there and find yourself a girlfriend."

"But who'd be interested in a middle-aged guy who's never around at weekends?" replied David.

"Well, you never know until you try," insisted Sophie. "You might meet someone who works awkward shifts. It might suit them very well. And you're not old. In fact you're even quite good looking!"

"Oh, I wouldn't quite go that far!" giggled Kezzie.

"Thanks a bunch!" laughed David.

"No, but you are!" continued Sophie. "There must be lots of women who would like you."

"She's right actually, Dad," agreed Kezzie, "but don't go for anyone under forty-five!"

"Why not?" asked David.

" 'cos I couldn't cope with you seeing anyone of our age. It's, um, a bit yukky!"

"God, you're so immature!" cut in Jeremy. "And to think that you're the oldest one here. How come you can't bear the thought of Dad with a younger woman? Why shouldn't he?

Kezzie squirmed in her seat. "Well, I'd rather not say in front of Freddy, but, well, you know, it's all a bit, um, yukky."

"So you said," barked Jeremy.

"Well," said David, looking very serious, "I appreciate the concern you have for me, Kezzie, but I'm just fine actually, and I've been meaning to tell you that I've written off to a marriage agency for a Thai teen bride. Apparently they're queuing up to meet Western men like me. In fact I'm meeting one next week."

"You're not!" screamed Kezzie. "I don't believe you!"

Jeremy laughed. "He's pulling your leg, Kezzie," he said.

"All I am saying," continued David, "is that there is still life in the old dog yet. So watch this space. I'm sorry if you find the notion of inter-generational copulation yukky Kezzie, but there it is. And anyway, you'd be the first one to complain if I disapproved of someone you met simply because of their age, or the colour of their skin. Think about it!"

"Well said, Dad!" said Sophie.

"Well said, Dad!" mimicked Freddy, from under the table.

"Shut up, Freddy!" laughed Sophie, "or you won't have any ice cream."

* * * * * *

David sat with a cup of tea and reflected on the day. He'd dropped Kezzie off at the station, and Sophie and Jeremy at their respective flats, and Rachael had collected Freddy. Suddenly, the house was quiet again.

He reflected on all the talk about joining an opera group and finding a girlfriend. He knew they meant well, but maybe they under-estimated the dislocation the Leeds trips would cause to his life. It would be impossible to have any regular commitments at least until Freddy had grown up. Freddy needed his company, and that took a lot of time. He had always put his family first, and that wasn't about to change. The idea of seeing an escort occasionally would fit the bill perfectly. Just a stop-gap for a few years until his commitment to Freddy was less time-consuming. No commitment, no burden, no fuss. And maybe, in the meantime, he might just have that chance encounter, but while he was waiting, he need not be alone every evening . . . purely medicinal, as John would say.

* * * * * *

"Hello? Is that Victoria?" David was on the phone.

"Yes."

"Oh, hello, this is David. From Westley. We spoke last week."

"Oh, yes. Hello David. And how are you?"

"Fine, fine. I was just wondering whether you had been able to find someone for me."

"I certainly have. I was waiting for you to call. There's good news, and bad."

"Oh?"

"The good news is that I"ve found just the girl for you. I think you'll be very pleased this time."

"Good. And the bad news?"

"She's in London until next week. She won't be available until a week on Monday."

"Oh." David was disappointed. Eight days to wait. "Can you, um, tell me something about her?"

"I certainly can. Her name is Miranda. She's twenty-one – a genuine twenty-one! – and five feet eight inches tall."

"Oh, quite tall then."

"Yes, she's done a lot of modelling apparently."

"Really?"

"Yes. She's very slim, with a firm figure, and a very lively personality."

"Has she done much escorting before?"

"No, only for about a month. Don't worry, she's not a hardened professional, like Geraldine."

100

"Oh, well, that's a relief."

"No. I think her modelling work has dried up a bit and she simply needs the money. So, is it a 'yes' then?"

"Yes. Next Monday will be fine. Just call me to confirm will you, and then we can arrange a pick-up place."

* * * * * *

David handed Miranda a glass of Archers and lemonade.

"Thenk-cue! You're soo sweet! Mwa, mwa," she mouthed, in a high pitched, sing-song voice, as she took the glass.

He had met her, as arranged, in the shopping centre underground car park, and had at once been startled by her enormous, smiling mouth, and breasts, large, prominent breasts, scarcely covered by the plunging neckline of her tiny dress, which was so short that it fell barely an inch below her bottom. David was relieved and somewhat stunned. Miranda was every man's dream of a page three girl, certainly John's dream, but perhaps David's ideal was something a little less obvious. The breasts were slightly too large, the mouth and eyes too wide, and the lipstick too heavy. As he drove Miranda home, he resolved to put aside his reservations, and enjoy himself.

Miranda walked around the sitting room, taking a close interest in the paintings and photographs on his walls.

"I hear you had a bit of a disappointment last time. Am I more to your taste?"

She opened her eyes impossibly wide, and moved very close to David. He breathed in the scent of her perfume.

"You're lovely," he said. He meant it. "You're really lovely."

"Thenk-cue!" she said again, and leaned forward to kiss him on the cheek. David reached forwards to put his arms around her, but she had already turned back to the pictures.

"Is this a real painting?"

"No, no, just a print. Well, a daguerreotype, actually."

"Lovely!" she sang. "And did you take this photograph - this bird?"

"Yes. It"s a blue heron just taking off. I took it on the Galapagos Islands."

"Soo sweet! Lovely!"

All her sentences climbed a musical scale, descending sharply on the last syllable.

"I must say," stammered David, "you're very attractive. Your figure is superb." He felt embarrassed to hear himself talking in this way.

"Thenk-cue!" she said, an octave higher.

"I hear you've done some modelling."

"Quite a bit actually. I've been in The Sport twice. Do you read it?"

"No, I'm afraid I don't. But I have a friend who does glamour photography. He's not very good though. I reckon I could do better."

"Dyou want to shoot me then? I don't mind."

"Really? Could I?"

"Of course! I'm yours for the hour. Whatever you want. So long as I get a set of prints. Would that be OK?"

"Of course. Yes, I wouldn't mind having a go."

"Fine, we could do it here. The furniture is lovely. It's a good set. Do you have any lighting equipment?"

"Oh, no, I don't. I do all my photography outdoors. But I've got some lamps we could use. Trouble is I've only got a long lens. That's what a use for photographing birds outside, you see."

"Well, you'll just have to use it for photographing this bird inside, won't you."

Miranda loved her own joke, and followed it with a laugh not far short of top C. David winced, and left the room to fetch his camera and lamps. When he returned, Miranda was draping herself over the edge of the settee. "How's this?" she asked.

"Oh, fine, just fine. Look, you just move into any position you think best," he said. "You know far more about this than me."

Miranda sat, kneeled, stood, turned and twisted, while David scurried around, trying to get the best angle each time.

"Want some topless?" asked Miranda, slipping the front of her dress down to her waist before he had the chance to answer. Despite loosing the minimal support of the dress, Miranda's breasts remained high and motionless, as if held in place by some invisible force. David stared.

"You've got very nice, um, breasts, haven't you!"

"Thenk-cue!" chirped Miranda. "I had them done last year. Changed from A to D cup. They told me it would make my fortune, but I'm still waiting," she laughed, squeakily.

"Oh, so they're, um . . ."

"Silicon! Yes. Here, have a squeeze!"

She grabbed David's hand and placed it flat across her left breast. David gently applied a little pressure."

"Go on! Give them a good squeeze! It doesn't hurt!"

David pressed slightly harder. "Yes, very nice. Very firm, I must say."

"They make me feel like a real woman!"

"I imagine they do," said David, quietly removing his hand. "Very nice indeed!"

"Thenk-cue! You're soo sweet!"

Now topless, she went through another series of provocative poses, and David found himself enjoying it more than he expected. He turned lights on and off, and began to decide for himself the positions he wanted her to adopt.

"You're good, darling!" grinned Miranda, lying on her front with her bottom up in the air.

Now it was David's turn to say thank you.

"Knickers off now?" she asked cheerily, rolling onto her back, lifting her hips and sliding her knickers down over her knees, before flicking her foot and sending the knickers across the room." Hope you don't mind me being shaved."

"Oh, no, that's just . . . fine."

"But I won't do any continental shots though. Only artistic."

"Continental?"

"Legs wide open."

"Oh, no, of course."

"Not very refined. Too obvious."

"Yes, I agree," muttered David.

A few minutes later Miranda sat up. "We've only got half an hour left. I don't want to rush you or anything but I do have another appointment later on. So why don't you take your clothes off now and come here and sit next to me on the carpet?"

David quickly removed his clothes, feeling slightly embarrassed about his obvious state of excitement.

"OK," said Miranda, now dropping her voice to a pitch more easy on the normal human ear, "I do hand relief for sixty, French for seventy, and full personal for ninety." She leaned close, pressing her breast against his shoulder and placing her hand on his penis. "So what's it to be?"

"Oh, um, well, the full a la carte, please!" grinned David, nervously, leaning to kiss her.

"Oh, you want kissing too?" she said, pulling back slightly. "I don't normally kiss, but since it's you, well maybe for a little extra . . ."

* * * * * *

David said goodbye to Miranda and a hundred and fifteen pounds, but he was not unhappy this time. He'd thoroughly enjoyed himself. The conversation had been somewhat limited, and her voice had become irritating very quickly, but the rest of it had been wonderful. There hadn't been quite enough kissing, and perhaps not quite the right sort of kissing he'd hoped for, but the actual sex had been marvellous. The feel of her young, firm body wrapped around his was a memory he thought would satisfy his desires for a long time.

But the next morning he awoke with Miranda on his mind, and the craving had returned. Taking photos had been fun, and very erotic. The photos! He had to get the photos developed quickly. He decided to take them to the twenty-four hour service at the local pharmacy.

* * * * * *

John climbed into the front seat of the Bentley next to David.

"Watcha, mate! Feeling fit then?"

"You bet!"

"Well, I"ve got something to show you after the game," said John.

"And I"ve got something to show you too, actually."

"What?"

"You"re not the only one who can take pictures you know," grinned David.

"Oh, not more of your bloody pigeons and blue tits!"

"Pink tits"

"What?"

"Big ones!"

"You're joking! You've taken pics of some bird?"

"Not just some bird, John, Miranda."

"Who the fuck's Miranda?"

* * * * * *

"You dirty old bugger!" exclaimed John, as they sat later, in the bar. "She's fucking gorgeous. Where did you find her?"

"Truth?"

"Truth."

"She came from an escort agency called 'Gentlemen Prefer Blondes'."

"She's an escort?"

"Yes."

"Not a model?"

"She's done modelling too."

"I can see that. But she's an escort?"

"Yes."

"You didn't shag her too, did you?" David grinned sheepishly, and sipped his beer. "You did, didn't you? You lucky bugger! Must've cost you a fortune, a stunner like that."

"A hundred and fifteen."

"Jesus, that's more than 'er at 'ome gives me in pocket money in a month!"

"Rubbish. It's probably not as much as it costs you to hire a model and a studio for an hour, and anyway, what's all this about 'er at 'ome. Anyone would think you were under the thumb."

"I am, I am!" protested John. "You don't know the half of it. I haven't had sex for six months!"

"What? I thought you had sex with all your models."

"Poetic licence, mate, poetic licence. No, it's so long since the missus was in the mood that I think it's healed up!"

They looked at the photographs again.

"Actually, these aren't at all bad," said John. "The lighting's crap, and you've got a bit of red eye on one or two, but for a first time, they're pretty damn good. Nice framing and angles. They're quite artistic."

"As opposed to continental, you mean?"

"Oh, very technical. No, actually, I wouldn't mind having a session with this lady myself. Can I have her number?"

"You'll have to save up your pocket money then!"

"Oh, I"ll manage it, somehow. The missus can go without food. It'll do her good."

* * * * * *

David saw Miranda twice more during the next ten days, and found her as vivacious and energetic as ever, although he began to see cracks in her performance. She was just a little too professional, too detached. He didn't delude himself into thinking that he might find an escort who would actually get pleasure from having sex with him. It was just a job for them, after all, but he hoped that one might let down her guard a little. That would never happen with Miranda. Clearly she was just there for the money, and always thinking about getting to her next job. Perhaps it might be possible to see someone new to escorting, who was still unable to detach sex and love-making from emotion, who might even show genuine feeling. Was that too much to hope?

Over the months David saw escorts at least twice a week, and sometimes even more often. Occasionally, he saw the same one two or three times before, as with Miranda, becoming disillusioned, hoping always that the next one would be different. Some were very beautiful, but cold, and others much plainer, but affectionate. On many occasions he ended up taking photos of girls who had photogenic features, and who seemed keen to prance in front of a camera, but he never forced the issue. He always gave the girl a set of prints, and stashed his copies in an old cardboard box, where they lay, undisturbed. His enjoyment was in the taking of the photographs rather than to look at them or display them afterwards. To some women, he gave his phone number in case they left the agency but still wanted to see him, and others said they had friends who might like to try escorting, and who better to start with than a 'nice man' like David, now well-known as a gentlemen, and good payer, by escorts far and wide.

But David recognised that the craving had become an obsession and, as with many obsessions, he now suffered periods of gloom. He became excited with the anticipation of meeting a new escort, and always went through the same rituals of preparation before each meeting. Conversations for the first half hour were inevitably identical, and the second half hour often became a sweaty rush to complete the task. An hour was never enough, and overnight stays were prohibitively expensive. He invariably ended up after a meeting, alone in the pub, thinking 'so what?' to himself.

He tried giving up escorts for a few weeks or a month at a time, only to surrender to temptation when a particularly captivating voice came on the phone asking to meet him. After a year, he reached the stage when the next one was always going to be the last one. He wanted to get this thing out of his system and return to a normal life, whatever that was. Perhaps, after all, he should take his daughters' advice and join an opera group.

But then, one day, he had a call from someone called Delores.

* * * * * *

"Hello? Yes, speaking... Oh, I see..."

It was a woman calling herself Delores. David sat down and spoke into the phone.

"But who gave you my number?...Oh, right. So are you another agency?... Well, they all say they have girls like that but, to be honest, most size eight super-models are size fourteen housewives the wrong side of thirty. In any case, I haven't been seeing anyone lately. I'm afraid I'm not really interested...Really? Oh well then, go on, describe her...Well, she sounds too good to be true. She sounds just perfect...Well, maybe... How old is she?... Oh, no sorry, I think that's a bit too young. I really don't think I want to meet girl who'd be shy and uncomfortable with a much older man... Really?... But good conversation is also important too . . .Well, you're very convincing. But what if I say 'no' as soon as I see her?... OK, that sounds a good idea. Yes, all right then. Would tomorrow at seven be possible?... Fine... No, no I would prefer to come to collect, if you don't mind... No, I don't know it, but I'm sure I can find it. I'll be in a green Bentley... Yes. OK. Bye."

Could the woman with all her aitches in the wrong places she be believed? An eighteen-year-old? David thought himself mad to be doing this, but the girl's description sounded exciting. Tall and very slim, very pretty, and intelligent, said to like older men. Was all that possible in a girl just eighteen? Why was she doing escort work if she was so outstanding? He often asked himself that question, but several of the students he met, many of whom were heading for the professions, had explained that they could earn as much in one evening doing escort work than they could in a month serving in the local pub. So it made sense. He was giving them the opportunity to earn good money. Girls of his era would never have dreamt of doing such a thing, but these were modern times. Sex no longer held the same taboos for the younger generation. Virginity was a social stigma rather than a virtue, so why shouldn't a girl use her assets to earn money if that's what she wanted to do?

He wasn't quite sure why he was going through all these old arguments again. Was he trying to justify the fact that, yet again, his resolve had weakened, and here he was about to meet another escort? Justifying it on the grounds of altruism or magnanimity was fools' territory. The plain fact was that he had become addicted to young pretty women, and there seemed an endless supply wishing to meet him.

* * * * * *

So it was that he sat in his Bentley in the car park of The Cock and Bull at ten minutes to seven the next evening. With the pub behind him, he looked across the car park and into the road, which climbed steeply up a hill. Would they come? He had been let down many times before. He had become philosophical about it. If they didn't turn up, or were late, then that told him all he wanted to know about their characters. Reliability and punctuality counted a lot for him. His whole life had been shaped by it. He couldn't make exceptions for escorts, unless the excuses rang true. But he

110

need not have worried this time. Just as the minute hand of his car clock moved on to the hour, he noticed two figures at the top of the hill walking down towards him, one old, very thin, and slightly bent, walking awkwardly, and the other, short and plump, her thighs rubbing together. As they got nearer, David looked away, hoping that these were not the women he was waiting to meet. But they crossed the car park, and headed towards him. The older woman was looking directly at him, the younger one, her face red with the exertion, was now trailing a few yards behind. David shifted in his seat, uncomfortably, but rolled down his window.

" 'ello? Are you David? I'm Delores. And this 'ere his Avril."

Avril stood slightly behind Doreen, looking embarrassed. David quickly looked her up and down, noticing her blotchy skin, and fat thighs, accentuated by a pair of ridiculously ill-fitting pink shorts.

"Um, hello. Uh, look, I'm sorry, but I'm going to have to say no. Your young lady isn't to my taste. Please don't take offence, but . . ."

Doreen moved close to the open window and spoke quietly. David noticed that she had no upper teeth, and her face seemed to have collapsed into her mouth. Deep lines were gouged into her cheeks, and her breath smelt heavily of strong tobacco.

"Oh, no, hit's hall right, David. I didn"t hexpect you would like Avril, see? Mandy's on her way. She was slightly delayed. She'll be with us at hany moment. Do you think I could sit in the car and wait?"

"Oh, um, well if you're sure she's coming," said David, reluctantly.

Doreen walked around to the passenger door and opened it.

"Get in the back, Av," she said. "Oh yes, she's coming hall right", she said, as she climbed in the front, next to David.

"So, um, who was it gave you my number then?" he asked.

"A girl called Stacey. Met you through an agency. Pretty girl."

"Oh, yes, I remember Stacey. I caught her stealing from me, I'm afraid."

"Yes, she told me. She's very sorry about that. You know "ow hit is. Some of these girls can't 'elp themselves. I blame the parents myself. Don't bring 'em hup right. Poor 'omes. You know. You won't have that problem from Mandy. She's well brought up, she his. Known 'er hall my life, I 'ave. She's a good girl"

* * * * * *

Mandy had refused to walk down the hill with them.

"It's too fuckin" obvious!" she had said to her mother. "I'm not walkin' down that fuckin' 'ill with Avril dressed like a blow-up doll, and you in them shoes what's too tight for yuh. Everyone in the fuckin' road will know whass goin' on. We should've said we'd meet 'im in town. Look you two go first, and I'll come a few minutes later."

The truth was that Mandy wanted to make a grand entrance. She knew she looked good, and that her walk always attracted a lot of wolf whistles. The last thing she wanted was to be cramped by her mother on one side and Avril on the other. Besides, it sometimes paid to keep men waiting – just a little while. She wanted to heighten the anticipation. To make him slightly desperate, to take him almost to the point where he wanted to give up, but then to

112

arrive and fawn all over him with apologies. It was always a good ice-breaker.

She set off down the hill. It was a pleasant summer evening. At the last moment she had decided to put on a long open waistcoat to match her skirt, but which would float open as and when needed to reveal the skimpiness of her white top. The incline of the hill forced her weight forward in her shoes, giving her slightly more bounce than usual, and she could feel her breasts rising and falling with every step.

David could tell from the moment he saw the distant figure coming down the hill that she was exceptionally beautiful, even long before he could discern any features. There was something in the way a young and beautiful girl walked that spoke a language of its own. When driving, he had often noticed girls walking with their backs to him, and he always thought he could tell whether one would be attractive simply by the way she walked. As Mandy came closer, his initial impression was confirmed, and the closer she came, the prettier she seemed. He could see that she walked loosely and neatly; that her hips were narrow and her legs extremely long and slim; that her breasts were full and high; that her hair was long and wavey, and shone in the evening sun. And by the time she reached the car park, he was marvelling at her large almond-shaped eyes, and perfect complexion. When she drew near, she smiled at him, and he found himself smiling back. She walked to his side of the car, and put on her best accent.

"Oh, hello, David. I'm so sorry I'm late."

She stooped and pushed her head through his open window and kissed him lightly on the cheek.

"This is Mandy," said Doreen, proudly, baring her gums in a sickly grin. "I 'ope you're not still disappointed."

David looked at Mandy. They both smiled.

"No, not at all," he said to Doreen, without looking away from Mandy.

"Right, we'll leave you to it then," said Doreen. "Come on, Avril."

Avril's thighs squeaked on the leather seat as she twisted to clamber out of the back of the car. Doreen held open the front passenger door for Mandy, who walked around and slid in gracefully, next to David.

"OK, thanks, Delores," said Mandy. "See you later then."

Doreen turned to go, her arm firmly gripping Avril, as they started to climb the hill.

" 'Oo's Delores?" Avril could be heard to grumble, and she began panting again.

* * * * * *

David sat still for just a moment, watching the two figures going awkwardly up the hill. He turned to Mandy and smiled again. She smiled back, but neither spoke. He reached forwards, turning the key in the ignition, and steered out of the car park onto the road. The hydraulics gave out tiny puffs and hisses as the wide tyres crunched powerfully over the uneven surface.

Mandy sat in the middle of the big leather seat, and looked down at the walnut facia and silver knobs. The big car rolled like a silent ship. Around her open-toed shoes Mandy could feel the thick lambs' wool caressing her toes. She stretched her legs into the deep footwell.

David drove on. He couldn't resist glancing sideways. Mandy was sitting very upright. She moved her legs, stretching them forwards, and seemed to be rubbing her feet gently against the rug. Her waistcoat hung down loosely and, from the corner of his eye he could see her breasts pushing forwards, with just a small inverted triangle of thin white cotton material covering her nipples.He called to mind the statuette of Marianne, which had been modelled by a young Brigitte Bardot in the nineteen fifties, and which had adorned every town hall in France for nearly half a century. It showed a very slim torso with full, perfectly-formed breasts, and a face with a tiny nose, large eyes, and generous, pouting lips. If ever there was a rival for this image, it was the girl now sitting next to him.

He turned onto the ring road, and the car came to a standstill in the outside lane of two lines of traffic.

"Looks like there's been an accident or something," he said. "Nothing's moving."

Mandy sat forwards and leaned across him to look past the vehicle in front. As she did so, she briefly placed one hand on top of his thigh.

"Never mind," she said. "We're not in a hurry, are we?"

Every time he looked at her, he couldn't stop smiling, and she always smiled back in a big wide smile, her pink tongue and small white teeth teasing and arousing him. "Well, I'm not, if you're not," he said.

"Would you mind if I take off my shoes?" she asked.

"No, of course not. Take off whatever you like!"

He wished immediately he hadn't said that. It sounded crass, but she just smiled again. Instead of bending forwards to undo her shoe, she lifted one thigh and then the other, up to her chest, and reached forwards with both arms to release the buckles in front of her, with each foot in the air. David looked down at the long underside of her thighs, now revealed to him all the way to her bottom, and saw the small strip of her white knickers between her legs. Mandy dropped her legs and pushed her feet forwards into the thick lambs' wool, and wriggled her toes.

"It's lovely and soft!" she said. "I'll just slip off my waistcoat too, if that's OK. It'll get creased if I sit on it too long."

She slipped each arm out of the waistcoat and lifted her bottom to pull it free, before twisting around towards him, and placing it on the rear seat. As she turned, David glanced down at her breasts again, now just inches from his face. Each breast strained against the skimpy top, which was clearly unable to cope with any degree of movement without spilling its contents.

Mandy turned back. David now noticed the split running all the way up her skirt, and saw that two of the fastening rings had become detached from their eyes at hip level. Here, the skirt puckered, and he could see inside. The traffic moved on a few yards, and then stopped again. David pulled the automatic gear lever into drive, and inched forwards to close the gap.

"Would you mind if we had some music on, David?"

"No," he said, 'help yourself."

Mandy twiddled with the controls of the radio. As she reached forwards, the thin strap on her right shoulder slipped down, and her right breast fell loose. David looked, and was unable, this time, to look away when she saw him looking. She pretended not to realise that she was exposed. She smiled again, and continued to tune the radio. "Is this OK?" she asked, turning her head sideways. She had found Classic FM, and one of Mozart"s Violin Concertos was playing.

"Fine. But are you sure you like it?"

Mandy sat back and looked down at her naked breast. She lifted the strap back onto her shoulder, smiling again.

"Whoops!" she said. "Do you like it?" He grinned, looking back at her breasts, now covered. "The music, I mean," she said, her eyes twinkling.

"Yes, I love it," he said.

"Then so do I. Very peaceful."

She looked at his lap and smiled when she saw the effect her teasing was having on him. "Would you like me to give you a blow job?" she asked.

David broke into a loud laugh. "What? Here?"

She edged close to him and immediately started to undo his trousers with her nimble, thin fingers. "Why not?" she said.

"But someone might see. That guy in the lorry next to you has been looking down at you for the last ten minutes as it is. He'll see what's going on."

But despite his protests David was hugely excited, and made no attempt to stop her.

"Let him see! I don't care. Let's give him a free show!" she giggled, pulling David's erect penis free of his trousers, and lying down with her head in his lap. "You just concentrate on the road, and I'll concentrate on you."

She kissed and licked him slowly, and David moaned with pleasure.

"It's very nice," she said. "Smells good. Nice shape. Big too. Umm. I can't wait to feel this inside me." She slowly slid her mouth over and down his penis. He tensed slightly, surprised that she took him so deeply. She shifted her position so that she was now kneeling on the seat with her bottom in the air, and David reached across with his free hand to gently stroke her back and bottom.

"You'd better stop before it's too late!" he gasped.

She lifted her head. "It's all right. I don't mind. I want you to finish – if you want to. I'd like you to. I want to taste you."

"What? You don't mind if . . ."

"I want to . . . just relax, David." She turned back to her task and, in less than a minute, David arched his back and groaned, as Mandy expertly brought him to climax. "You taste nice. I knew you would," she said, her head still in his lap.

The traffic moved forwards again, and a loud horn sounded. Mandy sat up and looked sideways. The lorry driver was grinning and gesticulating with his fingers. The jam had cleared, and now, they were moving at speed.

"Should I turn around and take you back?" said David. "It's been quite a long time, and we've already, you've already . . ."

The corners of Mandy's mouthed turned downwards, and she looked disappointed. "Oh. You don't like me then, after all."

"Of course I like you. You're absolutely gorgeous. Stunning. I've never met an escort like you. In fact, I've never met any woman like you. But my time will be over before we get to my house, and . . ."

"Please don't take me back, David. Not yet. I'm enjoying myself. Unless you want to, of course. But if I can come back with you, well, I'll do anything you want. Anything. Or if you don't want to do anything, that's OK too. Whatever you say."

"I'd love to take you to my home, really. I just thought my time was up, and that you'd need to get back."

"Thank you, David. You won't be disappointed."

"I know that, Mandy. You've already exceeded my wildest expectations. Anything else is a bonus."

Mandy reached up with her right arm and put her hand behind David's head, stroking the nape of his neck with her long fingernails. She rested her head against his shoulder, and took his free hand, and kissed and slowly sucked each finger in turn, before placing the hand between her thighs.

David parked the car in front of the garage, and then walked Mandy around to the front door. She slipped her hand into his as they walked. Once inside the large hall they stood facing one another. He put his hands on her hips.

"Gosh, with those heels on, you're almost as tall as me!" he said, drawing her close.

"Yes," she said, smiling, "but my waist is higher. I have longer legs but a shorter body. We can have sex standing up!"

"I think I'd rather get you to the bedroom for that!" he laughed.

She put her arms around his shoulders and drew herself close. He felt her breasts and hips pressing against him. He leaned to kiss her and she opened her mouth wide, pushing her tongue in deeply. It was a long kiss.

"You kiss!" he exclaimed, pulling back. "Some girls don't kiss. Well, certainly not like that!"

"I don't kiss anyone. Kissing is special. Just for you, David."

"I'm very flattered."

He looked her up and down again. She stood, just enjoying his admiration.

"Seen enough?" she laughed.

"No way! I could never tire of looking at you. Tell me, what modelling have you done? Delores said you were a model."

"Oh, well, that was a bit of an exaggeration, I'm afraid. I haven't done any modelling. I'd really like to though."

"What?" David was genuinely shocked. "I just can't believe that you haven't been snapped up by some modelling agency. I'll be honest with you, Mandy, and this isn't bullshit,

I think you're really very beautiful. You're quite exceptional. Surely you've been told that a hundred times."

Mandy smiled. "Well, yes, but not by anyone like you. I'd like to model, to act, anything like that. I'd love to be famous. But I don't know where to start."

"Well, first you need to get a portfolio done and then go to model agencies, I guess."

"But don't the portfolios cost a lot?"

"They can do. I'd do it for nothing, but I'm not a professional photographer."

"Would you? Would you really? You'd take photos of me?"

"Mandy, men would fall over themselves to take photos of you, really! Of course I will. I'd love to, but I really don't think I'd do you justice. You really need proper studio shots."

"But will you take some first, so that I can just see them? I've never had any done before."

"Of course I will. No problem."

Mandy looked around the hall. "It's so big! Can I have a guided tour?"

"Sure. What, the whole house, you mean?"

"Yes please."

"OK, well let's start with the downstairs."

He took her into the sitting room, and she gasped. "My mam's whole house would fit into this! And it's so clean and tidy. All those nice pictures and ornaments! You've got a lovely 'ome, David." When they came to his study she gasped again. "So many books! Shelves and shelves of them. Have you read them all? We haven't got any books in our house."

"What, none at all?"

"Don't think so. I haven't seen any."

David frowned. He walked towards the shelves and took down a book. "Here, Mandy, this is you."

"What?" She moved beside him and looked at the pages as he flicked through.

"It's Manga art," he explained. "Cartoon girls with impossibly large eyes, impossibly small noses, impossibly wide mouths. Tiny chins. The slimmest of rib cages, breasts to die for, and legs that go on forever."

"They're lovely, aren't they? But my tits aren't that big!" protested Mandy.

"You'd be deformed if they were," he laughed, "but you're the nearest thing to a living Manga girl I"ve ever seen. I mean, just look at you! Unlike the Manga, you're real! My real little Manga girl."

Mandy smiled. "Cool. I like it when you say I'm your girl."

"Well, you are. Here, you keep this book. Take it home with you."

Mandy gasped. "For me? To keep? As a present, you mean? Oh, David, thank you. That's so nice. I'll always keep it."

As they were walking out of the room Mandy picked up a small wooden statuette of a naked girl, and ran her fingers over it.

"This is nice! Where did you get it?"

"Brazil."

"Oh."

"In South America."

"Oh. Do you go there a lot then?"

"Well, I've been there a couple of times. I go abroad quite a lot."

"I've never been abroad. I'd love to go."

David frowned again. "Well, I'm sure you will. I hadn't been anywhere much when I was your age. When you're a famous model, you'll go everywhere."

Mandy laughed. "Well, I haven't been anywhere at all yet. D'you know, I haven't even seen the sea. Not in real life."

"But didn't your parents ever take you on holiday?"

Mandy laughed again. "Holiday? No. I grew up with my mam. Never knew my dad. She couldn't afford it."

"Oh, well, that's a shame. Well, why don't I take you to see the sea?"

"What? Would you? Would you really?"

"Why not? It's only a two-hour drive. We could have a day at the seaside. I'd like to see you in a bikini on the beach – or preferably not in a bikini!"

Mandy threw her arms around him. "Thank you, David. I'd really love that! Come on then, show me the rest."

They finished wandering around the remaining ground floor rooms and then headed for the stairs. Mandy climbed the stairs with David close behind, watching the way the cheeks of her bottom moved beneath her tight skirt. Just before she reached the top step he placed both hands on her bottom. She stopped, and leaned back towards him, pausing.

"Sorry, Mandy, but I"ve just got to do this," he said. "I can't resist it."

He dropped both hands to the hem of her skirt and pulled it briskly upwards, exposing her naked bottom. Far from objecting, she bent forwards, putting both hands on the top stair in front, inviting him to continue. Her bottom was at his face level, her legs slightly apart. He gently kneaded her cheeks with his hands, kissing and licking her at the same time.

"That's nice," she said. "Don't stop!"

Encouraged by her enthusiasm, he pulled apart the cheeks and licked her deeply with a long slow action. She trembled, and her knees started to buckle. He twisted her around and pushed her back, so that she was lying on the landing, with him still on the stairs. He lifted her legs onto his shoulders and his mouth came to rest against her small tuft of soft, dark, pubic hair. Using his thumbs, he very gently opened the lips of her vagina, and pushed the tip of his tongue against her clitoris. She trembled again, and put her hands around his head, grasping his ears. He continued to lick her as her thighs locked around him.

"Oh, David, David. No one's ever done that to me. Oh, it's, it's, ohhh . . ."

David continued for several minutes, while she moaned and sighed.

"David! I want you to fuck me. Please, fuck me. Now! Fuck me 'ard!"

David kicked off his shoes and quickly dropped his trousers. Mandy reached down for him and gabbed his penis firmly with both hands, drawing him toward her, her long legs spreading wide. He placed both hands under her bottom, and lifted her hips, as he slid into the wet warmth of her, and she trembled again as she felt him enter. Now he was on his knees, pushing and thrusting against her, and Mandy was calling out.

"More, David! Come on! More!"

He removed his hands from her bottom and placed them under her legs, lifting them high until her knees were pinned down on each side of her head. Her hands grabbed at his back and bottom, her fingernails digging in deeply, as he drove her backwards across the landing carpet, and in a very short time, she shuddered as she felt him climax.

They lay quite still.

"That was my first time," she whispered.

He lifted his head. "First time? What d'you mean?"

"The first time I've ever cum. Except in the shower, by myself."

"That's unbelievable. Really?"

"Yes, really. Thank you."

"No. Thank you. It wasn't my first time, probably my ten thousandth time, but, my god, I don't remember a time like it before. Mandy, you are truly amazing."

"Yeah, I can die happy now."

David chuckled. "You can say that again. Shag Mandy and die – a variation on the Venice theme. We didn't make it to the bedroom, after all! Come on, let's go for a shower. Look at the state you're in!"

She was now naked except for her shoes and the remains of her skirt and top, both now hanging around her waist.

"You can talk. You didn't even take your socks off!"

He put his hands under her, and she clung to him with arms and legs as he lifted her up and carried her towards the shower.

"There you go," she laughed. "You're still in me! I said we could do it standing up!"

* * * * * *

"Can I wear this?"

Mandy walked into the bathroom where David was still drying himself. She had been into his wardrobe and was wearing one of his shirts.

"Of course you can. Why is it that girls always look so sexy in men's shirts? Mind you, I guess you'd look sexy in an old sack! You're just a clothes horse, aren't you? Are you hungry?"

"Not really. Maybe a bit. Are you going to eat now?"

"Maybe just a nibble. Why don't I rustle up something? We'll go into the sitting room and talk about taking some photos of you. Unless of course, you need to be going now. God knows how much this is costing me," he said laughing.

"David, please don't."

"Sorry? Don't what?"

"Please don't keep asking me if I want to go, and please don't talk about money, OK?"

David looked serious. "Oh, um, well, maybe we need to get that straight though because I don't want there to be any embarrassing misunderstandings later."

"David, shut up. There won't be, OK? Please. Now, can I help you in the kitchen?"

* * * * * *

Fifteen minutes later they sat in the sitting room in the middle of the large Chinese rug, nibbling salt biscuits and salad. Mandy drank lemonade from a champagne glass.

"Are you sure you don't want anything stronger?" David asked, as he poured himself a beer.

"No, this is fine. I don't like alcohol. So what do I do then? Does it all happen on that settee where the lights are shining?"

"Well, we can do some outside while it's still light enough. You'll have to pop your clothes on again, or I guess you could just wear some of my stuff if you want."

"That would be funky! Maybe a bit of both. I wish I'd brought more clothes with me."

"We don't have to do it all today. Next time, you can bring whatever you like."

"OK. So today we can concentrate on taking the nude ones then, yes?"

"Nude? If you want to. It's up to you."

"Course I do. I reckon I'm as good as them girls, uh, those girls you see in the Star and the Sun."

"Better. Much better."

"Well, there you go then. Let's do some really dirty ones!"

David laughed.

"I love your sense of adventure, Mandy. You just don't give a damn, do you? It's so exciting. So sexy."

"Is it? Good. OK, Mr Photographer, how d'you want me then?"

* * * * * *

An hour later they sat drinking coffee. Mandy hadn't bothered to put any clothes back on, and was sitting cross-legged on a large Victorian arm chair. David was removing the last film from his camera.

"Have you got a video camera?" she asked.

"Yes. Why?"

" 'cos I"d like to film us having sex, then watch it on TV afterwards. Could we do that?"

David burst into laughter.

"I"m not sure if the battery is charged up, and even if it is, I think my own battery is completely flat."

"What d'you mean?"

"Mandy, I'm an old man."

"Fuck off! Course you're not! You practically killed me upstairs, you were so strong and powerful. Old man, my arse!"

David laughed again. "What I mean is that tonight, for the first time in about thirty years I've had two orgasms in the space of about an hour-and-a-half, and now you're suggesting that I do it again. Sorry, sweetheart, but I just can't manage it."

Mandy smiled, licked her finger, opened her legs, and played with herself, provocatively.

"I bet you can. Come on, me 'oneypot''s getting wet again."

David shook his head, smiling.

"Look, I know I will shoot myself tomorrow for this, but I really can't. The spirit is willing but the body is weak."

"Well, you're wrong, and I will prove it to you. Get the video camera – please."

David grinned, and went to do as he was told. He set the camera on a tripod, pointing towards Mandy, and turned it on.

"The battery is fine. OK, it's rolling. Action! Take one."

Mandy giggled. "Hi, Mam," she said, looking at the camera, "this is your naughty little girl here, playing with her pussy, and in a minute, that big bad man over there is gonna come over and stick his big thing in!"

She used her fingers to spread herself wide, and made a series of panting noises.

"Very good!" laughed David, clapping.

"Come over here, big boy," she beckoned.

David sauntered over and kneeled down in front of her.

"Are you sure you haven't done this before?" he asked. "You're very good."

She deliberately misunderstood him. "Oh no, sir, I'm just a pure little virgin! Please be gentle with me! Don't hurt me will you? This is my first time."

David pawed her in a half-hearted fashion. Mandy stopped acting, and looked at him.

"You're not really into this are you, David? Here let me help."

She kneeled in front of him and began removing his clothes. She then made him lie down on his front while she ran her fingers up and down his back, taking care to end each stroke between his legs, where she paused, allowing the tip of her fingers to brush against his genitals. She followed this by doing the same thing using her tongue, licking slowly down his back and ending between his legs, her long hair and breasts brushing lightly against his back and bottom as she moved down. As she buried her face into him and reached out with her tongue, David squirmed and groaned with pleasure.

When she was sure he was responding, she beckoned him to turn over and began the same procedure on his front, finishing each action at his now-erect penis. David moaned and sighed constantly. Eventually, Mandy stood each side of his hips, taking his penis between her hands, and slowly lowered herself onto him, going into a deep squat while remaining on her feet. From this position, she began to bounce up and down on him, placing her hands firmly on his chest, and allowing her hair to dangle in his face. David reached forwards and held her thighs as they moved. Soon Mandy was panting and moaning as much as David, and at the moment of his climax, she pushed down on him hard, rotating her hips and feeling him pulsate deep inside her. They both yelled out, and then she collapsed on top of him.

A tear rolled out of the corner of one of David's eyes. Mandy saw it, and licked it off.

"Well, old man, how does that feel? Thought your battery was flat?"

"You're fucking amazing, Mandy. Fucking amazing," moaned David."

Mandy laughed, causing a strong contraction which expelled David from her.

"Ooo, sorry," she said, "that's messy! Where are the tissues?"

She wiped them both clean and they showered again, before cuddling up on the settee to watch the video.

"So cool!" exclaimed Mandy. "You can see everything. You look enormous. How does it go in there?"

"You look gorgeous!" he replied. "Look how slim you are! Look at the way your breasts move. You're so fit and slim. Watching you do that is like watching ballet. You're so light and strong."

"I could be a porno movie star!"

"Sweetheart, you ARE a porno movie star!"

"Will you show it to anyone?"

"Not on your life. Never. This is private. Between me and you. I'll keep it safe so that one day I can watch it and remember the sexiest evening of my life. I really mean that, Mandy. Thank you."

"My pleasure, sir. Glad to have been of service."

* * * * * *

As they were about to leave David opened his wallet and began counting out money. He handed her a wad of notes.

"Thank you for a wonderful evening, Mandy. I do hope we can make this a regular thing."

"No, David. I don't want any money."

"What? Don't be silly. You've been with me nearly five hours. Any other girl would be charging me a fortune for that."

"Well, I'm not any other girl. OK, so I came for money, that's true, but I've had a lovely time, and you've taken my photos and said you'll take me to the seaside, and given me a book, so I just don't want money from you as well. Maybe I am being silly, but that's the way it is. Anyway, maybe you won't believe this, but that's the first time I've really enjoyed sex in my life, so perhaps I should pay you."

"I just don't know what to say. I . . ."

"Just take me home, David, before I jump on you again!

* * * * * *

"Mandy? You in there? Come on, bab, get up! You got a punter waiting downstairs, an' another comin' at two o'clock."

It was the next day, and Mandy had locked her bedroom door.

"Mand?" called Doreen, again. " Can you 'ear me? Open the fuckin' door!"

The door opened a few inches, and Mandy put her head in the gap.

"What d'you want?"

"You knows what I want. You ain't deaf, gel. Now come on. Get some nice gear on, and I'll send 'im up."

"Oh, Mam, tell Avril. I'm still sleepy."

" 'e won't go with Avril."

"Well, I'm sorry, but I'm not seeing anyone today. I really can't be bothered."

"Really can't be bothered? Oh, 'ark at you, you little madam! Wass with all the posh talk then? You ain't with your Mr David La de Dah now, yuh know."

"It's how I like talking."

"Since when?"

"Since now!"

Mandy slammed the door and Doreen heard the bolt click.

"You fuckin' little cow! We'll lose a regular customer. I needs 'is twenny quid. Fuck you!"

* * * * * *

David awoke and thought it had all been a dream. Had he really made love three times to the most beautiful girl he had ever seen? And was he fooling himself to think that she seemed to enjoy it, or was she just an extremely good actor? But she hadn't even wanted money. Then again, maybe that was just a clever ploy, almost like a free trial before he was expected to pay enormous sums once he was hooked. No, he was being too cynical. She wasn't that devious, was she? Or had she got even greater designs on him? Surely she didn't think that he'd want her to move in? No. She was far too young. It wouldn't work. How could he explain her to his family? Ridiculous notion. But he knew he had to see her again, and as soon as possible.

He dressed and took the films to the pharmacy. He couldn't wait to see them. He hoped that some would be good enough for a portfolio, but if not, it would provide a good excuse to take more. He could go on taking photos of Mandy forever.

* * * * * *

"Hello, is that David?"

The phone had rung several times that afternoon and each time David had rushed to pick it up, hoping that it might be Mandy. So stupid, he thought, cursing himself for acting like a lovesick teenager. So when it really was her voice, he felt his heart beating fast with excitement.

"Yes! Hi, Mandy. I was hoping it was you."

"Were you? Really? So last night was all right then? So you want to see me again then?"

131

"You bet. As soon as possible."

"I could come tonight, if you like. I could come now!"

"Oh, sweetheart, don't tempt me. But I can't, I really can't. I'm playing squash this evening, and tomorrow I'm off to Leeds for the weekend."

"The weekend?" Mandy sounded disappointed. "So you don't want to see me until next week?"

"I want to, Mandy, but I just can't. I'm back on Tuesday morning. Are you free on Tuesday evening?"

"Yes. So you do like me then?"

David was bemused by her lack of confidence. The night before she had been so full of herself, so much in control, she could do anything with him, and she knew it. Now she seemed uncertain. She obviously needed reassuring.

"Listen, Mandy, not only are you the most attractive girl I've ever met, but you're lively, funny, exciting, good company and incredibly, amazingly sexy. If I don't see you on Tuesday, I'll go crazy, I really will."

"We'll both go crazy then," she laughed. "What would you like me to wear?"

"Nothing!"

"No problem."

"You mean that, don't you! Well, you'd better wear something – at least, until you get in the car."

"OK, I'll see if I can find a bit of dental floss. See you Tuesday!"

* * * * * *

After the squash game David and John sat in the bar, David with his back to the door. He had said nothing about Mandy, or told John much about his escorts recently, and had only showed him the photos of one other, besides Miranda. It was clear to him that John's talk about girls was all wishful thinking, and David didn't like boasting about the women he'd met. In any case, these girls weren't conquests, so there was nothing to boast about. They were simply business arrangements. Nevertheless, he knew it would make John jealous if he talked too much, and he wanted to preserve their friendship. Far better to let John go on with his boasting, and keep him guessing.

John was in the middle of explaining how David could improve some of his squash shots when he stopped mid-sentence, his mouth open.

"Will you look at that! No don't, she looking."

"Who?" asked David.

"The most incredible girl. My God, just look at that figure. That's unbelievable. Oh my God, watch out, she's heading this way."

David twisted around in his seat. It was Mandy. She was wearing tight waistless trousers, slung very low across the hips, and with a dip at the front to a point several six inches below her navel, and which clung tightly between the legs, showing every contour. Her midriff was bare and she wore a flimsy bra top, little more that two tiny pieces of cloth and held together with string, so that only the tips of her breasts were covered.

She smiled when she saw David, walked straight up to him, and sat facing him with her legs either side of the arm of his chair, and her back to John.

David was so surprised that he showed no emotion, not even recognition. John's eyes had glazed over. A small dribble had run from the corner of his mouth, and was making its way down his chin.

"Hello, darling," said Mandy, taking David's head in her hands, and kissing him noisily and wetly on the mouth. "I was just passing, and I remembered you were playing. Your face is so red! Must've been a good game. D'you like my easy-fuck trousers?"

She lifted one leg up, placing her foot on the arm of his chair, allowing him to inspect her crotch from very close quarters. David looked down and now noticed a split between the legs of her trousers. He could see that she was not wearing knickers, and the lips of her vagina protruded through the slit. His mouth opened, but he said nothing. Behind him John had turned to stone. Mandy continued.

"Oh, I see you're busy, so I won't stay. See you on Tuesday. Bye."

She got up and walked out, all eyes following her bottom, as she went briskly back across the room to the door.

"Who the hell was that?" asked John, after a silence of several seconds. David didn't reply. "This has got to be a wind-up," continued John. "How much did you pay someone for that, you dirty bugger! She's a strip-o-gram girl, isn't she? Well, I'll be fucked! She can strip my gram any day! She was real class. Top class. Did you see those trousers? They were so low at the front, you could see the top of her pubes, you really could! And those boobs. Oh my God. What a doll! What I wouldn't do to her. Come on, what's it all about? Who's birthday is it?"

David smiled. Mandy had done this deliberately. He'd told her he was playing squash, and she'd come all this way just for that little performance. Any brief feeling of being angry with her for doing this in front of John quickly passed when he thought about the sheer audacity of it. She was so exciting. So cheeky. So sexy. And what was she trying to tell him?

"Birthday?" he said at last. "Mine, mate. Mine"

* * * * * *

David could hear a magpie squawking. He opened his eyes. What day was it? And then he remembered. He turned his head, and looked at Mandy, sleeping next to him. She had stayed the night. He put his hand around her tiny waist and stroked her, moving it over her hip and the down around the curve of her bottom, before slipping his fingers between her legs. She stirred and rolled over towards him, lifting her arm up, and putting her hand around his neck. He leaned down and carefully placed his mouth over one nipple, sucking it slowly up into his mouth.

Mandy murmured. "You ready again, you sex maniac?" she said, sleepily. "Can't a girl get no rest?"

"Get any rest," he corrected. "I'm just admiring the view."

"And 'elping yourself."

"That's right!"

"Well, you'll just have to 'ang on a mo – I need a pee."

She threw back the duvet and bounded out of bed into the bathroom. He lay back listening to the splashing noise.

"Can I come and help?" he called.

"Help what?"

"Help you pee?"

"If you like."

He jumped up and went in to kneel in front of her as she sat there. He pushed his hand between her legs, allowing the urine to trickle between his fingers.

"You dirty old pervert!" she laughed. "Stop it!"

He took some tissue and wiped her dry before washing his hands.

"I've never done that before," he said. "Just suddenly thought of it."

135

"Was it nice?"

"Actually, it was warm, and really sexy. Look what it's done to me!"

"Oo yes, so I see. Well, we'd better do something about that. Can't waste it."

* * * * * *

Afterwards, David lay on his back with Mandy nestling into him.

"Why did you come to the Leisure Centre last week?" asked David.

"Just wanted to see you. Just felt like it."

"I was cross at first, then I felt really pleased. You looked sensational. John, the guy I was with, wouldn't stop talking about you. Said he could see the top of your pussy."

"He could! I pushed the trousers low deliberately. And he would have seen the rest too if he looked through the split! But that was for you, not for him. I was just winding him up."

"You wicked girl."

"I was going to wear a micro mini with a see-through top, but I thought they might not let me in."

"John would've died from a heart attack if you had. So would I, probably. I love the way you're so daring."

"Good."

They were silent for a few minutes.

"D'you hate me being an escort?" she said, suddenly.

"No! Of course not. How could I? You wouldn't be here otherwise. We wouldn't have met. Who am I to make judgements, anyway? I've never had a problem with women using their assets to earn money. Why shouldn't they? Some use their brains, others use their bodies. It's as simple as that. In any case, show me the woman who hasn't used sexual allure to get a favour out of a man, and I'll show you a liar. And I read that over seventy-five percent of men use a prostitute at some stage in the lives, but get them to admit it! So many hypocrites! Transactions for gain using sex have always gone on and always will. So, how long have you been working?"

"Well, you're my first escort job."

"Really? But you're obviously very experienced. When did you start?"

"Don't ask."

"Sorry. None of my business."

"It's OK. I'm just not ready to tell you everything yet. Is that all right?"

"Mandy, you don't need to tell me anything if you don't want to."

"I do want to, but not yet."

"OK. Look, the main thing is, that what you do you're just brilliant at, but I guess you'd rather do it for pleasure than for money, am I right?"

"Well, they're just different things. Normally, it's just business, that's all. I don't do it for pleasure myself, but I get pleasure from doing it well, if you get me. It's usually OK. I like acting up, which is what it is really. I used to enjoy teasing my teachers. It's fun. I've met some nice guys, and some nasty ones. There's good and bad. I s'pose it's the same in any job. But that's why I didn't want money from you. It was different with you."

"But you need money to live, so I'm going to give you money. But why was it different with me?"

"Well I s'pose I just thought you would be like the others, but maybe pay more, that's all. But I've never met anyone like you. I mean, you're kind, and you treat me well, and you talk about all sorts of interesting things. An' it's really nice coming to your 'ouse, riding in your car and that. More like a proper date than just a quick job."

"But I imagine you'd meet other nice guys if you did more escort work. And maybe younger ones too, more handsome."

"I don't want younger guys. I've always liked older ones. They treat you better. And you treat me best of all. An' a man's looks aren't all that important. I mean, I don't like fat men or smelly ones, but it's the way a man behaves and that. And the way he talks. That's much more sexy than some of these young guys who think they're God's gift 'cos they've got big pecs. No thanks!"

"So I'm not too old for you then?"

"No way. An' you like girls young then, do you?"

"Of course! Well, for sex, yes. Sex is a physical activity, after all, so if you are fit and supple and energetic, you're bound to be more exciting than someone who isn't. You make it look and feel beautiful. That's what I go for."

"So what's your favourite age for a girl? How young?"

"Well, it's not the actual age that matters. Some women in their thirties and forties have still got amazingly young bodies, whereas some girls seem to over ripen in their late teens, and are really past it by twenty."

"But would you go with a girl under sixteen."

"Of course not. No way!"

"Why not?"

"I just don't need to. I know that lots of girls of fourteen or fifteen look years older, and are already having sex, but why break the law with an underage girl who looks older when you can have one who really is? It's just not worth the risk or the hassle."

Mandy looked sad. "But most men like schoolgirls, don't they? I'm always having to put on a school uniform. They really like it."

"Of course! There's a billion pound industry based on the forbidden fruit idea, you know, sexy school girl videos, the Lolita thing, and so on. The history of art and literature is full of it. Pop stars like Britney Spears have used it to sell records. It's always gone on, and always will. Trouble is we have a thing called the age of consent. Whether or not a girl is ready for sex it's illegal in this country if she hasn't reached sixteen. I'm just not prepared to break the law. Like I said, I don't need to. I'm only into girls who are sexually mature."

"It's a crap law. I know loads of girls who shag long before they're sixteen. Why shouldn't they, if they want to? It's their bodies!"

"Because the nanny State says they can't! It's naughty! The thing is, a lot of adults can't handle the idea of girls or boys under sixteen having sex, so they make laws to stop them. The idea is to protect them from being exploited. I don't have a problem with that, it's a good thing, but I agree that it's a bit stupid to fix one age for everyone 'cos everyone matures at different rates, and sex is all some kids think and talk about from about twelve onwards. But I don't know what the alternative is. In Shakespeare's time, it used to be twelve for girls and fourteen for boys, but now it's much higher, even though youngsters mature earlier. Crazy. In some countries the age is much lower; in others it's actually higher. Here it's sixteen, and I guess we're stuck with it."

Mandy's face had lost its colour, and she turned away.

"What's the matter, sweetheart? Come on, cheer up! I'll tell you what, if you don't want me to pay you each time we meet, why don't you just be my mistress, and then I can just give you money and things as presents whenever I like, how does that sound?"

Mandy turned back, smiling.

"Mistress? I like that!"

"Good. That's settled then."

"But if I'm your mistress, then I won't be seeing anyone else. I belong to you. Actually, I haven't seen anyone since I met you anyway."

David smiled. "Good. I'd be jealous."

Mandy sat up on one elbow, leaning her breasts against his chest. She looked at him closely. "Would you? Would you really?"

"Yes. But I won't hold you to it. I don't own you, and you must do whatever you want."

"But I don't want to see anyone else. My mam's not happy though. She wants me to go on working."

"Your mam? What d'you mean? Does she know what you do? Does she approve? That's unusual, I should think."

"Approve? You must be joking. She's been doing it herself for twenty-five years. My mam is Delores – Doreen, actually."

"What? She's your mother? Good God! I had no idea."

"Didn't you? Didn't you really?"

"Really. So she runs an escort agency, then?"

"No. She runs a brothel. Just her, and me and Avril – the girl who came with me to meet you."

"I see. So she hasn't got lots of models then? I must say, when I met her, she didn't quite seem quite the type. It's hard to believe you're her daughter though – she's small and um, well . . . you don't look like her daughter, I have to say."

"Well, I am. And I've got two brothers, but we've all had different fathers, so none of us look alike. I've no idea what my dad looked like, so maybe I take after him. My mam doesn't even know which one he was," she said, laughing.

"Well, you certainly don't take after your mother. Oh, look at the time! I really must be moving. I'll drop you off, if that's OK."

"Can you drop me in town? I'd like to get a photo album to stick the photos in. Can you let me have a couple of quid?"

"Of course I can, you silly! Get one by all means, but I should wait for the next photos to be developed, if I were you. They'll be ready tomorrow. I think they will be better than the first batch."

"But the first ones are lovely. I really like them. All of them. Especially the really filthy ones!"

"You would, you nympho! But they're not really suitable for a portfolio. Wait until the others are ready before you choose. But take the first ones with you anyway. Why don't we take some more next time, then you'll have masses to choose from for your album. Now come on, we'd better get up."

* * * * * *

A week later David went into the pharmacy to collect the prints from the third photo session with Mandy. As usual, he couldn't wait to see them and he looked forward to giving her a new set of prints that evening. As he left the shop, he suddenly felt a hand on his shoulder. He turned, thinking he'd left something on the counter, and that the assistant had run after him, but he came face to face with a man he did not recognise. Another man moved in behind David, taking hold of his arm.

"What's this?" asked David, surprised.

"Andrew David Bates?" said the first man. "I am a police officer, and I am arresting you for taking indecent photographs of children. You do not need to say anything, but anything you do say will be taken down, and may be used in evidence against you."

* * * * *

The Police

"Children? What children? What d'you mean, children?" asked David, as the police officer took from him the package containing the photographs he had just collected from the pharmacy.

"Come with us, sir."

What was happening? This was some sort of mistake. They've made a mistake, thought David. Been misinformed. Got the wrong person. This would be sorted out.

Passers-by watched as David was escorted to a nearby police car. The officers walked close beside him, each holding an arm. The rear door of the car was opened, and a hand was placed on his head as he was lowered into the car. The door slammed, and the two officers walked around to climb into the front seats.

David was in shock, but said nothing. The car drove off and, as they went, he glanced back at his Bentley, still parked in the bank car park. Where was he going? To the police station, he realised. This was all a terrible misunderstanding. Indecent photographs of children? What children? It wasn't illegal to take photos of a young female adult, was it? His mind was confused. OK, so there were many naked ones in the batch, but was that against the law? Surely not. Was it? Had he done something wrong without realising it? Had the pharmacy staff been offended and called the police? But the photos were in a sealed envelope. Maybe the processing firm had reported him. But what for? Taking naked photographs of an eighteen-year-old? This was just nonsense. Surely? Or was she eighteen? What if Mandy was only seventeen? Could she be? Is that why she was asking him whether he liked younger girls? Now that he recalled the conversation, he remembered her being a bit upset. She had been defensive and had gone quiet. Maybe she was seventeen after all. He'd never have guessed. Sometimes she looked twenty. She certainly behaved much older. Would her being seventeen make any difference? It would mean that she is legally a child? Was it against the law to take naked photographs of a seventeen-year-old? He didn"t think so. Was it?

At the police station he was led through a large iron door, and told to sit down on a wooden bench facing a long counter, where various police officers were busy filling in forms. His arresting officers disappeared through a door. No one seemed to be taking any interest in him. Two other men sat further along the bench, smoking, and drinking coffee from plastic cups. Around his feet were numerous cigarette ends. The room smelt stale. After well over an hour he was called to the counter. The desk officer was writing in a ledger, and spoke to him without looking up.

"Mr Bates, you have been arrested for taking indecent photographs of children. Would you like to see a solicitor?"

"Look, there's been some sort of misunderstanding."

The officer looked up over his spectacles.

"Would you like to see a solicitor?" he repeated.

"I think I'd better."

"Request noted. You are allowed one phone call."

"One?"

"One."

David thought. He'd better phone Sophie, but she wouldn't be home yet."

"Can I do it later?"

"Yes. Right sir, I need you to empty out all your pockets, money, keys, everything, and shoelaces, and then go with this officer."

"Shoelaces?"

"Yes sir."

David was led away, through a passage, and into a tiny room with a bench across the end wall and a toilet without a seat in the corner. This is a cell, he thought. I'm being locked in a cell!

On the bench were two dirty blankets, each with strands of black human hair adhering to the fabric. As the door banged behind him David turned to look at it, and felt a wave of nausea sweeping through his body. He sat on the bench and looked around. On the floor by his feet he noticed the remains of a meal spilling from a cardboard container. How long was he expected to wait? What was there to do? There was nothing to read, nothing even to look at. The four walls were bare. He tried to think. What on earth was going on? How had the police known he was going to the pharmacy? No one knew. He hadn't decided himself until the last minute. Was it just a coincidence that they were there, or had they been waiting for him? But what was all this about children?

He noticed a communication button on the wall above the toilet. Should he press it? Had they forgotten him? No, he had asked for a solicitor. Presumably one would come soon. He had to wait. He stood up and paced the room, for want of something better to do, and sat down again ten minutes later. Every so often, he repeated the routine.

After two hours, he realised that Sophie would be home. He needed to speak to someone. He pressed the button, and waited. Nothing happened. Over the next hour, he pressed it several times, but there was no response. He heard shouting which he presumed was from another cell, and then the noise of heavy doors unlocking and locking. Still no one came. He lay down on the hard wooden bench, and waited.

Suddenly, he heard a small noise outside his door, and realised he was being watched through a spy-hole.

"Excuse me?" he said, standing up quickly and going to the door. "I was told I could make a phone call. Could I make it now? And is my solicitor coming soon?"

"You can make your phone call now, but you're not being interviewed until tomorrow, so the solicitor will see you then."

"Tomorrow? Oh, so can I go home now and come back tomorrow?"

"No, 'fraid not. You're here for the night."

"The night?"

This was monstrous! What the hell was happening? He was taken back to the counter and handed a telephone.

"Sophie? It's Dad. Listen, sweetie, look, there's a problem. I'm at the police station. No, I can't go into any detail now. Just some awful misunderstanding. But I'm going to be here all night. No. No. I don't know. Look, don't worry, I just had to call someone, that's all. Didn't know who else to call. No, there's nothing you can do. No, don't come. I'll call you again tomorrow. Yes, I'm supposed to be going to Leeds tomorrow night. Yes. No, don't call Rachael. But could you ring Bob – you know, the guy who did your windows – just tell him that I can't make our meeting tomorrow morning and I'll get back to him to re-arrange. No. Sorry about this, sweetie. Yes. I'll call you tomorrow. Thanks. Don't worry. Everything's fine. Bye."

Back in the cell, David looked at his watch. Nearly seven. He was supposed to be meeting Mandy. She'd be waiting and he had no way of contacting her. She might think he was standing her up. Poor Mandy. The photographs! Would the police know who she is from the photos? How could they? So how could they say the photos were of a child? The whole thing was falling apart. They couldn't know who she is, could they? So if they didn't know, how could they know her age?

So what children? He had taken photos of other girls in the past, all much older than Mandy, so it couldn't be them. The more he thought about it, the more certain he was that this was a mistake. Someone would pay for this. He'd make a complaint! Sue the bastards! How dare they arrest him like this!

He lay down on the bench again. He had been brought a cold and tasteless meal which he found inedible. He closed his eyes and tried to sleep. Must sleep. Morning would soon come if he could sleep, then the nightmare would be over. But the bench was too hard. He found himself getting numb where his body made contact with the unyielding wooden surface, and he kept turning over. The light in the ceiling shone in his face, and he tried pulling the blanket over his eyes, but the stench was too much for him to bear. From time to time he fell into a doze, jerking awake when he realised where he was.

Morning eventually arrived, and he was escorted to some washbasins, and told he could freshen up. The officer on duty knew nothing of his case, and could not answer any of his questions.

At midday the door was unlocked, and he was led away to an interview room where he was told the duty solicitor was waiting for him.

"Right, Mr Bates," said the very young-looking, rather intense female, who faced him across the small table, "they're going to release you on police bail pending further enquiries. They've searched your house and . . ."

"Searched my house?"

"Yes, and they seem very interested in some photographs they have found in a cardboard box. They have taken away a number of items from your house. You will be given a list."

"What am I supposed to have done?"

"They think that some of the photographs are of girls under sixteen."

"But they're not! Most of the girls are well into their twenties. One or two are nineteen. None are under sixteen. It"s complete nonsense."

"How do you know that, Mr Bates?"

"Because they told me! They're all escorts, you know, working girls."

"A lot of working girls are under sixteen."

"But these aren't. I'm sure of it."

"How did you meet them?"

"Like I said, they're escorts. I met them through escort agencies. I can probably find the phone numbers of some of them."

"I think you should volunteer as little information to the police as possible. If some do turn out to be under sixteen, it is better that you do not condemn yourself by leading the police to them."

"Oh, I see, but I'm sure they're not. But even if they are, what would happen to me? I mean, if they've lied to me? I mean, I acted in good faith. But they simply can't be under sixteen. I just don't believe it. You should see them! They all look older than you, if you don't mind my saying."

If the young solicitor was annoyed or offended by his comment, she showed no sign of it. She continued to look straight at him.

"Have you published or distributed any of the photographs in any way?"

"No, of course not. Except that almost all of the girls were given copies. Some wanted to be models, you see. That's why they were taken."

"In that case, the consequences of simply taking photographs of children are not so severe as they might be if you had distributed them."

"Why does everyone keep saying 'children'? Young women, no younger than eighteen, not children."

"If they are under eighteen, they are legally children, and if any are under sixteen, as the police suspect, then you are breaking the law. You can be prosecuted under both the Sexual Offences Act and the Children's Act."

David's face had drained of colour.

"What? But none of them is under sixteen. But . . . but . . . what if one is seventeen?"

"Why?"

"Oh, it just occurred to me that one might have been seventeen. The one whose photos I was carrying when I was arrested. She told me she was eighteen, but now I begin to wonder . . . but all the others were much older."

"There is no problem if the girl is seventeen. But if the police can prove that any are under sixteen, then we do have a problem. What could be even more serious is if one could be persuaded by the police to make a complaint against you."

"What d'you mean?"

"Well, did you have sexual intercourse with any of them?"

"All of them! They were escorts! That's what escorts do!"

"Oh, well, I have to tell you that the maximam sentence for having unlawful sexual intercourse with a girl under sixteen is two years' imprisonment. And there is no defence."

"What do you mean, no defence? Surely, if a girl says she is eighteen or more, and looks and behaves older, then that is a defence?"

"The fact that you didn't know a girl's age, even if she lied to you, is not a defence you can enter. It doesn't matter whether you didn't know you were committing an offence, or didn't intend to commit it, there is no defence available to you. It's called strict liability. In law, you are strictly liable."

"But that's monstrous! Is there no protection?"

"The law says that it's the girls who need protecting, Mr Bates, not the offender."

"So what's going to happen now?"

"The police will try to identify all the girls in the photos, and if it turns out that any are under sixteen, they will almost certainly charge you. It all depends on how strong their evidence is, how explicit the photographs are, and whether it can be proved that it was you who took them. Or if a girl makes a statement of complaint against you, that will also constitute evidence. If an under sixteen-year-old complains that you had sex with her, then you will most likely be charged both with taking photographs and with unlawful sexual intercourse."

"Complains? But they came of their own free will. They were paid. Why would they complain?"

" 'Complain' is a legal term in this context. It means making a statement to say what happened. In that case, they become the victim, and you are the one accused of committing an offence. Well, that's all we can do today. Here is my card. If you wish me to act for you when you return in two months' time, I will be happy to do so. There is no cost to you while you are at the police station. Or you can appoint your own solicitor. The police will now process you, and let you go."

"Process me?"

"Take your fingerprints, photograph, and a DNA sample. It's standard procedure. Oh, and just one more thing, whatever you do, do not try to contact any of the girls you have photographed. The police may be watching you, and not only might you end up leading the police to the girls, but it could also be interpreted as interfering with witnesses."

An hour later a big iron door was pulled open and David was released from the rear of the police station into the bright afternoon sunshine, clutching a sheet of paper which told him when he was to return, and threatening instant imprisonment if he did not. It was almost exactly twenty-four hours since he had first been arrested. He walked the two miles back to his car, stopping to buy a local newspaper en route. Immediately, he noticed a small column on the right of the front page:

Paedophile Ring Unearthed in Westley
Police last night swooped on a large Georgian house in Grensham Heights, Westley. A police spokesman confirmed that a fifty-three-year old man had been arrested, and that a large quantity of child pornography and computer equipment had been removed.
A man was last night helping the police with their enquiries.

* * * * * *

One afternoon three weeks earlier a young girl was standing on the edge of a pavement with her jacket slung over one shoulder. It was a warm day and she wore a loose-fitting, very short skirt, and a halter-neck top. She stood with one leg slightly in front of the other, and one hand on her hip. As each car drove past, she flexed her front knee and dipped her head, looking into the car. If it contained a single male, she smiled, and turned her head as the car went past. If it did not stop, she turned her head back to wait for the next car. From time to time, she also glanced across the road into the railway goods

151

yard where, behind a pile of railway sleepers, a car was parked. The two men in the front seat watched her.

"No, take it from me, Derek, said PC Phil Watson, to the man sitting next to him in the front seat of the car, "you're on to a good number here. The Super has given us a very long lead to do whatever it takes to get a high conviction rate. With all that Government money pouring into the project, he's got his bosses on his back to get results, so he's on ours. And if we have to cut a few corners and bend a few rules, that's OK by the gaffer, just as long as we cover our tracks."

"Well, Phil, it's all a new game to me," confessed Derek. "In the Force I was with, we did everything by the book." PC Derek Bostock had just been transferred from rural Shropshire and was still finding his feet in the city.

"But you're a country bobby, Derek, no disrespect intended. This is the urban jungle. They fight dirty, and you've got to fight dirty too. Get your retaliation in first!"

Watson laughed loudly at his own joke. He was enjoying showing off to his new oppo. He loved to shock and play jack-the-lad. Bostock smiled, politely.

" 'ang on, Derek, she's nodding," said Watson, looking across the road at the girl. "Start the engine."

They watched the girl walk down the road and get into the car which had just parked.

"We'll give her two minutes' start so's she can get him up there and ready for us, then we'll move in."

"Has she done this before then, Phil?"

"Oh yeah. But we can't use the same girl too often in case we come against the same magistrate. The courts would get wise. Anyway, she'll be sixteen next month, so she'll be no use after that."

Derek wasn't sure about this. He knew that there was a big problem with teenage prostitution in the town, but to deliberately set one up - 'sprat to catch a mackerel', was how Watson had explained it – made him feel uncomfortable.

A few minutes later they pulled up behind the Corsair, which was parked between some disused garages.

"All right, Derek, you go and fetch him back here. This will be fun."

Bostock got out, walked up to the driver's car, and tapped on the window. There was frantic activity inside the car and, eventually, the driver's window was wound down.

"Would you mind stepping out of the car, sir?"

He led the man back to the unmarked police car and told him to get in the back. Watson turned around to look at the man, who sat with his head in his hands.

"Do you know why you are sitting here, sir?" asked Watson, toying with his prey.

"Um, yes," whispered the man, struggling to get his words out.

Watson was going to enjoy telling him anyway.

"You were observed picking up this young woman on Station Road at approximately two-fifteen, and we followed you to this place, where you were further observed to be engaging in sexual activity with her."

"Please, please, let me off!" implored the man. "My wife . . . my children . . . I'll lose my job . . ."

"Really, sir?" sneered Watson. "Well, perhaps you should have thought about that first. Do you know how old this young female is?"

"Um, no."

"Well, I"ll tell you sir. She is well known to us. She is, in fact, fifteen years old, sir."

The man went very pale, but remained silent.

"Right, sir, let's take down some details, shall we?"

As the man drove away to begin his nightmare, Bostock brought the girl over to the police car.

"Get in the back, Louise," barked Watson at the girl.

They drove back towards Station Road.

"Very good, Louise. Now we need you to come down to the Station tomorrow to make a statement. All right?"

The girl was sullen and silent.

"All right, Louise?" he repeated.

"Yeah," she said. "Now can I get back to work "cos I gotta pick me baby up at five, and I ain't got no money for food yet."

Watson smiled. "Like I said, love, you help us and we'll help you."

They pulled up at the side of the road and Louise got out, walking quickly away without looking back.

"Tomorrow morning at the Station!" called Watson, after her.

"Her baby?" asked Derek. "She doesn't look old enough to . . ."

"Oh she's old enough all right. Lots of these girls have babies in their early teens. But she hasn't got a baby. It died. It's her pimp she's worried about. He's on our list. We'll have him one day, but for now, we're concentrating on the punters. We need a few high-profile cases to let the public see how successful the project is. Nick a few fat cats, and we're all in clover. Then we can start flushing out the pimps. The girls don't like shopping the punters, but they know we won't let them work if they don't co-operate. When we get around to the pimps, the girls'll be falling over themselves to help us. The pimps are the real bastards in all this but, to be honest, I don't care who goes down just so long as we meet our arrest and convictions targets."

"So how many girls co-operate like this?"

"Most of them, if they know what's good for 'em. But that's just the tip of the iceberg. We've got a good network going now, and it's getting bigger every day. We've got contacts all over, not just on the streets, but in massage parlours, the strip clubs, the escort agencies, the small ads columns, and so on. We've got someone in most places. Then there's the video surveillance, and the phone tapping. Surprising what you get from that."

"Phone tapping? Isn't that illegal without a special warrant from the Home Office?" asked Derek, looking surprised.

"Is it?" replied Watson, feigning ignorance. "Well, dear, dear me! I never knew that. You learn something new every day in this job, and that's a fact!" he said, tapping the side of his nose, and winking.

"So where're we heading now, Phil?" asked Bostock, as he drove towards the industrial part of town.

"Oh, just another little call. A flat on the Newby Estate. You been to Newby yet then Derek?"

"No, but I heard about it. A bit rough, is it?"

"Rough? I wouldn't go down there after dark without armoured back-up, but at this time of the afternoon when all the kids are coming out of school, it's fairly quiet. And it's a good time to call on our Sharon. Some of the girls from the comprehensive school will be arriving about now to do a bit of homework, if you get me."

"Homework? You mean...? Really?" Derek was shocked. "What, ordinary young schoolgirls just . . . well, so will we be arresting Sharon then?"

"Oh, no, nothing like that. Never managed to pin anything on her, but she knows I'm breathing down her neck, so she does me favours when I need them."

They pulled up into a car park at the base of a large tower block, taking care to steer around broken glass and the body of a dead cat.

"It's a bit grim!" winced Derek.

"Oh, the outside is quite pleasant. You just wait until you get inside."

They pressed the concierge button to gain entry and Derek recoiled from the smell of urine that hit him as he entered the hallway. A small boy looked at them, and ran into the lift, quickly shutting the door.

"Bugger!" said Watson. "We've been seen."

When they reached the twenty-second floor, Sharon's front door was open and they walked in.

" 'ullo, Phil!" said a big woman with frizzy black hair. "What a nice surprise."

"I'm sure it is," grunted Watson, looking down as the small boy ran past him, and down the stairs. "That kid one o' yours, then?"

"Neighbour's. Just runnin' an errand, 'e is."

"I'll bet."

"You wanna cup o' tea then?"

They walked in and sat down, clearing a space on the littered sofa.

"This your new oppo then? 'andsome, ain't 'e?" cackled Sharon.

"PC Bostock, from Shropshire," replied Watson. "Just showing him 'round the patch. So, who you got working today then, Sharon? No schoolgirls, I hope?"

"Whadya take me for, Phil? Course not! Would I ever? No, I got two o' me cousins staying with me that's all. From

Leicester. Donna and Donna. So, 'ow d'you like yuh donna kebabs then, Phil? Tender lamb or spring chicken? They're in the other room, if you want to interview 'em. Do your oppo here wanna interview one too?"

"No, I can handle this. You keep PC Bostock company while I check this out. Just drink your tea, Derek, and hold the fort, will you?"

* * * * * *

"He's been a long time," ventured Derek, half an hour later.

Sharon continued looking at the television as she replied. "Very thorough is Phil. Always takes down all the girl's particulars, 'e does. I'm sure you'll learn a lot from 'im."

Ten minutes later, Watson emerged, looking flushed. He nodded at Sharon, and made for the door.

"Everything in order?" asked Sharon.

"Yes, until the next time. Be seeing you, Sharon."

As they drove off, Bostock was silent. Watson sensed his unease.

"Listen, Derek, on this patch, you see what you want, hear what you want, and you scratch each other's backs. That's the way it works, OK?"

"What d'you mean?"

"Back there. One of the perks of the job, understand? Some for you too, if you want it, all right?" he grinned, nudging Derek in the side.

Bostock smiled, uncertainly.

"Right!" said Watson. "Now we're off to a much nicer part of town. A pharmacy in Westley. Must get there before it closes."

"A pharmacy?"

157

"Yes, another of my contacts. I've got a few pharmacy assistants around town on the look-out for dirty pictures. I had a call yesterday from this one, and we're going to have to see what she's found for us. She says she's got a guy who started to bring in some very naughty stuff for processing. Says he's some bigwig ex-local government officer. Rich bastard with a big house and fancy car. We know he's been using escort agencies and now he's taking dirty pictures. A very big fish, he is. A good catch if we can hook him."

"But what's he done? Seeing escorts isn't illegal is it, or taking pictures?"

"Derek, Derek, my son, listen. It's not very nice though, is it? Respectable man, pillar of the local community an' all that, shagging prostitutes and taken pictures of them? What would the neighbours say? Better still, what would the papers say? Tut-tut!"

"But if he hasn't done anything wrong . . ."

Watson was enjoying this. "It's not what he's done. He may not have committed an offence, yet, but he's obviously very close to the line, and we can always arrange to give him a little push over it. This shop assistant thinks that the girls in the pictures may be underage. She's just being public spirited. And think about it – why's he taking the pictures? What's he doing with them? If they're just for his 'own use' as they call it, then maybe we could help spread them around a bit, and then have him for distribution."

"What? You mean, frame him?"

"Derek! Would I?"

"You don't like him, do you?"

"What makes you think that? I've never met him. But no, of course I don't like him. It's nothing personal! I just hate all these fucking rich bastards who can just snap their fingers and all the girls come running. I'd like to see 'em all locked up for good."

"You're just jealous!" ventured Derek.

"Jealous? Course I am! Aren't you?"

Derek forced a smile, but he wasn't enjoying his first day of attachment to PC Phil Watson.

In the pharmacy, the assistant took them through to a back room.

"He brought these in yesterday and I told him he'd missed the collection, so they wouldn't be ready until tomorrow. I haven't looked at them yet, but the last ones were, well, horrible!"

Watson looked at the plump and very plain young woman and wondered whether she was still a virgin. He eased open the first packet, and spread the photos on a table.

"What's this?" he growled. "Bloody sparrows?"

"Blue Tits, actually," corrected Derek.

"What?"

"They're Blue Tits."

The assistant blushed. "I'm sorry," she said, "Perhaps I should have opened them first. The last ones were, well, they were very rude. Of a girl. Showing . . . everything. And she looked very young. Very young indeed. But he came to collect them before you could get here."

Watson looked at her. She might be just wasting his time.

"So how young do you think the last girl was then?"

"Oh, I'd say fourteen or fifteen."

"Really?"

"Yes, or maybe sixteen or seventeen."

"Or eighteen or nineteen?" suggested Watson.

"Well, possibly. It's so hard to tell these days, isn't it?"

"And the photos," continued Watson, coldly. "What could you actually see?"

"Things you shouldn't see. They were very rude."

"Very rude?"

"Yes."

Watson sighed. "It's not actually illegal to take very rude photographs of girls over sixteen, you know, madam."

"But there have been several different girls. It's not right, is it, a man like that? And you can see, well, breasts, and down below."

"Down below? Below what?"

"You know. Below."

"Oh. Right. OK, well, we're very grateful to you for your continued assistance. Please do phone me again, but it might help next time if you just take a quick peep at the photos first, and if you're sure that the girl looks under sixteen, and if you can see down below, then give me a call. But do make sure that they're not sparrows."

"Blue Tits!" said Derek.

"Yes, thank you, PC Bostock, Blue Tits."

* * * * * *

A week later PC Bostock was just arriving at work when he met Watson coming out of the door.

"Come on, Derek – let's go!"

Bostock turned in his tracks and followed his partner into the car pound.

"What's on?"

"It's that pharmacy assistant. The one with the Blue Tits. She says that the bloke brought in another film yesterday and was keen to know whether the prints would be ready by today."

"And has she looked at them?"

"She has. Nearly a hundred of 'em. And this time she's says she's very shocked indeed."

"But I got the impression she shocks easily. Aren't we wasting our time?"

"Well, maybe, but it's worth checking out."

In the back room of the pharmacy the assistant left them alone, and they began to thumb through the prints.

"D'you know her then, Phil?" asked Bostock.

"Not sure. She's vaguely familiar. Something about her. Certainly haven't seen her recently, but these girls can change a lot in a few months. She might be city girl. Or even an outsider. We get quite a bit of passing trade from Wales and runaways from the North. They come for a few weeks, then move on. She's young though, I'd say."

"Hard to tell. Doesn't look under sixteen. Eighteen more like. A year either side, I'd say. Pretty though, isn't she?"

"Derek, you shock me!" mocked Watson. "You're not supposed to notice that."

Bostock blushed. "Oh, um, sorry."

"Only kidding, mate. She's fucking gorgeous! That's why I hate this bastard. What right has he got to be shagging this girl? He wouldn't get a cracker like this out of her knickers if it wasn't for his money and his detached house. That's why we're going to nick 'im."

"But we don't know who she is. She's probably over sixteen."

"She might be. She might not be. But we can still nick him pending further enquiries. If we take these pictures to a magistrate, and I know just the one, there will be no problem getting a search warrant to turn his place over, then who knows what we might find there? We might even find a few things that weren't there in the first place."

"You mean . . .?"

Phil tapped his nose again and grinned malevolently. "Right, ask the assistant if she can rustle up some coffee. We'll just have to sit it out until our Mr Bates comes for his photos. I can see why he wanted to get them back quickly. He must really have the hots for this one."

* * * * * *

When David got home from the Police Station, Sophie was waiting for him. She looked tearful and worried. Jeremy arrived an hour later, and sat holding his hand as he told them the story of his arrest. David was acutely embarrassed that his children were hearing all this. Despite having developed a rationale to justify to himself why using escorts was acceptable, it was still painful to be sharing this aspect of his private life with his children. He had always wanted them to think the best of him, and now, perhaps illogically, he felt ashamed.

They were angry and upset, with him for 'playing with fire', as they called it, and with the police, the girls, the system, and the world in general for the unfairness of it all; but they were also very supportive and promised to phone or call to see him every day until this thing was over, which both of them believed it would be in no time at all. Kezzie was less forgiving, and kept her distance, as David thought she might. She was less mature about these matters than Sophie or Jeremy, and found it difficult to visualise her father in any sort of sexual situation, left alone with a prostitute.

On the kitchen table they had found a list of things taken from the house by the police. As well as the box of photographs, they had taken his computer, his telephone answering machine, and family video tapes that he had compiled over the years as the children had grown up.

162

"But why my computer?" asked David, of no one in particular.

"I think they often do that," suggested Jeremy. "I guess they'll be checking your e-mails and looking at the websites you've visited. They're probably hoping to find you've been trading your pictures."

"But that's preposterous!"

"Calm down, Dad! They're just checking."

"But I need my computer for my work. All my files are on it. I can't operate without it."

"Have you got hard copies of anything?" asked Jeremy.

"Some of it. And a few back-up disks. I suppose I can last for a while if I can pop 'round to your flat from time to time and use yours, but I will be sending out new contract paperwork in a few weeks. I'll need my templates for that."

"You'll probably have it back by then. Don't worry, Dad. We'll manage."

"But what about the family videos? They're irreplaceable. What if they lose those? They contain all your birthdays and Christmases and things as you grew up."

"I'm sure they'll just look to see what they are and then return them," suggested Sophie. "Judging from the newspaper report they think they're on to some sort of organised group so they're obviously going to look hard at everything."

"Yes, I suppose you're right," said David, feeling reassured. "But I really don't know what the neighbours are going to make of all this. They're giving me very strange looks already since they saw the police here and read the newspaper. I suppose I'll have to talk to them soon."

"No, Dad", insisted Jeremy. "Don't say anything. You don't know who you can trust. Just try to carry on as usual.

Let them think what they like. If this all blows over, you could
end up regretting having told them things."

"Jeremy's right, Dad. Just try to carry on as usual."

* * * * * *

For the following two days David was alone, and stayed
in. Was this 'carrying on as usual'? What was 'usual' since
Rachael had left? Being alone, or entertaining escorts? Well,
that had got to stop immediately. The neighbours would be
watching whenever they saw him in his car, so he dare not be
seen with a young female passenger. And he supposed that
the police might be watching as well.

It was the weekend, and he had forgotten that Rachael
had taken Freddy to camp, so his usual trip to Leeds was off.
He knew that on Monday he would need to call a solicitor and
take advice. Slowly, he descended into a deep depression. His
excursion into the world of escorts had given him a brief,
sometimes exciting, period of escape from his loneliness,
which now flooded back with increased darkness and
hopelessness. Meeting Mandy had been a truly wonderful
experience, too good to last, he had thought at the time, and
now ripped away from his grasp. He badly wanted to see her
again, and yet he knew he dare not. The police would be
trying to find out who she was, and he had to avoid leading
them to her, if only to protect her from their attention. He
wondered what she was thinking had happened. There had
been no messages from her on his mobile phone, and he dared
not ring her.

* * * * * *

Mandy couldn't understand why David didn't ring her. She lay on her bed with the door locked. She definitely wasn't going to ring him after he failed to show up for their date the night before. It was up to him. Maybe her mother had been right. Just a bloody punter, after all. Bastards. Set you up and then drop you when they get bored.

After their last meeting she had returned home to find Doreen in the kitchen, talking to Avril and Stacey.

" 'ere she comes, gels, love's young dream!" laughed Doreen. "Thought you was never comin' 'ome, bab! All right?"

Mandy nodded, but said nothing, helping herself to a drink.

"Yuh stopped the night then! " 'e must like yuh, bab!" said Doreen.

"I knew 'e would," said Stacey. "Is 'e in love with yuh then?"

Mandy shrugged. "Maybe."

"Maybe, she says!" scoffed Doreen. "Well, I'll tell yuh something, Stace, our Mand 'as certainly got the 'ots for 'im."

"You ain't, 'ave yuh, Mand?" said Stacey, looking surprised. "That ain't a good idea, Mand."

"She's a silly fucker, that's what she is," hissed Doreen. "No good'll come of it, you mark my words. There'll be tears over this."

"Oh, just stop your foul language!" protested Mandy.

"Oo, 'ark at 'er, Miss Posh Knickers!" sneered Stacey. "Look, Mand, 'e's only a fuckin' punter. You don't wanna get involved. I'm surpised at yuh, Mand. You was always so cool. You 'ad 'em wrapped 'round yuh little finger. Wass gone wrong with this one?"

"He's nice. He's lovely."

"Fuck off, Mand!" screeched Stacey. " 'e's just a mug like the rest of 'em."

"No, you fuck off, Stacey, you bitch. Go on. Fuck off out of 'ere."

Doreen shrugged her shoulders, as Stacey turned towards the door.

"All right, I"m goin". But don't forget who found 'im for yuh, you ungrateful cow!"

Stacey left, slamming the back door.

"She's trouble, she is. You wanna watch 'er," warned Doreen.

"She stole from 'im. How could anyone steal from 'im, mam?"

"You 'ave got it bad, ain't yuh, bab? Wass so special about this geezer then? You ain't never bothered about it before. It's just business. I don't like seein' yuh like this, Mand. It worries me."

"I'm fine, Mam, but I ain't, um, I'm not seeing anyone else now. I'm his mistress."

" 'is what?"

"His mistress. He said so."

"Now you listen, my gel. If you was 'is mistress 'e'd be settin' you up in a flat an' that, an' payin' all yuh bills, and givin' yuh a store card, and whatever."

"Well, maybe he will. Soon. He makes me feel beautiful."

"You are beautiful, bab."

"But special. Intelligent and that. He's interested in what I say. He makes me laugh, and that. Anyway, I'm seeing him again tomorrow, and I got a new dress to wear. D'you like it?"

She fished in her bag and brought out what appeared to be a knot of string. She shook it loose and held it out for Doreen to inspect.

"Dress? That ain't a dress, bab. That looks like the leftovers from a crocheted purse! You can't walk down the street in that? You be fuckin' naked!"

"But I know he'd like it."

"I'm sure 'e would, bab. Any man would! I reckon as 'ow this geezer would like you even if you wore a boiler suit!"

"You reckon?"

"I do."

* * * * * *

But despite Doreen's warning Mandy had put on the string dress and ran the gauntlet of wolf whistles as she made her way to the pub car park the next evening to meet David. She was surpised, and felt uncomfortable about the fact that he was not there when she arrived. Before, he had always been early, but now she had to wait in the car park and endure invitations and crude remarks from every male entering the pub.

After nearly an hour, she gave up and rushed home.

"What you doin' back?" asked Doreen, as Mandy burst in through the back door.

"He hasn't come!"

"Why not?"

" 'ow the 'ell do I know?" thundered Mandy, bursting into tears, and running upstairs.

"Fuck me!" muttered Doreen. "I don't never remember that girl cryin' since she was about eight. What the fuck's got into 'er?"

* * * * * *

Now it was the next day, and there was still no word. Perhaps he had been involved in an accident? But if that was so she still could not phone him because his family would be there. More likely he had grown tired of her and found another girl. They did that, these punters. Now it was the weekend, and he'd be visiting his son in Leeds. No, she'd give it until Tuesday, and then phone him to tell him just what she thought of him.

But by Sunday lunchtime, having not slept for two nights, she persuaded Doreen to make the call for her.

"Hello, is that David?"

"Yes."

"Oh, um, hello David, this is Delores speakin'. Hi 'ope you don't mind me phonin' but hi was wonderin' hif you'd like to see Mandy again."

"Sorry, Delores, I'm afraid I can't. I've got a personal problem at the moment. I really can't."

"Oh, um, would you like to see another girl then?"

Mandy frowned and dug Doreen in the ribs.

"Oh, no, no. If I saw anyone, it would be Mandy."

"Oh, well, I'll be honest with you, David, I got one very upset girl here. She really took to you. Very upset, she is."

"Really?"

"Yes, Very."

"Look Delores," said David, " I'm really, really sorry. But I can't. I just can't. Tell Mandy I would love to see her, and maybe I will one day, but for the time being, I can't see anyone. I can't explain. Please, don't phone me again. When I've sorted out my problem, I'll phone you."

"Fuckin' bastard!" said Doreen, after she had put down the phone. "It's what I told you, Mand."

"But I didn't get me last batch of photos."

"What photos?"

" 'e took loads of photos of me. Naked an' that."

"He fuckin' didn't! What for?"

"For me portfolio."

"The bastard! An' 'e ain't give 'em all to yuh? The cunt'll be sellin' 'em. Makin' money out o' yuh, bab. We'll 'ave to sort him, Mand. Bastard."

"Whadya mean?"

"You'll see." "Now then, Mand. I got a very nice punter comin' in half an hour. What say you sees 'im?"

"I dunno."

"Oh, come on, Mand. You gotta get this fuckin' David out of yuh mind. " 'e's no good for yuh. Now, come on, gel, see this punter for me, will yuh?"

"S'pose."

"Thass my girl. Now, don't you worry about that David no more."

* * * * * *

That evening Doreen went out.

"It's like this, Wayne," said Doreen, sitting in the corner of the Cat and Whistle, clutching a gin and tonic, "there's this geezer what's really flush, fuckin' rollin' in it, 'e is, and I got somethin' on 'im. But I needs your 'elp."

Wayne looked at his mother, weighing her up. What was she up to, the old bag?

"Wass in it fuh me then?" said Wayne.

"Could be a lot. A grand or more. No knowin, an' there's no risk, 'cos like I say, I got somethin' on 'im."

"What you got then?"

"Well, you know 'ow our Mand's always wanted to do modellin' . . .?"

Wayne interrupted. "If I find you been workin' that girl I"ll fuckin' skin yuh!"

"I ain't, I ain't. I swear to God. I swear on me fuckin' mother's grave I do!" Doreen took a deep breath and calmed down. "No, listen up, bab. It ain't like that. No. No."

"Kev thinks you're workin' 'er"

"Kev! Wass 'e know? 'e don"t know nothin'. No, bab, listen, there's this geezer what takes photos. Picks girls up outside school gates 'e does. An' outside children's 'omes. Proper nonce, 'e is. Fuckin' peedutrician, you know, real weirdo."

"A what? Paedophile, you mean, you stupid cunt!"

"Oh yeah, whatever. Only I didn't know that, see? I thought 'e was just a straight-up photographer, like. One o' the girls told me 'e was, see, an' Mandy, well, she wants to be a model, just clothes an' that, no porno nor nothin', know what I mean? So Mandy goes with this geezer to 'is 'ouse, and well, 'e puts one on 'er, don't 'e!"

"Whadya mean 'puts one on 'er?" shouted Wayne. "What, 'e fuckin' rapes 'er you mean?"

"No, no, nothin' like that, bab. Look, Mand don't know I come 'ere 'cos she's got a soft spot for this geezer. Thinks the sun shines out o' 'is arse, she does, so I come 'ere secret like, "cos I don't like wass goin' on."

"So what is goin' on then, you daft cunt. You ain't told me yet."

"Thass 'cos you keep interruptin', bab. Well, this geezer, 'e gives our Mand a few drinks like, and she ends up takin' all 'er clothes off an' 'e's there clickin' away, 'e is. She showed me some o' the photos and well, she's showin' it all, she is."

"I'll fuckin' kill 'im!" growled Wayne.

"But thass not all. Thing is, now 'e says 'e don't wanna see 'er no more, an' 'e's kept a load o' photos what she ain't seen, and I reckon as 'ow 'e's gonna sell 'em, like."

"Like on the Internet, you mean? Our Mand showin' 'er bits to all the fuckin' world? The bastard. I'm gonna cut 'im."

"No, no, bab, no need fuh that."

"So wass the angle then?"

"Well, 'e said not to phone 'im no more 'cos 'e says 'e's got some problem or other, but I reckons as 'ow 'e's just sayin' sod off 'cos 'e's got the photos 'e wants, and now 'e's onto some other girl."

"So 'ow do we get to the bastard then?"

"Well, I've got an idea . . ."

* * * * * *

" 'ello, is that David?"

It was Monday morning and David was just about to leave for an appointment with his solicitor.

"Oh, Delores. Look, please, I did ask you not to phone me anymore."

"I know you did, David, and I'm very sorry, but it's just that hi really need to see you."

David shuddered. Had the police got to Mandy already? How could they? Surely not?

"What's the problem?" said David, apprehensively.

"There's somethin' hi need to tell you about Mandy. Somethin' you ought to know."

"What?" said David, anxiously. "What is it?"

"I can't say it on the phone, David. Can you come over to meet me?"

David swallowed hard. What should he do? He had to know what this was about, but dare he risk further trouble?

Perhaps if he kept his eyes open, made sure he wasn't being followed . . .

"OK, I'll come over this evening. Is seven OK? Same place as before."

"Yes, that's fine, David. See you later then."

* * * * * *

David's own solicitor gave the same advice as the young woman at the police station. It all depended, he was told, whether the police could identify the girls in the photographs, and then whether any turned out to be under sixteen.

"What exactly was in this box?" asked George Crabtree, the silver-haired, distinguished looking senior partner at Simms and Simms, who specialised in criminal law.

"Photographs of the girls."

"That's all?"

"Yes, that's . . ." David suddenly went very red.

"What's the matter?"

"Oh, I've just remembered. There was a video tape in the box too."

"A video of what?"

"Of me having sex with a girl."

"Is it pornographic?"

"Oh, um, I'm not sure how you would define that."

"Domination? Bondage? Anal sex?"

"Oh no, just two people making love."

"Does it actually show penetration? Is it absolutely clear that full sexual intercourse is taking place?"

"I'm not sure if it actually . . . Well, yes, it probably does. Yes, come to think of it, I'm sure it does."

"Um. Well, providing the girl in the video is over sixteen, then there's no problem. You didn't make it for financial gain, I take it? You haven't made copies, or distributed it in any way, or shown it to anyone else?"

"No, of course not. Nothing like that."

"And you are sure she is over sixteen?"

"I was certain. Now I'm not certain about anything anymore."

"Well, the problem we now have that if she turns out to be under sixteen, the video tape could provide the prosecution with prima facie evidence of unlawful sexual intercourse. There'd be no need for her to make a complaint, or even to be called as a witness."

"No, no," frowned David. "The girl in the video is definitely over sixteen. You should see her!"

"Well, if the tape ever becomes evidence, then I will, in due course. If you end up being charged with anything, all evidence must be disclosed to us so that we can prepare our defence. Look, Mr Bates, there are one or two things you need to do now. Firstly, on no account make contact with any of the girls. Secondly, change your phone numbers. We don't want any old 'friends' phoning you up, do we? And be careful about who you phone, particularly on your landline – you never know who is listening."

"Can they do that?"

"Officially, no, and they certainly couldn't enter overheard conversations as evidence, but it could lead them to the girls. Whatever you do, you must avoid giving the police further opportunities. For some reason they think they're on to an organised paedophile ring and they'll be doing everything they can to catch you out. Oh, and by the way, change your car."

"What? My Bentley? But I've had it for years!"

"Well, it's up to you, of course, but it's far too conspicuous, and you really don't want to be drawing attention to yourself, do you?"

David left the solicitor"s office in a daze, and walked through the shopping mall towards the car park. The place was crowded with people, laughing and chatting, seemingly without a care in the world. David noticed several young teenage girls in summer tops and mini skirts, and he found himself trying to guess their ages, but looked away quickly when he realised he was staring. "How old are you, Mandy?" he said to himself. Despite his solicitor's advice, he knew he had to meet Doreen that evening. He just had to know.

** * * * **

At ten-to-seven David parked at the back of the car park and waited. Soon he would know. Had the police been asking questions already? Was this just to warn him, or was it some sort of blackmail? No it couldn't be. Mandy was definitely over sixteen. She acted years older. She just looked young. But not that young. No, that wasn't it. Perhaps this woman just wanted to persuade him to see Mandy again.

He saw her approaching down the hill, recognising the bias in her gait from their previous meeting. She reached the passenger door of the car, and seemed to hesitate, looking to one side as she opened the door.

"Hello Delores, look, I'm really sorry about . . ."

Before he had chance to finish his sentence, a male figure suddenly jumped out from behind some bushes and pushed Doreen to one side. Pointing a gun at David he climbed into the car and pushed the barrel of the gun hard into David's ribs. At the same time, another man appeared, opening the rear door and getting in behind. David felt another gun in the small of his back. He involuntarily raised his arms, and noticed Delores scuttling back up the road.

"Put yuh fuckin' arms down! Put 'em down!" shrieked the man next to him. David lowered his arms and turned his head to look at the man. He was in his early twenties, small, thin, unshaven, a yellow complexion, and with a tattoo on his cheek.

"Don't look at me, you cunt!" screamed the man. David looked forwards and could see the other man in his mirror. Slightly younger. Brown frizzy hair. Both of them looked very scared. David's mind raced. What should he do? Without the guns he felt he could take them on, but one didn't argue with guns. And they seemed so nervous that he guessed it would take very little provocation for one of them to fire. He suddenly thought of Freddy, of Sophie, Jeremy and Kezzie. He had to survive this. No heroics. He decided to co-operate.

" 'and over yuh money!"

David reached into his pocket and drew out a wad of bank notes, handing them to the man next to him.

"Now give us yuh fuckin' cards you bastard, or you'll get a bullet in yer leg."

"Cards?" asked David. "Credit cards? I haven't got any on me," he replied, truthfully.

"You must 'ave fuckin' cards."

"I haven't, I swear!"

" 'e's fuckin' lying', Wayne," said the man behind. "Put a bullet in the fucker, an' less go."

"Shuddup, Kev!" replied the man in front. "Where's yuh fuckin' cards then?" he said to David.

"At my house."

"In fuckin' Westley?"

"Yes."

"Right. Take us there. An' don't you fuckin' try anythin'. You make just one fuckin' mistake an' I"ll fuckin' let you 'ave it. Right! Drive! Drive!"

David started the car and drove forwards with both guns still pushing painfully into his torso.

"I 'ate fuckin' bastards like you," continued the one called Wayne. "You know what you are? You're a fuckin' nonce, thass what you are!" he shouted, venomously.

David didn't know what a nonce was, or what the man was talking about. He just looked ahead and drove on.

"That little girl what you touched up," said Kevin, from behind, "I'll fuckin' kill yuh! That was my fuckin' sister, that was!"

"Like 'is fuckin' sister," corrected Wayne. "Just like your fuckin' sister, wasn't she, Kev?"

"Yeah. Just like my fuckin' sister. Known'er all me life, I 'ave. Just like a fuckin' sister to me, she is."

David realised that they must be talking about Mandy.

"What d'you do to 'er then, you fuckin' nonce? Come on, what d'you do to 'er?" growled Wayne, pushing the gun harder into David.

David hesitated. "I . . . we . . ."

"Don't talk, you bastard," said Kevin. "We know what you did. Well, you're gonna fuckin' pay for it."

" 'oo's in your 'ouse?" demanded Wayne.

"Oh, no one," replied David. "I live alone."

"So there's no one there then?"

"No."

"You got cash in your 'ouse, 'ave yuh?"

"Yes."

" 'ow much?"

David remembered he had collected rents just before the weekend, much of it in cash.

"About eight hundred I think."

"Good. And cards? You got cards? Don't lie to me, you fuckin' nonce."

"I've got a cash card and a credit card."

The men fell silent and David drove on.

" 'ow much further?" asked Wayne,

"About ten minutes."

"Go faster, you fuckin' bastard!" spat Kevin, into David's ear.

"If I go faster. I'll set off a speed camera or I'll be stopped." David had recovered from the initial shock and was beginning to gather himself. He felt able to reason with them. "Look," he continued, "I'm co-operating. You'll get what you want. I don't want trouble. You make me go faster and you might attract the attention of the police. We might be stopped."

"You're a fuckin' cool customer, you are," said Wayne.

"Yeah," agreed Kevin. "They're normally shittin" themselves when they see the guns, ain't they, Wayne?"

They both laughed, nervously.

"Look, I don't want trouble," continued David. "I just want to get this over, all right?"

"Aint you fuckin' scared, you cunt?" said Kevin, smacking the rear of David's head with his open hand.

"I just want to get this over with," repeated David.

* * * * * *

When they arrived, Wayne got out and looked around. Satisfied there was no one else there, he told David to get out, and pushed him in front. Both of the men took off their small jackets, which they then used to hide their guns, staying close to David as they moved towards the front door of the house.

David opened the door, and stepped inside. Wayne and Kevin had become much more nervous again.

"The cash! Take us to the fuckin" cash!" said Wayne, into David's ear.

David took them upstairs and removed a wash bag from a bedside cupboard where he kept spare cash. He handed it over.

"Any more?" said Wayne.

"No."

"Cards? Where's the cards?"

"Downstairs."

He led them downstairs and took his wallet out of his desk drawer. Wayne ripped it from his hand and emptied the contents on top of the desk.

"You got loads o' fuckin' cards 'ere, you fuckin' liar!" he growled.

"No, look," said David, " these are mainly store cards. This is a video card, and this is a blood donor card. This one is from the DIY store. None of these are any good to you. This is the cash card. You can get money out with this."

"And what about this one?"

"That's my credit card. I don't use it for cash. I don't know the pin number."

"Give us the pin number for the cash card. Write it down."

David took a scrap of paper and wrote down the number. Briefly, he considered writing a false number, but decided not to risk it. They seemed satisfied to take just the cash card,

"What else you got?" asked Kevin, looking around. "Gold? Jewellery?"

"No, nothing like that."

"Any other valuables?"

"No. Just some antique furniture, but it's too big for you to take."

"What's this?" Wayne had picked up David's video camera case.

"It's a video camera."

"What's it worth?"

"Not much. It's quite old."

"Take it anyway!" said Kevin.

They looked around from room to room, but decided that there was nothing else worth taking. In Freddy's room, they saw toys and drawings spread out on the floor and the bed.

"Thought you said you lived alone. Who's is this?" asked Wayne.

"It's my son's room. He only stays occasionally.

"Right!" ordered Wayne. "Now you're takin' us to the nearest cash point!"

"OK," agreed David. For a fleeting moment he wondered whether he could drive straight to the police station and try to make a run for it. But perhaps they would still shoot. In any case, they were Mandy's brothers, and if they were caught, then he would have led the police straight to Mandy. No, he would just have to see this out by co-operating.

He parked near the cash point. Wayne waited until there were no people around.

" 'ow much will it draw out in one go then?" he asked.

"Um, £300, I think," lied David. He knew his daily limit was £500.

"Stay with 'im Kevin!" said Wayne, getting out of the car and walking towards to cash point. He seemed to take a long time. When he returned, David noticed him secreting some of the cash beneath his belt before showing Kevin the remainder. He had obviously drawn the full five hundred.

"OK, drive!" he ordered. "When can I use this again?" he asked, holding up the cash card.

"After midnight," answered David.

"Right," said Wayne. " 'ere's what we do. You drive us back, and you don't report you've lost this card until after nine tomorrow mornin'. An' if you do, we'll be back. We know where you live, and we know you've got a kid, an' we're not afraid to use these guns, understand?"

"Yes", said David. "I'll just say I lost my card. Will that do?"

"You're getting' the idea nicely," replied Wayne.

"Don't trust 'im Wayne!" protested Kevin. "The fucker'll be onto the filth as soon as we've gone."

"I won't," said David.

"No, 'e won't. 'e don't want no trouble with the cops anymore 'n we do, the fuckin' nonce, and 'e don't wan' us comin' back with our shooters, do yuh, Nonce?"

"No," said David.

"Well, I don't trust 'im," said Kevin. "Let's just lock 'im in the boot till midnight."

"It'll be all right, Kev. Believe me," said Wayne.

"Well, let's at least take 'is fuckin' car. We could get a lot for it."

"That wouldn't be a good idea," suggested David. "It's a rare car. You'd soon be traced. No on would buy it without its documentation. You'd have to prove ownership"

"All right Mr know-all. I knew that," said Wayne. "Leave it, Kev. Just leave it. We got what we came for. Keep it simple. Nothing traceable, right?"

As they neared the pub car park Wayne shouted for David to stop the car in a side street. Suddenly, they both jumped out and ran up an alley. David leaned over and pulled shut the doors that they had left open, reversed the car, and headed for home.

* * * * * *

"The dirty bugger!" exclaimed PC Phil Watson.

Watson and his junior colleague, Derek Bostock, were sitting in a small darkened room at the police station, watching a video.

"She seems to be enjoying it though," remarked Bostock.

"Bastard. We'll 'ave 'im."

"But we still don't know who she is."

"No, not yet, we don't," said Watson.

"What about the other girls, Phil?"

"Two traced so far. One twenty-four, and one nineteen, so they're no interest to us. I've sent copies of the other pictures up to Child Protection. They've got a data-base of children at risk, with photos."

"And what if none of them are there?"

"Then there's Social Services. A lot of working girls have attached social workers, so we might get a recognition there. Then there's the Beat. We'll keep copies in the car and show them to the girls on the streets. Someone's bound to know them. Bit by bit, we'll find them all."

Bostock picked up a handful of photos from the box and flicked through them. He came across one small black and white photo of a very young nude Asian girl. The words 'Nita Bains, aged ten' were written on the back.

"I never noticed this one before, Phil? This is disgusting. There's no doubting the age of this girl. She just a child."

"Oh, that one. Yes, I popped it in the box as a little insurance policy."

181

"What? So it's not his then?"

"Course not. But just in case we draw a blank on these other photos, we can have him for possession of this one."

"But Phil, we can't do that."

Watson looked irritated.

"Derek, my son, like I told you when you first joined me, we sometimes have to bend the rules and cut a few corners. This bloke needs nailing, yes? If we draw a blank on these photos, or it turns out that this little tart in the video is over sixteen, we need something else. We can't waste all this taxpayers' money on this investigation and then come up with nothing, now can we?"

"But it'll never stand up in court. He'll just deny ever seeing it. And it obviously wasn't taken in his house or with the same camera, was it?"

"No, but I've one or two other little tricks up my sleeve for our Mr Bates. It's just a question of putting little temptation in his way, that's all."

* * * * * *

David's bank manager was mystified by the fact that someone had simply found his card after he claimed to have lost it on a petrol station forecourt, and was able to withdraw a thousand pounds without knowing his pin number. He said it couldn't be done, and asked David to think hard again about whether he had ever given his pin number to anyone. But David stuck to his story, even when, at the bank's insistence, he was required to report the loss to the police a few days later.

He worked out that adding the cash taken from his pocket, home and bank account, together with the value of the video camera, Wayne and Kevin had relieved him of over two thousand five hundred pounds, which he knew he would never see again.

He had surprised himself about how calm he had been during the robbery; but events of the previous few days seemed to have numbed his reactions, and he felt able to cope with just about anything.

He decided not to tell his family for the time being for fear of distressing them unnecessarily, but he knew that now the police were involved, that he would have to tell his solicitor. What he couldn't decide was whether Mandy had played any part in the robbery. Clearly it had been set up by her mother, but presumably Mandy must have provided some information about him; or was it simply that her mother was an opportunist and had taken advantage of the situation? It must have been clear to her that he and Mandy had got on very well, and perhaps Mandy had talked about his house, giving the impression that he was worth robbing. But whether she had done it deliberately, and knew about the robbery, he doubted.

David parked his new car at the leisure centre where he'd gone for a squash match. He had joined the squash league so that he could play more games. Anything to keep him busy.

As he walked towards the doors, his mobile phone rang. It was a man's voice with a strong Northern accent.

"Is that David?"

"Yes, speaking."

"Ah, hello, David. You left a message on our answer machine a week or two back. Sorry we didn't get back to you but we've been away. What can we do for you?"

"Sorry, I don't know who you are."

"The agency."

"Agency?"

"Yes. Academy Escorts. You left a message saying you wanted an escort."

"I don't think so. There must be some mistake."

"No, no mistake, David. What is it you like? We can get anything you want, for the right price, of course. Where are you based?"

David was confused. He didn't remember phoning an agency. He was sure he hadn't. Had someone done it on his behalf? Some girl after a commission, who just gave his name and number?

"Um. Westley, but, uh look, I . . ."

"Oh, just down the M6. No problem. Now, listen, Dave, if you like them young and sweet, we can do that too. Fifteen, fourteen, thirteen, younger, just tell me when to stop. Just say the word, Dave, and we can fix it for you, tonight. Fresh little virgins, in their school uniforms if you like, untouched, but gagging for it."

David was stupefied. "Look, I don't know who you are, but I'm not interested. I didn't ring you, and please don't call this number again . . . hang on, how did you get this number? I only changed it this morning. What did . . .?"

The phone went dead.

David played the worst game of squash in his life. How did they get his number? Who was behind this? Was it the police? The man didn't sound like the front for an escort agency. Much too slick. Sounded more like a car salesman . . . or a policeman. And, in any case, no escort agency would say all that over the phone to a complete stranger. Had they been recording the conversation, hoping he would say something indiscreet, or even take the bait? It had to be the police. No one except Sophie and Jeremy had his new number.

* * * * * *

"So the shit has certainly hit the fan 'round your house," joked John, as they sat down in the pub for a beer the next evening. "No more nooky for you then!"

Typical John, thought David. Always the joker. But David needed a laugh. He couldn't go on worrying. It might never happen. "Yes. It's all very difficult?"

"Serve you bloody well right. I told you it would send you blind, all that shagging. I'm surprised your todger hasn't dropped off before now. Well, you know what 'er at 'ome always says, don't you?"

"What's that, John?"

"Abstinence makes the heart grow fonder."

"Really? So you must be really, really fond of one another then!"

"We're bloody ecstatic!"

They both laughed heartily. David felt better. "Thanks, John. You've really cheered me up. I've been pretty miserable about all this."

John looked serious. "I know, mate. Listen, it's all crap, take it from me. There's no way that girl's under sixteen. I saw her, don't forget. In fact, I thought she was about twenty. And I don't believe there's a single straight bloke who would turn her out of his bed on a cold night. She was definitely a fully-grown, nubile, sexually mature woman, and she fuckin' knows it too, judging by the way she flaunted it. If she's under sixteen, then my missus is Linda Lovelace, and there's not much chance of that now, is there?"

David smiled. This was just the reassurance he needed. He picked up the two empty glasses and headed for the bar.

* * * * * *

" 'ello? Is that David?"

David was just leaving for Leeds. He and Rachael had decided not to tell Freddy about the problem. He'd be told in due course if he had to know, and so David's weekend escapes to be with Freddy became more important. He could leave behind the spectre of the police investigation, and just enjoy being with Freddy, taking him to his rugby, for lunch to McDonald's, and for long walks with the dog.

But just as he was closing the boot of the car, the phone had rung.

"You may not remember me but I came to see you twice last year. Zoë."

"Zoë? Yes, I remember. How did you get my number?"

"That's why I'm phonin' you, David. You were very nice to me. I was a bit upset when you didn't wanna see me again, but that's your choice. Anyway, like I say, you were a decent bloke, and I think you ought to know that the cops are after you."

David swallowed hard and shuddered.

"Yes, I know."

"No, I mean, really after you. It's that bastard Watson. D'you know 'im?"

"Yes, I believe we've met."

"Well, watch 'im David. 'e wants you real bad. 'e's givin' out your phone number to all the street girls, an' 'e's showin' them photos of yuh. 'e's tryin' to set yuh up. D'you have a caravan site down by the canal?"

"Yes, I do. How d'you know that?"

"Listen, if you see a girl standing down there, don't go near 'er. Don't talk to 'er. She's wired."

"Wired? What d'you mean?"

"Look, I can't speak no more, David. Jus' watch out, thass all."

"Um, thanks Zoë. I will. Thank you very much. I owe you."

"Sure. Bye, David."

* * * * * *

The night before David was due to report back to the police station he went up to his mobile home site to meet a new tenant. As he drove through the gates he noticed a young girl sitting on a low wall. When she saw his car approach, she immediately jumped to her feet and smiled at him, invitingly. He drove on through the gates and parked beside the caretaker's van. Ken was outside, sweeping up.

"Who's the girl on the gates, Ken? I haven't seen her before."

"Good question. She's been coming up every day for a week now, always around teatime, and hangs around until it gets dark. She certainly doesn't live here. She doesn't seem to know anyone. If she wasn't so young I'd think she was on the game, judging by what she's wearing, not that she's hanging around in the right place to pick up any custom of course. You usually see girls like that down round the back of the station."

"Ask her to move on, will you, Ken?"

"What if she doesn't?"

"If she comes back tomorrow, call the police."

"OK, boss."

Ken was a bit surprised. Why didn't David just walk over and tell her himself? He'd been a bit funny recently. Still moody after his wife had left him, Ken supposed. Couldn't be easy.

* * * * * *

David sat waiting at the police station. He had reported to the desk nearly an hour earlier, and was told to take a seat. An officer would come for him. His fear and apprehension grew. What was going to happen? Had they found Mandy? What about the other girls? Would he be charged? An inner door opened, and his solicitor came in, clutching a bundle of papers under his arm. He sat next to David and spoke quietly in his ear, taking care that people nearby could not hear.

"They're going to re-bail you. They need more time. It means they haven't yet found anything to charge you with."

David tried to contain his relief.

"But don't let that fool you," continued the solicitor. "It means everything and nothing. These things always drag on. You just have to be patient. Oh, and they're giving you back your computer and all the other bits. They're only keeping the girls' photos and the video tape of you with Mandy."

"That's a relief. Not having my computer has been a nuisance."

"It's also good news. It means they found nothing on it to incriminate you further. If they had, they'd be keeping it as evidence. Oh, here he comes, our friend."

PC Watson appeared behind the desk and signalled for David to go over. Much to David's embarrassment, Watson spoke in a loud, clear voice.

"Andrew David Bates, I am arresting you for . . ."

Why was he saying all this again? Was it necessary to be so loud? Why here, in front of all these people. They're looking at me . . .

". . . against you," continued Watson. "Now come with me, Mr Bates, and the desk sergeant in the custody suite will give you the paperwork for your bail."

A short time later David sat in a small interview room with his solicitor.

"So I've got to come back in another three weeks. Why did he arrest me like that?"

"Well, that's just normal procedure. They have to re-arrest you when you surrender your bail, but I must say that our PC Watson is a particularly unpleasant character. The way in which he did it was completely unnecessary. I think your supposition that he has been trying to set you up is not unfounded. What you must do is to maintain a written record of all these occurrences, including the date and time, the names, and any other details. Some may just be a coincidence, but we need to be vigilant. It seems pretty clear that this Watson character is overstepping the mark, and we might be able to have him for abuse of process in the long run. That would cause any case against you to collapse. Have there been anymore phone calls?"

"Not since the last one I told you about."

"Well, let me know if the girl at the site is still there tonight."

* * * * * *

PC Watson watched David carrying his computer out of the police station, closely followed by George Crabtree.

"Cunt!" he muttered under his breath, and went down to the canteen, where he found Derek Bostock.

"Sod's not taking the bait. Being too bloody clever, he is. Just had a call from the girl Sharon gave me – the one I wired up with a recorder and a buzzer. She saw him down the site last night, and then the caretaker told her to bugger off. Bastard. Just renewed his bail. I made him fuckin' squirm though."

"So, he not playing then?" asked Bostock.

"Being too clever for his own good," replied Watson. "I got a friend from Manchester to phone him. Pretended to be an escort agency offering underage girls. Cool as a fuckin" cucumber, Bates was. Didn't buy it at all."

"Well, perhaps you've been wrong about him all along, Phil. We've just got nothing on him, have we?"

"No? Look, I can smell cunts like that from thirty paces. I know what he is. He thinks he can outsmart me? Well, it's time I started playing dirty."

"Sounds like you already have, Phil."

"That's not dirty, my son. I haven't even started yet. Anyway, what's the news from the Child Protection unit? They must have something for us by now."

"Yes, but it won't please you," said Bostock.

"Try me."

"They've identified two of the girls, and they're young."

"Great! So why won't it please me? They dead or something?"

"No, they're just not young enough."

"Bugger!"

"Two stepsisters. Social Services say they were found working on the streets when they were both fourteen."

"And?"

"That was six years ago."

"Fuck!"

"And anyway, they say they've never met this Bates bloke."

"Course they fucking have! They were photographed by him in his fuckin' house!"

"Yes, but they're not willing to confirm that. They won't make a statement against him."

"Bollocks! Anything else?"

"Yes, Social Services think that one of the other girls is in the hostel up Cemetery Hill."

"Yeah, I know it. Lots of working girls pass through there. Worth a visit. What's her name?"

"Kathy Richards."

"How old is she?"

"Eighteen."

"Well, let's go an' have a chat with our Kathy. And bring the photos. If she's been around the hostels, she might know some of the other girls.

* * * * * *

The door opened to the lounge at the hostel and the warden brought in a tall, extremely thin girl with long, fair hair. She sat awkwardly on the edge of a chair and fumbled in her bag for a cigarette. Her hands shook as she lit it. Watson eyed her suspiciously.

"How long have you been on crack, Kathy?" he said.

The girl went white. " 'ere, what's this?" she spluttered. "They told me you just wanted to talk about some punter."

Watson softened. "We do, love, we do. Just relax."

He opened a box and spread photographs across a low table in front of him. Kathy's was among them. She glanced at them, then looked away, nervously.

"Where d'you get them?" she gasped.

"Well, that's what I wanted to ask you, Kathy."

"Can't remember. Some geezer. Few months back. Can't remember."

He held a photograph up to the light. "Nice tits you've got, Kathy! Very nice."

"You dirty bastard!" she hissed.

"Now, now. I was just paying you a compliment, that's all. You've got the nicest pair of tits I've seen in a long time, don't you think so, PC Bostock?"

Derek glanced at the photograph, but said nothing. The girl looked away.

"Isn't that what he said to you to get you to pose for him, Kathy?" continued Watson. "I can just imagine it. He pours you a drink, and you sit down on one of his nice leather settees, and he speaks to you in his posh voice, and tells you what nice tits you've got and how you ought to be a model, and how he'll make you famous, and before you know what's happening, your bra just seems to fall off you, and there he is, snappin' away, click-click, click-click, and he's saying how good you are, and why don't you drop your knickers too, click-click, click-click. And then he throws a roll of notes at you, and you let the dirty bastard dribble all over you. Isn't that how it happened, Kathy?"

Kathy looked ready to explode. "You're the dirty bastard!" she thundered. "That bloke's worth ten of you!"

"Oh, so you do remember him after all then?" grinned Watson.

"Yes, I do, and it wasn't like that at all. Yeah, he paid well, but he was a gent. He didn't make me do nothing, or even try to persuade me. I wanted to do it. I enjoyed it, if you really wanna know. He was kind, and treated me like a lady. You wouldn't understand that, pondlife like you. You treat us all like shit. Everyone knows about you, you cunt! And if you think I'm making a statement against 'im, you can think again. You'll not find any girl to do that."

Watson grinned again. "Kathy, Kathy! Temper, temper! I'm not asking you to grass on him. After all, it was all legal, wasn't it? I mean, you're eighteen, aren't you? Everything you do is legal, isn't it ,Kathy? Well, almost everything."

Kathy frowned. "What d'you mean?"

Watson's face lost its smile and he looked menacingly at Kathy. "The crack, Kathy, the crack."

Kathy looked away and said nothing.

"My colleague here, PC Bostock, doesn't like drugs. Not one bit. He's from Shropshire, you see. They don't get much crack in rural Shropshire. And PC Bostock here, he's got a very strong sense of duty. Always feels obliged to go by the book. He's so keen! Not a soft touch like me. I mean, I can sometimes turn a blind eye to these things, but not PC Bostock. If he found a supply tucked away in your room upstairs, it could get you into so much trouble. You know how it is, love. The judges don't like crack pushers."

"Who says I'm pushin'?"

Watson ignored her. "Like I say, the judges don't like pushers. Usually hand down two years, even for a first offence."

Kathy sighed and her shoulders sank. Watson gathered up the photos, and handed the box to Bostock.

"Derek, I wonder if you'd be so kind as to take these around the other rooms, and see if anyone can put names to these faces. I'll just finish off speaking to Kathy by myself."

Bostock stood up, gave Watson a disapproving look, and left the room. Watson got up and strolled across to stand behind Kathy's chair. He leaned down close to her and placed his mouth against her ear. He reached over and, with a quick movement, plunged his hand down inside her blouse, roughly grasping one breast. Kathy jerked backwards, but was held fast.

"Ow, you bastard. That 'urts! Ged off!"

"Yes, very nice tits you got," he said, breathily.

"I ain't doin' that. Not with you!"

"You'll do what you're fuckin' told. You'll do what I want you to do. Understand?"

He squeezed her breast even harder.

"Yes! Ow! Let go!"

"That's better. But I don't want to fuck you, you dirty bitch. You crack addicts are all full of filthy disease. I wouldn't touch you with a fuckin' barge pole. No, there's something else you're going to do for me." He released her and walked around to stand in front of her chair. Kathy lifted up her knees and hugged them close to her body. "Now then, Kathy. This man who took the photos. He's not what you think. He's not very nice. In fact, he's a paedophile, Kathy."

"Bollocks!" said Kathy, rocking in her chair.

"No, really, he's taken photos of hundreds of girls. Hundreds. As young as thirteen, twelve, eleven. One is even eight. You should see them, Kathy. You'd be shocked."

Kathy stared at him.

"Trouble is, we need to nail him with some really good evidence. Catch him at it, so to speak. But like all these paedophiles, he's a really slippery customer. So we need to actually catch him with a young girl. The younger the better. Now, Kathy, you've been around, you know the scene. I bet you know one or two girls who would help us. There'd be money in it for you, and as for the crack, well, I'm sure I can persuade PC Bostock to look the other way . . ."

* * * * * *

"We've got one more lead," said Bostock, as they drove away.

"Really?"

"Yes. The pictures of the very petite girl in the black underwear. The one you said you were sure was only fourteen, remember?"

"I certainly do. And? Was I right? Who is she?"

"First name Sarah. They say she's working in a sauna in the city centre. Comfort Zone. Only, she's not fourteen."

"No?"

"No. She's twenty-three, and a single mother."

"You've got to be fuckin' joking!"

"No, really. Must admit I was surprised too, but the girl who told me used to be her next door neighbour. Has known her for years."

"Fuck!"

"Listen, Phil. I know you hate this bloke, but we're spending a lot of time on this investigation and we're getting nowhere. Every girl we've identified so far has been well over sixteen. This bloke doesn't seem to have done anything wrong."

Watson turned a deep purple colour.

"Now you listen to me, Derek. I'm getting a just a bit fed up with your whinging ways. I've been very patient with you so far, always looking so fucking disapproving and being so bloody green. This is the real world. If you don't like the heat, get out of the fuckin' kitchen and go back to helping old ladies cross the road in bloody Shropshire."

"OK, OK, calm down, Phil. No offence."

"All right, all right, none taken, mate. Sorry I blew it. It's just that this case is getting to me a bit, I admit it. I thought we were on to something big at the start, and nothing's coming out of it. But I have a gut feeling on this one. Just trust me. I've been around. I know a villain when I spot one. I'm not giving up on this one yet. Anyway, our young Kathy is going to help us."

"Kathy? But I thought she said she wouldn't make a statement against him."

"Well, let's just say I persuaded her to change her mind."

* * * * * *

"I"m afraid Kathy's gone, PC Watson."

Watson stood on the front steps of the hostel looking up at the warden. "Gone? Gone where?"

"I don't know. The other girls say she's gone up north. It was the day after you were here. She just packed her bags and went. I couldn't stop her. She's eighteen, after all. I have no powers once they pass seventeen."

Watson cursed and walked back towards his car. He felt sure he'd got Kathy in his pocket, but now she'd bolted. He'd catch up with her one day. They always came back, these girls. Every time it got too hot in one town, they'd move on, but they always came back, eventually.

But he was beginning now to think that his oppo was right. They'd found most of the girls now. All of them were over sixteen and not one would make a complaint. What had this bloke got, for Christ's sake? Was it just his money? He used the girls once or twice, and then just dumped them, yet they still stayed loyal to him. That wasn't like prostitutes. Most would sell their own mothers for a wrap of brown. But this bloke seemed to cast a spell over them.

There was one though who seemed to know more than she was saying. She'd shown a flicker of recognition when she'd seen the photos of the girl in the video. What was her name again? Tracey? No, Stacey. But she was as tight-lipped as the others. No joy there, and time was running out. The bail would be up in a week's time. He could always renew it, but the Super would need some persuading this time. And so far, he got nothing to charge the bastard with, except for being a bastard, of course.

Still, he'd given out Bates's phone number to loads of underage girls. Surely one of them would tempt him out of his shell. After all, he'd been used to seeing girls two or three times a week, so he must be feeling very sex-starved by now. And maybe he was also starting to feel a bit more confident. That could be his downfall . . .

* * * * * *

" 'ullo David, it's Stacey " 'ere."

"Stacey! Who gave you my number?"

"A copper."

"Not called Watson, but any chance, was he?"

"That's 'im."

"Why did he give it to you, Stacey?"

" 'e's givin' it to loads of girls. Showin' pictures of Mandy too. Wants to know who she is."

"Did you tell him?"

"Course not. I don't grass on nobody. Mandy's my mate."

"Thank you, Stacey."

"But Watson's tellin' everyone you're a paedophile. Wants to catch you with an underage girl, 'e does."

"Well, thanks for warning me, Stacey."

"Look, David. I'm sorry I was nickin' from you. It was stupid, I know. Look, I was wonderin' if you'd like to see me again. I'd make it up to you, honest I would. I could do anythin' Mandy did. An' better."

"Sorry, Stacey. I'm not seeing anyone. I can't risk it. I don't want to attract any attention from the police. It just isn't worth it. But I do appreciate you calling me. Really I do."

"But, David, OK, so you won't see me, but the thing is, I owe this geezer some money, an' I've gotta get it tonight, or I'll be in trouble. An' I've got no one else to ask. So could yuh borrow it me?"

"I'd like to help, but I'm afraid I can't. I'm sorry, Stacey."

"But it's really important, David."

"Sorry, Stacey. No."

"Alright then," said Stacey, with a sudden change of tone to her voice, "you let me 'ave an 'undred quid tonight or I"ll tell that Watson you asked me to get you a twelve-year-old. I swear to God I will."

David gasped.

"Why, Stacey? Why would you do that?"

" 'cos I needs the money, an' I needs it tonight."

"But, Stacey, I always treated you well. Why are you doing this?"

"I don"t give a fuck about you. I need that money. If you don't. . ."

David cut her off, and then turned off his phone to prevent her ringing back. Why was all this happening? He felt he was being attacked from all sides, and could never relax. He wrote down the details of his conversation with Stacey, and the next morning, he phoned his solicitor.

* * * * * *

"I think she's bluffing," said George Crabtree. "She knows you're under pressure from the police, and she's just using that to extract money. My guess is that she's feeding a drug problem, maybe hers, or maybe a boyfriend, and people like that will do or say anything to get money. I feel sure that you'll hear nothing from her again. You did well to stand firm. She'll have got the money from someone else, got the drugs, and will have forgotten about it already. People like her don't run to the police with tales. But tell me, she said she is a friend of Mandy. Did you think to ask her Mandy's age?"

"Shit! Oh, excuse me George. No, I was so shocked by her attempted blackmail that it didn't occur to me."

"Well, that's not surprising. Oh, well, never mind. I'm sure we'll find out in due course. You have to answer bail again at the end of the week. I doubt if they'll renew it this time, so it's either charge or release, I'd say."

* * * * * *

PC Watson put down the phone and smiled. "Got the bastard!" he muttered to himself.

Derek Bostock walked into his office, looking flustered.

"Phil, this report you asked me to write, well . . ."

"Never mind that. Get your coat, we"re going on a little trip."

"Where to?"

"The Nick. We've won the pools!"

Watson strode out of the office with Bostock scurrying after him. They were driving along the high road heading towards the city centre before Watson said anything.

"You ever woken up one day just knowing that everything was going to be just great, Derek?"

"Um, not often, no."

"When I woke up this morning, I looked out the window and it was grey and pissing with rain, and I just knew it was my sort of day."

"Yes?"

"Yes. I had that nice cold feeling inside me, and sure enough, we've hit the fuckin' jackpot!"

"Have we? How?"

"Turns out that our Mr Bates lost his cash card a while back."

"So?"

"Only, he didn't."

"Not with you, Phil."

"He didn't lose it. It was nicked, only he didn't want anyone to know that."

"No?"

"No. And you know why? Cos he didn't want the thief to be caught."

"Why not? Sounds stupid," said Bostock.

" 'cos the thief just happened to be the brother of our video star."

"Really? How d'you know that, Phil?"

" 'cos there was a camera at one of the cash dispensers when he withdrew the money, and it gave the bank a nice mug shot of him. He's got form. A lot of form. Name's Wayne Richards, and he's talking. Oh yes, he's talking. He's on remand at The Green. Up for sentencing next month. He wants a deal. Oh, I think we've got our Mr Bates now, my son. The bastard's gonna hang, he'll fucking hang."

"Um, don't think so, Phil. It"s been abolished, remember?"

* * * * * *

Wayne drew deeply on his cigarette and sat back, watching PC Watson's pen scribbling across the page. When Watson had finished, he gathered all the sheets together and tapped them into line.

"Right Wayne, I'm going to read all this back to you and then ask you to sign the top and bottom of each page. You know the drill."

" 'ang on a bit. You sure this is gonna get me off? I don't trust you bastards."

"Well, it's like this, Wayne, said Watson, "you're up for sentencing on the supermarket job next month and you're expecting a two stretch. If we proceed against you for kidnap and armed robbery, you could be looking at an extra eight, so you don't have a lot of choice, do you? It wouldn't be difficult for us to accidentally lose the bank photo of you providing you sign this statement. We want to nail this bloke, Wayne, 'cos he's a nonce. You're not a nonce-lover, are you Wayne?"

"Course I'm fuckin not."

"No, I thought not. You're just an honest villain, aren't you. Just a bit of robbery with violence, that's you, isn"t it? Nothin' serious like sex crimes."

Wayne nodded. "Course not. I 'ate fucking' nonces. Castrate the bastards, and feed their balls to the dogs, that's what I say."

"Good, so I think we understand one another, don't we, Wayne?And we want this bastard Bates behind bars, don't we, so decent lads like you can cut 'im up a bit while he's doing stir, isn't that right?"

Wayne grinned, and picked up the pen.

* * * * * *

David sat in the small, sound-proofed room with two tape recorders running, watching PC Watson pulling photographs out of a box.

"So you're saying, Mr Bates, that you met these girls through escort agencies?"

David looked sideways at George Crabtree, who was busy making notes. Behind Watson sat PC Bostock, his arms folded.

"That's right," answered David.

"But you can't remember the name of the agency?"

"I didn't say that. What I said was that the agencies tend to come and go. Their names or their telephone numbers change quite frequently."

"So how do you find out about the agencies in the first place?"

"From the personal columns in the local paper. There's several column inches of similar adverts every day. I'm sure you will have seen them."

"And is there any other method you have used to meet girls for the purpose of having sex with them?"

David frowned at the bluntness of the question. "Well, if I met a girl I liked, I sometimes gave her my phone number so that she could ring me."

Watson put his hand into the bottom of the box and brought out a small business card.

"Do you recognise this, Mr Bates?"

"Yes, that's my business card."

"And that's what you would give to a girl you wanted to meet again?"

"Yes."

"Rather an unusual business card, isn't it? I mean, just your name and telephone number? No address, and this little design on it. Strange design don't you think? Looks like a vagina."

"Vagina? I think it's meant to be a telephone."

"Funny telephone, if you ask me."

"Well, I really can't see how you think it"s a vagina, either!" retorted David.

"Does anyone else you know also carry cards like these?"

"Pardon?"

"Do you know any other men who carry cards like this?
Are you a member of an organisation which distributes these
cards to its members, containing this symbol? Is this a sort of
membership card?"

"No, of course not. I got the cards printed on the
machine in the shopping centre. The design is simply one of
the options you choose. It has no significance whatsoever. I
just happened to choose a telephone because I wanted to have
a card with my telephone number on it to give out to business
clients."

"And to young prostitutes?"

"Um, yes."

"For the sole purpose of enabling the girl you have met
to contact you again."

"Yes."

"So you don't ask the girls to recruit other girls for you
then?"

"No, I don't ask for it, but it has happened."

"What has happened, Mr Bates?"

"Well, sometimes, a girl would phone me to say she had
a friend who wanted to meet me."

"Why would her friend wish to meet you?"

"To be an escort."

"To have sex with you, you mean?"

"Yes."

"And do you ever ask for a particular type of girl?"

"Well, they know the sort of girl I like."

"And what is that, Mr Bates?"

"Well, I suppose I like what most men like. Slim,
attractive, shapely . . ."

"And young?"

"Yes, young."

"So when you contact an agency, or speak to a girl you've met, you ask for a girl who is young?"

"Yes."

"And why young, in particular?"

"Oh, well, I suppose it was because to start with I was sent women who were older and less attractive. Not so slim."

"And what is wrong with that? You're a middle-aged man. What is wrong with a woman who is, say, in her thirties or forties?"

"There's nothing wrong with them. I just happen to find younger women more sexually attractive, that's all. I mean, you don't get older women winning beauty contests, do you? I know some men like older women, or plumper women, or whatever, but that's not my taste. You don't drive a Reliant Robin if you can afford a Rolls Royce, do you?"

"Sorry, you'll have to explain that."

"All I'm trying to say that is when you buy something, you buy the thing that attracts you most, and the best you can afford. Since I was paying for female company, I knew I would enjoy it more if my companions were sexually attractive to me, and my preference is pretty normal, I'd say. Like most men, I am attracted to young, slim, pretty females.

"Normal? You say you think you are normal?"

"Yes. Of course. Whatever normal means, in this day and age. Normal, typical, call it what you like."

"So, let's see about that. How young is young, Mr Bates?"

"Well, most of the women I met were in their early twenties. A few were in their late teens."

"Mr Bates, I want you to think carefully before you answer this question. Have you ever asked for girls who were under sixteen."

"No. Never."

"You are quite sure about that?"

"Certain."

"Did you ever ask the escorts how old they were?"

"Yes, sometimes."

"Why? Did you think some might be under sixteen?"

"No, of course not. I think I asked just out of interest, and because the agencies sometimes lie about the girls' ages."

"So you thought it possible that some of the girls might be a lot younger than you had been told, but you still went ahead and had sex with them?"

"No, not at all. It was the other way around."

"What do you mean?"

"Some girls were a lot older than I had been told."

"Never younger?"

"Not that I was aware of."

"But they could have been."

"I don't know. Maybe, by a year or so."

"So you could quite easily have had sex with a girl who was under sixteen, and it didn't bother you?"

"No, I didn't say that. As far as I was told, the youngest I ever saw was eighteen. I am certain that none were under sixteen."

"And if you thought a girl might be under sixteen, what did you do?"

"It never happened."

"So you're a good judge of age then, are you, Mr Bates?"

"Well, I think I would know if a girl was under sixteen."

"And how would you know that?"

"Well, from the way she behaved. From her general maturity."

"And from her looks?"

"Yes, although obviously some girls look older than their years, and some look younger."

Watson reached into the box and took out the photograph of a blonde girl."

"And how old would you say this girl is then, Mr Bates?"

"Uh, twenty, I think."

"And what was her name?"

"I'm sorry, I can't remember. It was last year when I met her. Even if I could remember, it wouldn't help because many girls don't use their own names. They have working names."

"Well, Mr Bates, would it surprise you to know that this girl is, in fact, nineteen, which means that when you met her she was eighteen? That's two years younger than you thought at the time."

"Well, I said I thought she looked twenty in the photograph. I can't actually remember what she said at the time. It may have been eighteen or nineteen, and it was only nine months ago, so it could still be right."

"And what about this one?"

"Um, twenty-two."

"No. She"s nineteen."

David felt unsteady. "Well, you picked two who may be slightly younger than they look, but there are others who are much older."

"Really? Well, let's look further, shall we?" Watson spread the photos across the table between them. "So which ones are older then, Mr Bates?"

"This one! Look! I can't remember her name but she was twenty-three. She had a young child. I think she looks much younger."

"Strange how your memory is so selective, Mr Bates. You can remember the ages of all the girls, but you can't remember any of their names."

"I have a poor memory for names."

"Very convenient. What about this one?"

Watson pushed all the photos to one side, and now began covering the table with pictures of Mandy. Despite his nervousness and discomfort, David couldn't help but notice again how beautiful she was, and realised how much he was missing her.

"Surely you remember this girl's name? After all, these were the photos you were carrying when we arrested you, so you took them very recently, didn't you, Mr Bates? So what is her name?"

David looked down at the pictures and remained silent.

"Well, let me help you, Mr Bates. Her name is Amanda Kinch. Did you know that?"

"I didn't know her full name. I just knew her as Mandy."

"And how old is Mandy, Mr Bates?"

"Eighteen. She told me she was eighteen. And her mother told me that too"

"Her mother? Are you telling me that you met her mother?" said Watson, feigning surprise.

"Yes. Her mother was running the agency."

"Are you seriously asking me to believe that this girl's mother was prostituting her own daughter?"

"Yes, apparently, although I didn't know that at the time."

"Would it have made any difference?"

"Um, I . . . I don't know. No, I suppose not. I mean, if she's eighteen, then it's up to her, I suppose."

"So where did you meet Mandy, then?"

"In a pub car park."

"Not outside a school?"

"No, of course not."

"And she told you she was eighteen."

"Yes."

"Well, Mr Bates, Amanda Kinch is not eighteen."

"No?" David felt faint. His pulse was racing.

"No, Mr Bates. In fact, she is fifteen years and nine months old, Mr Bates."

David's head dropped. George reached sideways and put his hand on David's shoulder. David looked up at Watson's triumphant face.

"No, no, she can't be," said David. "I don't believe it. It's not possible."

"And what is more, Mr Bates, we have a witness who has made a statement saying you knew her age, that you picked her up outside her school gates, that you regularly pick up girls from a local children's home, and that you have asked Amanda's mother to find you girls as young as ten."

"That's complete and utter rubbish!" blurted David. "It is just not true. It's outrageous! Who is this witness? She's lying."

"She? Did I say she?" he turned to Bostock. "Did I say she, PC Bostock?"

Bostock remained motionless, and said nothing.

"And with these photographs, Mr Bates," continued Watson, "we found a video tape. Do you know what was on that tape?"

"Yes."

"And what was on the tape, then, Mr Bates?"

"It was a recording of me with Mandy."

"Made by you?"

"Yes."

"In your home?"

"Yes."

"And it showed you having sexual intercourse with a fifteen-year-old girl. Am I right?"

"I didn't know she was fifteen at the time."

"No, so you say. But can you confirm that you are having sexual intercourse with Amanda Kinch in this recording?"

George leaned forwards and whispered in David's ear.

"No comment," replied David.

"Oh, right then, moving on," said Watson. "I notice that she is drinking champagne. Was it always your practice to get girls drunk before you had sex with them?"

"No, of course not. That's a gross distortion of what happened. I usually offered girls a drink, yes, just as a matter of courtesy, that's all. And Mandy wasn't drinking champagne. She just happened to be using a champagne glass. She was actually drinking lemonade."

"Drinking lemonade from a champagne glass? Really?"

"Yes."

"And she was quite happy to go along with what happened?"

"Yes."

"Are you sure? I mean, there was no coercion on your part?"

"None at all. She was completely happy with everything that happened. Enthusiastic, even."

"Well, Mr Bates, we have watched this recording several times, and listened to it carefully. In one section, Amanda is saying, and let me quote: "Oh, no sir, I'm just a pure little virgin! Please be gentle with me! Don't hurt me will you? This is my first time." Now, does that really sound like a girl who is completely happy, and enthusiastic?"

"But she was acting!"

"Acting? A fifteen-year-old?"

"Yes! She was just playing around. It was a just a game. Anyone could see that."

"Really, just like anyone could see that she's eighteen, you mean? Right, well, our time is running out, and I am going to draw this interview to a close. Mr Bates, we have evidence that you have deliberately set out to ensnare children for the purposes of your own sexual gratification. Today, we intend to charge you with offences relating to Amanda Kinch. You will be bailed to appear before magistrates in two weeks' time and, in the meantime, our investigations will continue."

* * * * * *

While waiting to be formally charged, the solicitor took David to one side.

"Listen, David," he said, "I know how you must be feeling, but it's no more than we expected once they found that one of the girls was under sixteen. They will charge you with taking photographs of a child, and with what they idiotically call taking 'pseudo' photographs, which refers to the video."

"But isn't that the same as taking photographs?"

"No, it will almost certainly be a separate charge. They have a habit of duplicating charges to make something stick. I'm afraid it also looks as though you will be charged with USI."

"USI?"

"Unlawful sexual intercourse. We don't know if the girl has made a statement, but if the video is as explicit as you believe, they'll charge you anyway, because the video itself will suffice as evidence. But as I've said before, whatever you do, don't contact the girl."

"Don't worry, I won't. But what about this other witness?" said David, glumly. "This business about children"s homes and schools? It's all complete rubbish."

"Are you sure you've never been in those places?"

"Of course I haven't, George! Don't you believe me?"

"It doesn't matter what I believe, David, I . . ."

"It matters to me. Listen, George, What I have told you is the truth. Everything. I know you're just doing your job, but it's really important to me that you believe everything I have told you. I would feel much more confident about you representing me if I knew you believed me."

"I understand that, and of course I believe you, David. Absolutely. Actually, the police may be bluffing about those sightings. They're still trying to bracket you with the predatory paedophiles, and my guess is that they think by frightening you they may get you to tell them more than they already know."

"But that's so underhand!"

"Are you surprised, after all that's happened? Look, I have to be leaving now. They'll read out the charges to you shortly. Just say 'no reply' to each, and bring the charge sheets into my office tomorrow. They won't ask you any more questions today. You'll get bail until the court hearing."

"And will that be the end of all this?"

"Oh no, just the beginning, I'm afraid. You'll then have the charges read out in court, and that will be adjourned, and you'll get bail again. It will go on and on until the Crown Prosecution Service has gathered all the evidence, and is ready to proceed. The trial will be at the Crown Court because of the seriousness of the offences."

"Seriousness?"

"Well, obviously you haven't murdered anyone, but it's more serious than a parking offence. Any offence which carries a possible sentence of more that six months in prison goes to the Crown Court. But look, let's not think about that yet. We'll fight this all the way, don't you worry. But it will almost certainly take a year before it comes to trial."

"A year! Oh my God!"

"Sorry, David, but that's the way it is. Look, just call me if there is anything you need to know."

* * * * * *

"I'll see if I can catch him, Mr Bates. I think he's just left the office."

David had just arrived back home from the police station and needed to speak urgently to his solicitor.

"David? You just caught me," said George Crabtree. "Everything all right?"

"I'm not sure. You were right about the charges – it was the three you mentioned, but I was interviewed again after you'd gone."

"What? They can't do that. You should have refused."

"It wasn't about my case. It was to do with the theft of my cash card."

"What happened?"

"Well, I was just about to leave when I was approached by another officer. He'd been waiting for me. Said he was investigating the loss of my card. Apparently, the man who stole it was photographed by the cash machine, and they know who he is. So I was asked if I wanted to make a new statement."

"And did you?"

"Yes. Well, they know who Mandy is now, so I didn't see any point in continuing to pretend that I'd simply lost the card. I apologised for having misled them, but explained that the men had threatened both me and my son."

"OK. Well, presumably they will be charging him. It might help your case because Mandy and her mother may be accomplices to the robbery. The whole thing could be interpreted as a conspiracy against you."

"I don't think so. The policeman who took the statement let slip that it was Mandy's brother, Wayne, who made the witness statement against me. He's the one who identified Mandy and who said I'd picked her up at her school, and so on."

"Oh dear, I think I can see what's going on here. They"ve done a deal with him. He becomes their main prosecution witness in exchange for them overlooking the robbery."

"Can they do that?"

"It happens all the time. In your case, they are so keen to prosecute you that they are willing to overlook a much more serious crime of kidnap and armed robbery. There's obviously a strong political motivation behind this. It probably because of the government-funded project to clean up the city's underage prostitution. Continuation of the project's funding depends on a high arrest and conviction rate. Unfortunately for you, this has all happened at the wrong time. A few years ago the police didn't give a damn about underage prostitutes. They were all treated like criminals. Now they're all victims. My guess is that our PC Watson is eager for promotion, and he really doesn't care how he gets it. Look, I'll pass you back to my secretary. Make an appointment to come to see me next week, and we'll talk about this in more detail. We need to start thinking about a defence strategy."

* * * * * *

No sooner had David put down the phone, than it rang again. It was Sophie.

"Dad, Dad, have you seen the paper? What's happened?"

"I've been charged. What's in the paper?"

"A small report giving your name, and the road you live in, and your age."

"Oh no."

"But can they do that?"

"I suppose so. They wouldn't do it otherwise."

"But why?" said Sophie. "You haven't been found guilty yet. It's trial and conviction by newspaper!"

"Well, I suppose they would justify it on the grounds of public interest."

"But what kind of people are they writing for? How can someone else's misery be of public interest?"

"That's the way newspapers sell copies, Sophie."

"Well, it's sick. Just sick. Everyone will know. All my friends."

"I know. I'm so sorry."

"So what happened? Did they find that some of the girls were under sixteen?"

"Just one – so far. They're still investigating. But I feel sure that there won't be any more."

"You said that before, Dad. You were sure that none were under sixteen."

"I know. I'm sorry. I'm so very sorry."

"No, it's you I'm worried about. What's going to happen to you? Will you go to prison?"

"Oh, I'm sure it won't come to that. We've a long way to go yet. My solicitor said it will take a year to come to court."

"A year? We have to live with this for a year?"

"Yes. I'm afraid so."

"Look, Dad. Just hang in there, OK? We're all behind you. Don't worry. I'll phone Kezzie and Jeremy."

"Thanks, sweetheart. I might just go out and get drunk."

"Well, don't go alone. Ring John. You need to stick close to your friends right now, Dad."

* * * * * *

Two weeks later David sat in his kitchen waiting for John to arrive. Their game was booked for six, and John was cutting it fine. The phone rang.

"David? Hello, mate. Listen, I'm not going to be able to make it again tonight. Parents' evening. Forgot all about it. Sorry it's such short notice."

"Oh, that's a shame. OK, well, what about Thursday? Shall I book a court?"

"Um, no. Look, I'll tell you what. I'll ring you when I can play. Wait for me to call, OK? Take it easy. See you later, mate."

"Hang on, hang on! What time does the parents' evening finish? How about just meeting for drink?"

"Can't, mate. She's trying a new recipe tonight. I'm under orders to be back by eight-thirty."

"Tomorrow then?"

"Can't, mate. I"ll ring you."

* * * * * *

But he didn't ring, so three days later David decided to pop around to John's house late one afternoon, when he knew John would be there alone.

"Are you avoiding me, John,?" said David, as soon as he was inside the door.

"What? Course not! What gives you that idea?" replied John, unconvincingly.

"Come on! What's the problem? Is it because they've charged me?"

John looked shiftily away, but then stepped forwards and grasped David by both shoulders.

"Listen, mate, I'm your friend through thick and thin, OK?"

David wasn't persuaded. "So why all the cancellations then?"

"Oh, listen, it's just been a busy time, that's all." There was an awkward silence. "Did they, um ask anything about me?" asked John, tentatively.

"Who?"

"The police?"

"You? Why should they?"

"You, um, didn't mention that I took photographs of Miranda then?"

"Of course not."

"Did the police speak to her?"

"They may have done, but, hey listen, this isn't about you. She was twenty-two or more, and you haven't done anything wrong. You're completely in the clear. You weren't mentioned."

"OK. Thing is, if it came out that I took glamour photographs, I could lose my job."

"I know that, mate. Don't worry. Believe me!"

"Well, as a precaution, I destroyed my entire collection."

"So, is this the reason you've been avoiding me?"

"No, well, the missus read the paper, and . . ."

"I get the picture. Look, if it makes things easier, let's just cool it for a while. Until this is all finished. Have a break from me until the court case is over. Would that help?"

"Oh, no, I wouldn"t hear of it," protested John. "No, I'm your best mate and I'll always be here for you. I'll call you."

But John never called, and David now realised that he wouldn't. John couldn't be seen socialising with someone accused of sex crimes against a child. He would be tainted by association. Despite being a joker, would-be womaniser, and pornographer, John was a devoted husband, member of the teaching profession, and had to put his marriage and career before his loyalty to a squash partner. David understood only too well. He didn't blame John, but it would make an enormous hole in his life. John would be missed.

It seemed to David that the collapse was just about complete. Only a few years before he'd been a happily married family man, with a diary crammed full of professional and social events. Life had been frantic, but satisfying and fulfilling. There had been so many invitations, that many had to be turned down. His Christmas card list ran into the hundreds. Now, nearly everyone had gone, except his children. Apart from Kezzie, at least they were still sticking to him and giving support. But there was limit to what they could do. He badly needed to have a very close friend, a confidante. A relationship. But who would want a relationship with a man charged with these offences? Whatever the outcome of the case, he felt his sentence had already begun. He felt stigmatised by the newspaper reports, which appeared every time he had to re-appear at the magistrates' court to answer his bail. He began to hate going out. Wherever he went, he feared people recognising him and pointing at him, or imagined they were saying things about him.

Every day the national newspapers seemed to contain more and more stories about sex offenders. Suspected paedophiles were the new bogeymen, and their public exposure was the modern-day equivalent of the medieval witch hunt. All those convicted were required to register so that their whereabouts could be constantly monitored. Would that happen to him? When he allowed himself to speculate on the future of his case, and concerned himself with public opinion, the more depressed he became. He had once been optimistic, energetic, and full of enthusiasm for life. Now he was reclusive, and lacked confidence. He found sleep difficult, often waking in the middle of the night from alarming dreams. His children did what they could, but David was reluctant to ask too much of them. He reasoned that they had their own lives to live and more often than not he put on a brave face, and reassured them that the whole thing was going to blow over. He even suggested that there was confidence that the charges would soon be dropped. But as the weeks and months went by, he began to feel desperate. He hated having to keep re-appearing in the magistrates' court, but George Crabtree assured him constantly that this was normal, that the Crown Prosecution Service were notoriously inefficient, and that no account was ever taken of the misery caused to the accused and their families by the very long delays. He obtained a small amount of comfort from the fact that there had been no further charges, and decided that the investigation must have been wound down because since being charged, the mysterious and often threatening phone calls had stopped. So everything hinged on the case against him concerning Mandy, and until the prosecution disclosed their evidence against him, he had no idea whether or not she had made a statement, or exactly what the nature was of the evidence against him, other than the photos and video. He talked to George about this.

"Well, if she hasn't made a statement," said George, "it means they can only use the photographic and video evidence."

"And could they convict me on that alone?"

"Yes, in theory, but they'd have no aggravating features."

"What does that mean?"

"I'm assuming that business about Mandy pretending to be a reluctant virgin was just play-acting . . ."

"It was!"

"OK, then the lack of aggravation makes a big difference when it come to sentencing. It means that although there is clear evidence that you had sex with an underage girl, and took photos and made a video, there is nothing to prove that you actually knew her age, or that you tried to procure underage girls. The witness statement they say they have regarding your being outside schools and children's homes would only be relevant if they could actually produce a statement from a girl who says she met you in that way, or if someone had actually recorded a date and time, with your car registration. So assuming there are no aggravating features, the result could be the difference between prison and say, probation."

For the first time in months David felt a slight lightening of the weight upon his shoulders. That night he slept well, and the next day he set off for Leeds, singing all the way. For so long he had resigned himself to the strong possibility that he would be going to prison, but now he had reason to hope that it might not happen.

* * * * * *

Nine months to the day after his original arrest, he attended what he thought would be another routine appearance at the magistrates' court. He sat in the dirty, stone-floored corridor while the clerk walked up and down taking names. The air was filled with smoke, and small, irritable children whined noisily.

Up until that day, every time David had attended court he had harboured a secret wish that he might be told that the charges had been dropped; that it was all over, so that he could rush out and tell his family. So when George Crabtree greeted him much more warmly than usual, and whisked him into a small conference room, David's hopes rose.

"I've got the advanced disclosure papers, and it's great news!" said George.

"Really?" answered David, expectantly.

George noticed his client's excitement. "Oh, not that great, sorry! They're still proceeding with the charges, I'm afraid, but I've had a quick glance through the papers, and there's no statement from Amanda Kinch."

Good for Mandy, thought David. She stuck by me, after all. "Oh, good," he said.

"Good? It's marvellous," said George. "It makes an enormous difference. And, as we suspected, the statement about you hanging around schools and children's homes comes from her brother, Wayne Richards, the man who robbed you. And it's all hearsay. It won't even get to court, I imagine. The only thing they can use it for is to establish her identity and age. The whole thing plays right into our hands."

"How?"

"Well, it contains information that Amanda was already working as a prostitute, which eliminates the corruption element that they might wish to level against you. It also confirms her mother's involvement in the robbery."

"Really?"

"So this is all very encouraging. Of course, further evidence could always be added later, but I think it's unlikely. Anyway, we've got eight weeks to study this and to decide on our strategy. They've included the photographs and the video, so we need to look at it all together, and then we come back here for a committal hearing."

"What's that?"

"Just another Magistrates' session – the last one, mind you – when they formally transfer the case to the Crown Court. Then, when we go to the Crown Court, we need to decide whether we are pleading guilty or not guilty."

David liked the way George always said 'we'. It helped to lift the burden and made him feel that someone else was sharing it with him, that he wasn't alone in all this. But at the end, he knew that it would be him alone, and not George, who faced the punishment.

The Prosecution

"As you know, we have no alternative other than to plead guilty," said Damien Fforbes-Brown, as he sat sipping tea in George Crabtree's office.

This was David's first meeting with his barrister, a high-flier from the Oxford and London circuits who, according to George, had a track record second to none, and who was the next best thing to a QC. 'Why pay all that money', George had said, 'when we can get an excellent man for half the price?' David hadn't been entirely convinced. He wondered whether a female barrister might be a better choice given the nature of the case, but he was happy, in the end, to be guided by George.

Damien Fforbes-Brown, was a small, thin man, in his forties, dressed in an over-sized suit, still crumpled from his train journey. Despite the fact that his briefcase bulged with seemingly disorganised papers, most of which had nothing to do with this appointment, David was impressed by his knowledge of the case. Some of the time he seemed not to be listening, but then he would turn and give a straight look with his steel-blue eyes which showed that he was obviously quite capable of concentrating on several things at the same time. In David's case, he had done his reading.

"It goes against the grain to plead guilty," continued Fforbes-Brown, "because I am a fighter, and I like nothing better than a good fight, but having looked carefully into what the prosecution has got on you, there seems little point. The photographs are there for everyone to see. It's quite obvious that they were taken in your house, and you've admitted as much. The video quite clearly depicts you having sexual intercourse with the girl, and her age has been established beyond doubt. The good thing we have is that there is no

evidence that you knew her age, and there are no other
aggravating features. But if we went for a not guilty plea, then
all this would have to be shown to a jury, and it would all be
reported in the local paper. I'm sure you wouldn't want that."

"No."

"No. Normally, I'm all in favour of letting a jury decide. I
work well with juries. I know how they think. But it's because
of that knowledge that I believe it would be a mistake in this
case. Imagine a jury with parents of teenagers, and people like
that squeamish pharmacy assistant, whose statement I have
read, watching that video? No matter what factual aspects are
in your favour, they'd take one look at that video and, well . . .
I'm sure you take my point?"

"Yes," said David, "so how are you proposing to
approach the case?"

"Well, the bottom line in this is that you could go to
prison, and you must prepare yourself for that eventuality."

"I have," said David.

"But bear this in mind: the maximam sentence won't be
more than two years, which means you'll actually serve only
one. In other words, you'd be out in no time, and this thing
would all be over. But that's the worst scenario. There are
other alternatives, including probation, community service, or
even just a fine; more likely, a combination of the three. I will
consider it a personal failure if you go to prison. What we
must now do is to prepare a factual basis for our mitigation
and see if we can get the prosecution to accept that in
exchange for a guilty plea. Then we supplement that with as
much other stuff as we can. Mr Crabtree has already
suggested you get a psychiatrist's report, I understand?"

"Yes. I went to see someone a couple of weeks ago. I
think it went pretty well. He said I'd been depressed

following my divorce, and that it had probably affected my judgment."

"Good. That sounds helpful."

"And he also concluded that he thought I was sexually normal, and that I don't represent a threat to women."

"That's excellent! That's exactly the sort of thing we need. Now, I understand you are to see the probation service next week to be interviewed for the pre-sentence report. That's a crucial interview because the judge places much importance on what they recommend when it comes to sentencing. So you also need to persuade them that you're not a risk. If we can get them to agree with the psychiatrist, then we're in a very strong position. The judge is unlikely to ignore both of them, although he could ignore one. Now, what else, George?"

"References?" suggested George.

"Yes, of course. Do you know people who would write you character references? They need to be sent to the judge."

"What sort of references?" asked David.

"Well, from someone who knows your sexual tastes and habits, for example. What about your ex-wife? Would she support you?"

"I think so. Yes."

"And a personal friend?"

"Not many of those left, I'm afraid, but I'm sure I could think of someone."

"And perhaps a work colleague?"

"Well, I'm self-employed now, but I think I could find someone who has done business with me over a period of time."

"Fine. The idea is to build up a picture of a responsible, caring, normal sort of man with an impeccable track record, who has simply made this one mistake."

"I get the idea. I'll approach them and have drafts sent to you for approval, before being sent to the judge, shall I?"

Before he could answer, Damien's mobile phone rang and he stood up and paced the room as he took the call. When he had finished, he resumed his seat.

"Sorry about that. Murder case. Being re-convened tomorrow. Very interesting. No body. Think we've won it actually. Right, so where were we? Oh yes. References. That's fine. Look, there's just one thing that bothers me slightly in this case"

"What's that?" asked George.

"It's this business about how old the girl is supposed to have looked. It's all very well them telling us that she's only fifteen, but we need to put up a fight here. What I'm not going to do though is to drag up her history: the fact that the girl has been a prostitute for years, that she appears to come from a thoroughly corrupt family, and all that. It could backfire in our faces. But what we can do is to get some independent opinion about how old she looks. That could provide strong mitigation. If we can get a medical person, or someone like that, to say she looks sixteen or more, then that would be a powerful weapon to add to our armoury. What d'you think, George?"

"Yes. Excellent. But who? Sounds like quite a specialist field."

"Well, I'll leave you to sort that out, George. You're the local man here. Anyway, Mr Bates, I'll be in touch if there's anything else. If you need to contact me about anything at all, George here will pass on any messages. Oh, and good luck with the probation officers."

* * * * * *

"Come in and sit down, Mr Bates. I'm Carmen Wills-Bennett, from the Central Child Protection Unit, and this is Rajinder Singh, your assigned probation officer."

David sat down. He remembered his barrister's warning about how important this interview was. It could mean the difference between prison and probation. It was just a question of persuading these two people in front of him now that this had been a one-off mistake, that he wasn't an habitual offender, and that there was no risk of his re-offending. Despite the importance of the occasion, David felt reasonably relaxed. It was almost like being back at work. He knew how professional people thought and acted. He felt at home with them. He knew their language, whether overt or codified. He recognised the signals. He had been part of it for years, having worked with all the statutory and voluntary agencies that meshed to provide public service. He knew how reports were compiled and written and presented. He understood what consultation really meant. He was one of the lads. He knew he could handle this. It was just a question of keying in to the right intellectual level, pressing the right buttons, using the correct body language, smiling at the right moment, showing empathy, just the right amount of guilt and remorse, not being too clever, but not appearing stupid.

"Right then, Mr Bates. It's David, isn't it?"

A good start, thought David. First name terms. A softly-softly approach. He preferred that. He'd used it himself, a thousand times.

"Yes," he answered, with a polite smile, and maintaining good eye contact with Carmen.

"Right, David, you know why you are here?"

"Yes. I do." Keep it simple. Don't offer any smart-alec answers. Take the lead from them.

"Well, would you tell us?"

The first trap. An invitation to dig a very deep hole, from which there could be no climbing out. Empathy stage one. Turn it around. Not why I am here, why you are here. Appear helpful.

"Right, it's so you can prepare a report for the court to assist the judge with sentencing."

"Yes, well that's part of it. But the most important part is to determine whether or not you fully understand the gravity of your offences, whether you are likely to offend again, and what factors led you to offend in the first place."

That's three 'offends' in one sentence. David didn't like that. Very heavy. They obviously wanted him to grovel a lot. Difficult, because he was hoping to get them to understand that he didn't know he was offending in the first place. Get their sympathy. He really didn't like this word 'offend'. It implied intent. He'd have to try to get them to understand that if he was going to make any real progress with this interview.

"Could I say something before we go any further?"

"Yes, of course."

"Well, although I have pleaded guilty to the three charges against me, I never intended to break the law, and I didn't even know I was doing it at the time. I mean, obviously I have no intention of offending again, and I'll never get myself in the same position again, but whilst I understand the seriousness of my position, I need to make it quite clear that what happened was entirely accidental."

"Really?" said Carmen, picking up and opening a file. "But it appears from the police evidence that you deliberately target young girls in their early teens. Your victim . . ."

She paused to look at a paper she was holding. Victim? Who the hell was she talking about, thought David. Mandy? My victim? This was going to be harder than he imagined.

This wouldn't be the open-ended professional discussion he'd hoped for. The agenda was obviously already set. Maybe the outcomes were too. This was the dogmatic jargon of someone who'd been on all the right courses. This was the sharp end of the new hegemony that had evolved from the early feminist assertions that all men were rapists. This was abuser/victim territory: everyone is either one or the other. This woman was on a crusade.

". . . your victim was only fifteen, and it seems that you ensnare your victims by waiting outside school gates and children's homes."

David was flabbergasted, and felt himself getting angry.

"I'm sorry but the statement containing that information is not in the prosecution's advance disclosure papers. It is based on hearsay evidence given by an unreliable source. There is no evidence to say I did those things. It is manifestly untrue. If we are going to discuss my 'offences' as you call them, I should be most grateful if we could stick to the evidence the court will see, rather than anything the police may have given you."

Carmen looked flustered, and fumbled with her sheets.

"We don't appear to have the full advance disclosure papers, but the police have provided us with all relevant documents, and also details of what they have found in their investigation."

"With respect, what the police may or may not have found does not constitute proof or even evidence. There have been aspects of the police investigation which have given my legal team much cause for concern. I would rather you didn't judge me on what the police may have told you, but simply on the facts as presented in the advance disclosure papers. And even they are still open to challenge in court."

"We have no choice but to respond to the information we have been given. In any case, the issue here is that you have pleaded guilty to very serious offences. We are not concerned with the detail, but with how you feel about your offending. So, are you denying that you are not attracted to fifteen-year-old children?"

Here we go again. Children. Another emotive word. Yes, technically Mandy was a child. But the word children to him conjured up primary schools, and brownies, and birthday parties, and adventure parks. To bracket Mandy with all that was a travesty.

"She was fifteen, yes. I did not know that. She behaved like a young adult. To call her a child is . . ."

"But she is a child, David, or do you see fifteen-year-olds differently to the rest of us?"

He could feel himself being trapped. He must stay calm and cool. He was being provoked.

"Yes, I agree that fifteen-year-olds are technically children, not adults, and are below the age of legal consent in sexual matters, but I think there is a big difference between a mature fifteen-year-old girl and a child of say, ten or eleven, whom everyone would recognise as a child."

"But the evidence against you also includes reference to an indecent photograph you have taken of a ten year old girl who, even by your definition, is a child."

"That photograph has absolutely nothing to do with me. I have never seen it before, and again, it has not been entered as evidence. Look, I have to ask you this, why are you referring to material which has not been entered as evidence?"

"It was found in your possession by the police."

"It was not, and I am sure it can be proved that the photograph was never mine. In fact, I understand the police have withdrawn it because it would be vigorously challenged in court."

"But it also says here that you had been using your computer to visit websites depicting child pornography, and that you therefore have an unhealthy interest teenage girls."

David took a deep breath.

"I'm sorry, but it doesn't say that at all if you read it carefully. The page you are referring to actually starts by saying that there was no evidence on my computer of any offence being committed. That means they found nothing to suggest I traded in unlawful pictures, or even visited those sorts of sites. What it does say is that the cookies showed that some sites containing teenage nudity had been accessed, and that links to these sites had arrived in the form of unsolicited e-mails. Everyone gets those these days, and some open by themselves. I am sure your own computer would show the same. My computer was not retained as an exhibit. This was simply a line of enquiry pursued by the police, and it revealed nothing. My interest in teenage girls is entirely healthy."

Raj interrupted.

"What we are trying to establish here, David, is whether you agree that a fifteen-year-old girl is unable to give informed consent to sexual intercourse."

"Well, it's not really a question of whether I agree or not is it? It's whether or not you think that the issue is an absolute. If you think the law is right, then there's nothing to discuss."

"Please explain yourself."

"OK. Well, the age of consent is purely arbitrary. The concept that someone is unable to consent when they are fifteen-and-a-half years old but is suddenly able to do so when they pass sixteen is just a nonsense. We all know that people develop and mature at different rates. The law concerning the age of consent has changed many times in the history of this country, and will probably change again. In other countries it's different. Does that make them wrong? Does the UK have prior claim to being right on these matters? There is no absolute or divine right in this. I understand that the age of consent is much lower in some European countries, and yet their figures for unwanted teenage pregnancies are much lower than ours, so maybe they're right and we're wrong. The point is that it doesn't matter what I think about the age of consent. The law in this country is that it is sixteen, and I've always tried to be law-abiding in everything I ever done. This time, I made a mistake."

"With respect, David, you haven't answered my question. We need to find out whether you recognise the vulnerability of someone under sixteen, whether you understand that they are simply unable to give consent in the way an informed adult can."

"I understand what you are saying, but I return to the point of this all hinging on chronological age. I read that there used to be an island on the Zuider Zee in Holland where, up until quite recently, once a daughter had started menstruating, she was put in a ground floor bedroom where the window was left open for the benefit of aspiring lovers, and with the full knowledge and endorsement of the parents. For them the onset of menstruation signalled a girl's readiness for sex. The same criterion is used in some African and South American communities. You may wish to argue that bodily functions can't be used as an indicator in that way, but in some countries, where they stick to a chronological determination for what you call 'informed' consent, they have chosen ages as low as fourteen, or even twelve. Maybe they're wrong too. Some fourteen-year-olds can, some seventeen-year-olds can't. Too much emphasis is being placed on chronological age. Mind you, I can't think of an alternative system, other than to have no age of consent at all, and to deal with every case on individual merit; but maybe that would be impossible to police, and could put even more children at risk. But the issue of consent is about much more than just sex. The Children"s Act specifically states that children must be consulted about matters that concern them and must have their views taken into account when decisions are being made. Why not in sexual matters? Why do adults insist on taking those decisions, but allow consultation on other matters?"

"So, do you think your case should be treated on its individual merits do you?"

"Of course I do! Isn't that what justice is about? We live in an open, free country. Mitigation should always be a factor in deciding innocence or guilt. That's why I have difficulty coming to terms with the fact that I am not allowed to offer a defence against unlawful sexual intercourse. It's fundamentally wrong. It's flawed. Even those charged with murder are allowed to offer a defence, so why not for unlawful sexual intercourse? It seems that our legislation discriminates against those accused of a sexual offence. It speaks volumes about our country's attitude to sex. It shows how moralistic and narrow-minded we still are. I think the law is wrong on this."

"Well, we're not here to discuss the pros and cons of the law. All societies throughout history have felt the need to control sexual behaviour. There's nothing unusual about that."

"But the main reasons for that control have been to prevent the production of children outside wedlock so as to protect the cultural and economic fabric of society. That hardly applies in this case."

"In some earlier societies, you would have been executed for what you have done!"

"And in others I would not have been charged with a crime at all. In most earlier societies there was a clear distinction between sex with children and sex with mature adolescents. You combine the two, and judge me alongside predatory child abusers."

"Well, we have to deal with the law as it is and the consequences of your offending. Don't you agree that a fifteen-year-old is bound to fall victim to the power you hold over her?"

"Power?"

"Whether you fully appreciate it or not, a fifteen-year-old girl is bound to be affected by the power you have over her, and therefore be your victim. Surely you understand that a young girl in the company of a much older man will be persuaded to do things she wouldn't normally do. She feels under pressure to comply. At best she wants to please you, at worst she is frightened by the consequences of not doing so. Think about it. This was a girl from an underprivileged background. You took her into your luxury car. It turned her head. You then took her to your luxury home. It was your territory, not hers. It was a ploy on your part, whether conscious or unconscious, to exert your power over her."

"Yes, I see that, but I really don't think the fact that she was a few months under the age of sixteen is a major factor here. Isn't it surely the case that this sort of thing happens in all encounters where sex or money or power or position is the goal? Don't we all try to impress with what we have and what we can do? Aren't we all trying, at some time or other, to get control of a situation, to use it for our own ends? It's not always as ruthless and as manipulative as you are suggesting. It's just human nature. It's just a matter of wanting to influence outcomes. In the sexual context it used to be called seduction. Is that such a dirty word?"

"But, David," cut in Raj, "you were over fifty and she was fifteen. Don't you think that was immoral?"

David gasped.

"Now hang on minute! I'm sorry, but I didn't think morals would come into this. In any case, aren't morals simply our prejudices which we insist others should follow? But here we are back to chronologically-dependent argument again. What is wrong about inter-generational sex? Why does it make so many people squirm? I am biologically conditioned to impregnate as many females as possible during my sexually active years, and females dress and make-up and act in accordance with their conditioning to encourage that to happen."

"You're saying that women, young girls, dress and make up just to tell you that they want sex with you?"

"No, let me finish. I'm not using that as an excuse for underage sex, or as a rapists' charter. I understand that civilisation and the laws of society govern the extent to which I can respond to my primitive urges, but what I am saying is that promiscuity is a biological imperative, no matter what religion or the moralisers may say. In my case, never mind how old I am, I happen to be attracted most to young females who are in their sexual prime. And I don't see why I should be ashamed of that. A pretty teenage girl in a mini skirt walks down the street and men of all ages look at her. Should the over thirties look away? My son, Jeremy, happens to be gay. I'm sure I would never hear you being so politically incorrect, in this day and age, as to suggest that he should be ashamed about that, but in the days of Oscar Wilde, he wouldn't dare admit it. It was morally wrong in Wilde's day, but now it is OK. So why should I be ashamed? Does the fact that the law changes from age to age suddenly make something morally right or wrong? I could name any number of kings or prime ministers or film stars or poets, who have had sex with fifteen-year-olds, and who were, and still are, regarded as more manly for having done it. But if it happens today, they're paedophiles. I just happen to be living in a time when such an act is now vilified. The Virgin Mary is supposed to have been only twelve or thirteen when she was impregnated by God. Does that make God a paedophile? If so, I'm in good company. After all, wasn't he the guy who invented morals? Look, I really don't think morals should come into this at all. My moral code isn't on trial here."

"So you do have a moral code then, do you?"

"Everyone does, whether they recognise it or not. Mine has nothing to with sex or religion. It's about respecting people, treating them decently, not causing harm . . ."

"So you didn't cause harm to this girl then?"

"Well, no, I don't think I did, actually. I know you say she was my victim, but it didn't feel like that. She hasn't made a complaint against me, despite the fact that I think the police have probably been pressurising her to do so, so I guess she didn't feel that way either."

"So you don't see yourself as her abuser then?"

David hesitated.

"Look, I understand what you're driving at, but this is where I ask you to consider this case on its individual merits. Of course I know that many girls who enter prostitution do so because they are neglected, abused, coerced, and so on. But some don't. And I know that it is fashionable to say that if there weren't men like me there wouldn't be any prostitution. But that, incidentally, is a chicken and egg argument. It negates the premise of the multi-billion pound advertising industry which functions on the basis that advertising creates demand, not fulfils it. A girl determined to sell herself can create a demand that may not have been there before she arrived. But that's beside the point. There has always been prostitution and there always will be. What I'm really trying to say is that there is an honourable side to it all. However girls get started in prostitution and, incidentally, I've met quite a few highly educated girls who chose it simply because it paid well, the girls are doing a job of work, and they deserve to be treated properly. I always did treat them properly, and with respect. They knew that, and liked it. They don't want to be looked down upon by their clients, or by the courts, or social workers or, dare I say it, by probation officers. They do not deserve moral condemnation simply because of how they earn their living."

"OK, OK," said Raj, "so are you really saying that you didn't suspect that this girl was under sixteen?"

"No. I didn't. And if you get the chance to look at the photographs and the video, perhaps you might ask yourself if you would have known too."

"Let me put it to you another way," said Raj. "When I drive to work I pass along the dual carriageway where the speed limit is forty miles per hour. If I'm running late, I push it on a bit, even though I know I am breaking the law. I think I'll get away with it. I think it's OK to go just a little faster. Now, in your case, you're with a young girl. You look at her, and you think, well, she's told me she's over sixteen, maybe she's a bit younger, but, what the hell, she's here now, so . . . isn't that how it happened, David?"

"You make it sound very easy, and not all that serious. I don't think much of your analogy, either. Frankly, it doesn't stand up. In your case, by speeding, you deliberately and knowingly break the law, and in so doing, endanger the lives of other road users. In my case, I did not knowingly break the law, and the most I did was to aid and abet a girl in her deception by allowing myself to believe that she was older than she really was. Unlike you, I didn't endanger life."

Raj looked away.

"But returning to the power and victim analysis, David," said Carmen, "you do seem to recognise that you manipulated this girl to achieve your own ends."

"Yes, as I have already acknowledged, I use strategies to get what I want. Just as we all do. But don't the girls use the offer of sex to get what they want too? Is it only men who manipulate? Didn't she also manipulate me to some extent? I don't blame her either! Isn't that the way humans interact? Can you yourself honestly say that you have only ever had sex with a partner where the motive was purely sexual enjoyment? Or was it, on occasions, to curry some sort of favourable response, whether or not that resulted in material reward?"

Carmen shifted uneasily in her seat. David continued.

"Isn't it the case that we are all manipulators and all victims at different times, and we all jostle to maintain or improve our position in order to get what we want? Even in this interview. We all know what's going on here. You're in the position of power. It's two against one. What you end up recommending could decide whether or not I go to prison. I'm like a puppet on a string, trying to give the right answers, trying to please. You pull, I jerk. It's a classic manipulator/victim model."

"Well, that's all very interesting, but the reason you regard us as having the power in the discussion is because you are the offender and we are the inquisitors."

"Yes, I accept that", said David, "except Raj here, who has just admitted trying to kill people with his car."

"That's a red herring, and you know it," said Carmen.

"It was meant to be a joke, actually."

"Very well, but the point is that I am far from convinced that you will not re-offend in the future. You attempt to justify your actions, and therefore may continue to represent a risk. You have tried to argue that what you did was not morally wrong, that it didn't harm anyone, and that you just happen to be in the wrong age or the wrong country."

"No, no, that's not the case. I was simply trying to provide a context, simply trying to show that this is not an absolute matter of right and wrong in moral terms, but that I recognise the law as it now stands. Look, there were particular circumstances that led me to begin using escorts. I was bereaved. I was lonely. I sought company. I admit I was foolish, maybe even a bit reckless, but I did not deliberately break the law. And I have not seen any escorts for nearly a year now – since I was arrested. It wasn't my first choice of companion. I have been married twice before and I was happy both times. I liked being married. I like focussing my love and attention on one woman. I want to be in love and to be in a permanent relationship, and when this is all over, that's what I will be aiming for again. I know escorts can't fulfil that need. I cannot begin to tell you the grief that all this has caused to me and my family, and the thought of going through it all again is all the deterrent I need. I will never again put myself in the position where there is any possibility that the sexual partner I am with could be under the age of consent. There will be no room for doubt."

"Right, well, I think we have covered all the ground" said Carmen. "Just one more question."

"Yes?"

"Would you be willing to attend a sex offenders' rehabilitation course? It is generally recognised now that sex offenders cannot actually be cured, but the course seeks to help them modify their behaviour."

"So you see me as an incurable sex offender, then?"

"Yes. Of course. We have men on these courses from all backgrounds, David. Yours is not unusual. Despite your spirited defence of your actions, the very fact that you are still in denial proves that you are an incurable offender."

"Sounds like the medieval ducking stool. Heads you win, tails I lose," sighed David. "So, is this course the alternative to prison? Is that what you're saying?"

"If the judge gives you probation instead of prison, then yes, it would be a condition of your probation."

"Then I accept. I can assure you that I will not re-offend, with or without your course, but I honestly believe that prison would serve no purpose at all. And it would cause untold further distress to my family, particularly to my young son. He would be the true victim in all this. Is that ever taken into consideration?"

* * * * * *

"I blew it, George," said David, when he visited his solicitor's office the following week. "I deluded myself into believing that they would listen to reason, that they would at least not have pre-judged the case. I couldn't have been more wrong. Right at the very end of it all, they simply told me that I was an incurable sex offender. They'd already made up their minds. Nothing I could say or do was going to change that. They just wanted me to grovel on all fours, and confess to being a wicked, manipulating abuser, and to acknowledge the harm I had caused to my victim. The only faint glimmer of hope is that they think that a sex offender's rehabilitation course will be better than prison. I had no idea that the hysteria against sex offenders had become so institutionalised.

It's a deep, deep hatred and revulsion, and the response is to cleanse, because a cure is impossible."

George smiled, benignly. "Just a fashion, David, and the tabloids don't help. Let's just go along with it. It's much more preferable to prison. From what I understand, the courses don't have an exam at the end. You simply have to attend, that's all. Let them have their pound of flesh, and you just hang onto your soul. Anyway, I've got some excellent news. Counsel has managed to do the deal with the prosecution. He sent them his factual basis for mitigation and, in exchange for a guilty plea, they accepted it in its entirety. Here's a copy for you to take with you. Basically, it states that you were deceived into thinking the girl was over sixteen, and that the statement made by her brother is a pack of lies, that her mother introduced her, that she was not under the influence of alcohol, as the police suggested, and that she dressed and looked much older than her years. The CPS have agreed not to challenge any of that."

"So what difference does it make?" asked David.

"A big difference. It means that they won't accuse you of hanging around outside schools or children's homes, or of having any knowledge that the girl was under sixteen. It establishes that things happened exactly as you say they happened, not how the brother told it, or how the police imagined it."

"I see."

"And I've also sent the photographs to a paediatrician who is an acknowledged expert in maturation rates and puberty, and has dealt with a lot of cases involving child abuse. Basically I've asked him to look at the photographs of Amanda and to say whether laymen like yourself could be expected to know that the girl was fifteen-and-a-half, or whether it was reasonable for you to think she was older."

"Don't worry, Dad," said Sophie, "it's not going to happen, but if it does, everything here will be fine."

David had given Sophie her final briefing. It was a week before the case came up for sentencing and he had prepared everything for the worst eventuality. Ken had gladly agreed to keep the site going and to oversee developments at the new site, and Sophie would attend to the banking and the post, and would also keep an eye on David's house.

"OK, so is there anything you want me to run through again? I've prepared letters for you to send out to the tenants saying that you're taking over for the time being. Obviously, you won't need to send them out if it doesn't happen. And I've made arrangements with the bank for you to be able to access the accounts. I can't think of anything else."

"Dad, Dad, we've been through it all. It's all just fine. I'll have no problems, believe me. But what have you told Freddy?"

"Oh, we just went for a long walk and I told him that I'd had young girlfriend but that she'd turned out to be much younger than I thought, and now I was in trouble with the police, and that I might go to jail for a short time, but that we all hoped I wouldn't. That's about it. I've always tried to tell you all the truth. Or at least, as much of the truth as you could handle."

"That sounds just about right to me. I'll phone him tonight and reassure him."

"Would you? That would help a lot. If I do end up in jail I'd feel a lot better knowing he was getting support from you other kids. I can't rely on Rachael. She grudgingly wrote me a supporting reference but I think she'd back right away if I went to jail. My biggest worry is that she might not want to bring Freddy to see me, or not often. Maybe you could help there."

"Of course I will. Freddy's my brother, after all. None of us have much time for Rachael, not after what she did to you."

"Well, we've all passed a lot of water since then, as John used to say!"

"That's a good one! Have you heard anything from John?"

"No, nothing. Trouble is, when all this is over it will be really difficult for him to re-establish a friendship with me. Too embarrassing. I think it's probably over for good. Another causality bites the dust."

"And what's happening about the house sale? Are you still trying to sell?"

"Well, I had an offer, but it fell through. I've withdrawn it from the market for the time being. I'll wait and see what happens next week."

* * * * * *

On the day of the sentencing George had arranged for a meeting with Damien, the barrister before proceedings started. Sophie was coming later to give support in the courtroom and, at Damien's suggestion, Rachael had been persuaded to come too. An ex-wife and a grown-up daughter, he had said, would look very good in front of the judge in a case like this.

"Well, its as we suspected," began Damien, now wearing his black gown and wig, "the pre-sentence report seems to have almost nothing to do with the facts of this case. I contacted the probation service earlier this week and asked them whether they would like to take on some amendments in view of the fact that the prosecution had accepted our factual mitigation, but they gave me short shrift. What they have produced is one of the most unprofessional pre-sentence reports I have ever seen. It's almost as though it's written about someone else. My guess is that it's just a re-hash of another report or, worse still, that it's just a template they use every time, and simply change the name of the offender."

"You really think that?" asked David.

"No, not really. Just being cynical, but they certainly haven't read the papers concerning this case. They still refer to you being a predator and to stuff the police showed them. I intend to demolish this report in front of the judge if I get the opportunity. The only problem is that it recommends probation, which is what we want, so I must be careful not to throw out the baby with the bath water. Now, moving on, we also have this report from the paediatrician which, again, isn't as helpful as it might be. I mean, it's all charts and diagrams about nipple growth and pubic hair. Have you read it?"

"Yes, I have," said David, "and I did wonder about the sample in the research he's quoting. I mean, I really don't know how he can talk about norms when he's referring to puberty. I've met women in the Far East who were in their early twenties and had almost no pubic hair at all. That would put them in his suggested first stage of development, which means, according to him, they couldn't be over twelve-and-a-half. And this stuff about breasts – again, don't some women stay flat-chested forever, whereas others have D cups before they're fourteen? I really don't see how this can help us."

"No, it's very confusing. He concludes by saying that he thinks Amanda couldn't be older than sixteen point seven but may be as young as fourteen point nine."

"Exactly! So what's the judge going to make of that?"

"Whatever he likes. That's the problem. He can pick out any quote from this to suit his purpose, and mood. If he's feeling lenient, he'll accept the sixteen point seven, presumably. I even wonder whether we should submit this at all."

"But," suggested George, "isn't the main point the part where he refers to what the layperson could safely assume, and that seems quite clear to me."

"Yes," agreed Damien. "He says that a layperson could not be expected to know from seeing the girl, even in a naked state, that she was under sixteen. That's pretty conclusive, I suppose. We must try to ensure the judge focuses on that."

The case had been scheduled for eleven, but lunchtime came and went without them being called. David sat with Rachael and Sophie in a corridor, watching barristers come and go, seeing people in tears, or sharing the laughter of relief. Conversation was difficult. David tried to talk about anything other than the case, but he could tell they weren't listening. The strain was beginning to show around Sophie's eyes, and Rachael clearly wished she was somewhere else altogether. But eventually, a clerk appeared and called the name Bates, and they all trooped into the courtroom. George and Damien were already there, sitting in the middle of a long bench. In front of them were piles of documents, tied up bizarrely in what David thought looked liked children's pink hair ribbon. Sophie and Rachael were directed towards the visitors' seating, and David found himself in the dock, standing between two prison officers. An usher called for everyone to rise, and the judge entered from a rear door, gliding noiselessly into his seat, high above everyone else. David was asked, as he had been at every court appearance, to recite his name and age, and to confirm his address.

He was then told to sit, and immediately the prosecution barrister was on his feet outlining the case. David listened intently and watched Damien making notes in the margin of his prepared response. It was a very factual presentation, outlining what had happened, the nature of the evidence, and acknowledging the fact that David's account of events was accepted fully. David was satisfied, but wondered if the judge had been paying attention. Throughout the presentation, he had tapped on the keyboard of a laptop computer, and never once looked up. Court ushers came and went, and people talked noisily in the wings. The prosecution counsel sat down. When Damien rose, a hush descended, and David was relieved.

He began by singing David's praises – what a fine upstanding member of society he had always been, how he had served the local community for many years, was a father, had no previous convictions – it was all rousing stuff, and David hoped the judge was getting it all down. Damien slowly got into the facts of the case, emphasising how the whole thing had been a ghastly accident, how he himself had a daughter of the same age, and that Amanda Kinch looked years older, and how on earth were men supposed to know these days, and how sorry David was. At this point the judge interrupted saying that he disagreed about the girl's apparent age, that he thought she looked fifteen, and why was she holding a champagne glass in some of the photographs? David's heart sank. Damien quickly pointed out that the drink was lemonade and that the prosecution had now accepted this, and moved on to the photographic evidence taken from the house which showed that David's taste in women spanned at least ten years, and was not restricted to teenage girls. This, he said, underlined the assertion that David did not go out of his way to meet underage girls; that his taste was wide and not restrictive; and he referred to the psychiatrist's report which agreed that David's taste in women was normal. The judge continued to quibble about the apparent age of Amanda, and so Damien decided, at that point to introduce the paediatrician's report. The judge called an adjournment so that he could study it, and the courtroom was cleared.

* * * * * *

"He's being bloody difficult," grumbled Damien, as the three of them sat huddled in a tiny room off the main corridor. "He's knows there is nothing aggravating in this, but he's turning old stones again just to check."

"How d'you think it's looking then?" asked David.

"Really can't say. He's being thorough, that's for sure. My guess is that he's having difficulty with this one. That report he's reading could be the deciding factor. I'll just have to make sure he's seen the layperson bit, that's all."

Twenty minutes later the court was re-convened and, as Damien suspected, the judge was having trouble with the report. He rightly pointed out that it could be used equally by the defence or the prosecution, but he wouldn't accept that David was a lay person. He was a parent, after all, the judge said, a man of the world, fifty-four years old, with professional qualifications, and if he couldn't determine a girl's true age, who could? Things weren't looking good.

Damien rummaged through his papers as though searching for inspiration. He'd fired all his big guns, but the judge wasn't convinced. He tried going back over old ground, drawing the judge's attention back to the reports, back to the photos, back to the fact that Amanda was dressed provocatively and wearing make-up and behaving in a way that belied her age, and ended by quoting the psychiatrist's conclusion that David wasn't a threat to women.

But the judge was one step ahead, and pointed out that the probation officers thought differently. This was the cue Damien had been waiting for. He picked up his copy of the pre-sentence report, took a deep breath, and rose to his full five feet six inches.

"Me lud," he said, with a voice more sonorous than Lawrence Olivier, "the psychiatrist is an eminent and revered expert in his field. He saw Mr Bates on two separate occasions before writing his report. The probation officers, however, saw Mr Bates only once, and whilst we agree with their conclusion that Mr Bates should receive a non-custodial sentence, we do not recognise many of the sections in their report as applying to Mr Bates's case at all. The comments take no account of the factual mitigation, which my learned friend has accepted in its entirety, and dwell on erroneous and unsubstantiated information supplied by the police during an early stage of their investigation. The report does not match in content what it finally recommends, and would appear to be a report belonging to the case of quite another person."

The judge sighed. "I have some sympathy with that view Mr Fforbes-Brown. I have to admit that the more I get into this case, the more difficult sentencing becomes. It is an extremely difficult case."

"It is, me lud," nodded Damien, wisely.

"So, is there anything else you can do to help me?" asked the judge.

Damien leaned towards George and whispered in his ear. David saw George nodding. George handed the clerk a sheet of paper which was taken to the bench, and Damien stood up and turned again to address the judge.

"Yes, me lud. There is one set of circumstances which has not been brought to your attention, but you may feel is relevant in helping you from the difficulty to which you most graciously admit. It is this, me lud. You have just been handed the copy of a statement made to the police by Mr Bates in which he describes how he was robbed at gunpoint of a very large sum of money by the two brothers of Amanda Kinch, a robbery that appears to have been organised by Amanda's mother. The police have not disputed the facts as laid out in the statement, or the identity of the assailants. Indeed, one was arrested but, to date, no charges have been laid. I hasten to emphasise, me lud, that there is no supposition by Mr Bates that Amanda Kinch played any part in this robbery or even knew anything about it. What we think it supports, however, is our contention that Mr Bates was a victim of a conspiracy by this family, both in the robbery, and in the earlier arrangement for him to be supplied, unknowingly, with an underage prostitute. In conclusion, me lud, may I reiterate that this case has no aggravating features. Mr Bates did not seek out an underage girl, he did not cajole or coerce, he did not ply her with alcohol, he did not sell or distribute her photographs, and he did not, as the police were suggesting at one stage, wait for girls outside schools or children's homes. What he did was consistent with what he has maintained throughout: that he used the services of escort agencies, and that of the many females he met, one, without his knowledge, happened to be a few months under the legal age of consent. Indeed, had Mr Bates thought what he was doing was an offence, he would hardly, being an intelligent man, have taken the photographs to be developed at his local pharmacy. Mr Bates is extremely remorseful about what has happened, and there is no question of his ever offending again. Thank you, me lud."

Damien sat down. David wanted to clap. The little man had earned his money. Now it was up to the judge.

With only a brief pause after Damien had finished, the judge announced that he was ready to give his summing up. David looked across at Sophie, who raised her crossed fingers, and forced a smile.

"This has been an extraordinarily difficult case," began the judge. Looking straight at David throughout, he continued: "You met a fifteen-year-old prostitute, took her to your home, had sex with her, and took indecent photographs of her. You also made a video recording of the two of you together. The facts are not disputed and are not in doubt. Your counsel claims that you did not know the girl's age. That is largely irrelevant because these are absolute offences for which Parliament does not accept a defence. I am asked by your counsel to accept your lack of knowledge of her age, and other factors, as mitigation. I do not need to do this before passing sentence, but I think the mitigation in this case does make a difference. But having looked carefully at the arguments put forward I conclude that you were, at least, reckless in determining the age of this girl, and you have admitted as much to the probation service. It seems simply inconceivable that someone with your background could not have guessed her true age, or at least been wary of what she claimed it to be, and that is where you were reckless. It is very unusual for a man like you to come before the courts. You have no previous convictions, you are fifty-four years old, you have the support of your family, and references from friends and others to which I pay great attention. I also pay attention to the psychiatrist's report, and to the helpful factual mitigation set out by your counsel."

David looked steadily at the judge waiting for an indication, a word, a movement, which would tell him what the outcome of this speech was going to be. So far, it seemed balanced. It could go either way. He had heard speeches like this: rehearsal of the facts, review of the evidence, the pros and the cons, and then, towards the end, the insertion of opinion which tipped the balance from neutrality into judgement. The judge was now talking about the local and national situation regarding prostitution, and the Government funded project aimed at reducing child prostitution which was up and running in the city. He said that he could not use case history for guidance on sentencing because times and attitudes had changed. David guessed this meant that someone let off a few years ago would be dealt with more severely today. But then he referred again to the difficulty he was experiencing in this case. How unusual it was, how powerful he found the personal mitigating circumstances, and referred again to the reports, particularly the psychiatrist's report, but . . .

David shuddered. That was the signal. The 'but' said it all. From that moment, David knew he was going to prison.

"Will you stand up now, Mr Bates," continued the judge. "It is with great sadness that, notwithstanding your age, character, background, and the very powerful mitigation advanced on your behalf, that it is my public duty to impose, in this case, a custodial sentence. For count one, having unlawful sexual intercourse, six months' imprisonment. For count two, taking indecent photographs of a child, three months' imprisonment, to run concurrent. For count three, taking a video recording of yourself having sex with the girl, three months' imprisonment consecutive, making nine months in all. You will serve half of this time in prison, and if you re-offend before the nine months have elapsed, you will go straight back to prison again. Your counsel will explain this to you in more detail. Before you are taken away, I am also

obliged to require you to sign the Sex Offenders Register, and
you will remain on this register for ten years."

David stood quite still, his body now just a shell
containing the bursting emotions within. While clerks and
other officers bustled around him, he glanced across the
courtroom, and saw Sophie wiping her eyes. Rachael looked
angry. He became aware that a hand was firmly gripping his
left arm, and that he was being told to sign a sheet thrust in
front of him. A door behind him opened and the hand holding
him gripped tighter, turning him and directing him through
the door. He glanced backwards just in time to see Sophie
raising her hand in a half wave, and he attempted to smile
back. Within seconds he was out of the large wood-panelled
courtroom, and standing in a brightly-lit basement, with
cream-painted brick walls, and thick green iron bars which
extended from floor to ceiling. Behind the bars sat three prison
officers, smoking and playing cards, around a small table.
Handcuffs were slipped over his wrists, and he was told to sit
down. A voice shouted 'Bates, nine months!' and a uniformed
officer sitting at a desk in front of him began scribbling on a
form. He was told loudly to empty his pockets, to remove his
tie and belt and shoe laces, and then led, clutching his trousers
to stop them falling down, into a small room. A young female
probation officer introduced herself and asked him whether
he was surprised by the outcome. David tried to speak, but
words would not come. His eyes filled with tears, and he
began to shake. The woman left the room. Minutes later two
men walked in, and he looked up to see George and Damien.
Damien looked flustered.

"I'm sorry, David. It's the best we could do. You'll be out
in four-and-a-half months, old man. Look, it's up to you, but I
think you should appeal. The judge kept saying what a

difficult case it was. That was signal to appeal. He was saying, basically, that the Appeal Court might take a different view."

David nodded, but was unable to reply.

"Look," said George. "Don't decide now. Think about it. I"ll be in touch very shortly and then you can decide. Next week will do. Tomorrow's Friday anyway, so we can't do anything before the weekend. They're sending you to Brandley. It's not too far away. I'll tell your family so that they know where you are. Chin up, David. It could have been worse!"

After they had gone David was taken through a series of iron gates and told to climb into a tiny cubicle in a big van. His knees pressed hard against the wall in front, and his shoulders were wedged tightly on either side. He realised that the whole van was subdivided into similar cubicles and, as he sat there waiting, he could hear other men shouting and calling from within the van, complaining about the delay. Eventually the van started moving and from his tiny window he could see the familiar streets and buildings of the city centre. He guessed that the window he was looking through was blackened on the outside, and he was relieved that no one could see him. As they left the city outskirts, he wondered how long it would be before he returned there, and then, suddenly, he was overwhelmed by an all-consuming need to be with Freddy. How he missed Freddy! The others could cope, but could Freddy? The tears began to flow. He had hoped he would be seeing Freddy this coming weekend, but now he wouldn't. How long would he have to wait before seeing Freddy again? What would Rachael be saying to Freddy? How would Freddy take it? David imagined the family phones ringing all evening as the information was passed around, opinions expressed, sympathy given. He knew, too, that other phones would be busy, once the

newspaper came out, and his neighbours and acquaintances
read that he had now been sent to prison for sexual offences
against children.

* * * * * *

The Prison

Nearly an hour later the vehicle came to a halt against some high walls with massive grey steel doors. David peered out, but his limited view prevented him from seeing the tops of the walls. The doors rolled slowly open, and the vehicle edged forwards through the narrow gap, stopping in a courtyard. David heard the banging of doors, someone shouting orders, and then there was silence. After a few minutes, from somewhere behind him inside the vehicle, a man was whining. Another began to shout:

"Come on you fuckin' screws! Open the fuckin' door! We're cookin' in 'ere, you fuckin' bastards."

"Fuckin' cook then," came the reply.

After about twenty minutes, during which other men joined in the shouting, more doors banged, then David felt a sudden gust of cool air, and the inside of his compartment was flooded with evening sunlight.

"Out!" snarled the guard.

David stood, and eased his way out through the narrow door, down metal steps, and into the courtyard, where he joined six other men who had also been occupants of the prison vehicle. They were led into the building, and through to a small, windowless room with no furniture. The guard went out, locking the door behind him. None of the men looked at one another. For a few minutes, they all stood, hands in pockets, heads cast downwards, like a storeroom of crumpled, forgotten statues. One man began punching the wall and cursing under his breath. Two others sat on the floor, their backs to the wall and legs sticking out, claiming more personal space. David looked up at the thin, dirty, fluorescent tube, and noticed hundreds of tiny insects crawling around it. Time passed.

After nearly an hour, keys rattled in the lock, and a guard stood in doorway. A name was called, and one man left. This routine was repeated over the next ten minutes until David was the last one.

"Bates?" screamed the guard.

David followed him out into a corridor and along to a reception area where two other guards stood behind a high counter.

"Bates?" asked one of the guards, looking at his clipboard.

"Yes?" answered David, quietly.

"Sexual offences, is it?" snapped the guard.

"Um, yes, that's right," answered David.

"Right," said the guard, brusquely. "You know that. We know that. They don't know that," he said, indicating the other prisoners who had moved into another room. "You tell 'em that, and you won't survive twenty-four hours, understand?"

"Yes," said David, falteringly.

"You're a nonce, understand? So you'd better think up a good story now, and stick to it. Fraud is the best one. All right?"

"OK," said David, immediately trying to think of what he could have done to be imprisoned for fraud.

"First time in prison?" growled the guard.

"Yes."

"You're gonna find it hard. Not just because you're a nonce, but because most inmates are less than half your age. I can put you in the isolation wing, if you like, but I wouldn't recommend it."

"No, it'll be OK," said David, taking the hint.

"Right then, keep your eyes skinned and your wits about you. Don't hide. Mix in. But if they suss you, go to the spur officer straight away."

"Spur?"

"You live on the spur. Each wing has three spurs."

"Right."

"Now, go through for your medical."

"Thank you," said David, out of habit.

He joined the other prisoners in the next small, airless room where, on a shelf, were paper plates containing cold meat pies and congealed mashed potato. None of the meals had been touched. A man saw David looking at the plates.

"Shouldn't try it, mate, if I were you. Been cooked hours ago. Probably reheated from yesterday. Don't want gut-rot on yuh first night, do yuh?"

David nodded, and smiled at the man.

"Bates!" came the cry, some time later. "Medical – through 'ere."

David followed the guard and was directed into another room where a doctor in a white coat sat scribbling notes. Without looking up he raised his free hand and pointed to a chair next to his table. David sat in it.

"Any worries about your health?" asked the doctor, still not looking up.

"Not really."

"Medication?"

"Yes. I take cimetidine at night. That's all. I had some with me, but they took it away."

"They would. You're not supposed to bring medication into prison. Well, you'll have to do without it tonight."

"But I have it every night. I get stomach pains if I don't take it."

"Then you'll get stomach pains. I'm sorry, but you're in prison now, and things have to be done in a certain way. Medication will be issued to you tomorrow evening."

He waved his hand indicating that the interview was over. David stood up and wandered back into the corridor, where the guard was waiting. Next he was sent into a long room where his photograph was taken, and then told to report to a hatch at the other end. He went to the hatch and placed his hands on the counter. The female behind the counter looked up.

"Stand back!" she bellowed. "Don't touch the counter!

David stood up, abruptly.

"Prison clothes," said the woman, thrusting a pair of jeans and a shirt at him. "In there!"

He went into an alcove, still in full view of the woman, took off his suit, and put on the overlarge jeans and shirt. He took the suit back to the counter where it was placed in a bag.

"You're allowed one phone call," snapped the woman. "Do you wish to make it?"

"Yes, please."

The woman handed him a phone card and indicated a row of three phones opposite. David dialled Sophie's number. She was in.

"Dad!" Sophie had been crying. "Are you all right?"

"I'm fine, sweetheart. Look, I'm in a place called Brandley. I've no idea where it is. It was difficult to see the way we were going, but it's not far. I'm only allowed one call. There's a notice on the wall here which says you can bring in some clothes and things. I don't know when visiting is. Go and see my solicitor tomorrow. Get him to sort it for you."

"Yes, yes, Dad, don't worry. We'll take care of everything for you. You just take care of yourself. I love you, Dad."

David struggled to overcome the lump in his throat, and fought back his tears.

"And, Sophie, Freddy . . . is he . . .?"

"Freddy's all right, Dad. Don't worry. I've already spoken to him. Listen, we'll come to see you as soon as they let us. Dad, please, just hang in there. We're all behind you, Dad. Be strong."

"I will. Don't worry. Bye, Sophie."

The phone card popped out and David walked back to the hatch.

"Excuse me, but can I use this again? Could I call my son . . .?"

"No. One call only. Didn't you hear me?" said the woman, holding out her hand for the card.

David re-joined the other prisoners, and they were led through a series of iron doors and barred gates, which were meticulously unlocked and re-locked by the guard, and they then walked along covered walkways until they reached a sign saying 'A Wing'. After passing through two more sets of doors, they were taken into a room containing bedding on shelves around the walls. Each man was handed a large plastic bag containing his bedding and a towel, and then led through further doors until they came to floor-to-ceiling iron bars, similar to the ones David had seen earlier that day at the back of the courtroom.

"This is your spur," said the guard, twisting the heavy key in the lock and pushing open the gate. "Follow me."

They walked along a steel balcony with a handrail over-looking a large, empty stairwell. Opposite the rail were rows of small iron doors which David now realised were cells. Each door had a peephole with a flap which could be opened from the outside. Above their heads were two more storeys of cells and, spanning the walkways at first floor level, was a steel suicide net.

In turn, each man was shown into a cell. On the top storey, the guard stopped and turned to David.

"Bates?" he said, looking at his list. "In 'ere."

David stepped forwards and through the door. It slammed behind him. He stood, clutching his plastic bag, and looked around. The room measured slightly less than nine feet square. There were two single beds taking up most of the floor space. Each bed was made of tubular steel with a thin sheet of steel for the base, and had a foam rubber mattress only two inches thick. At the rear of one bed was a toilet in a cubicle, and facing it, a small table with two chairs. There were also two small cupboards fixed to the walls, and a notice board covered in white blobs which, some days later, David discovered was toothpaste, the prisoners' version of glue, for sticking up pictures.

The small perspex window between the beds was barred, and the walls of the cell were painted a pale green. The floor, covered with grey lino, was littered with cigarette ash and other debris. The mattress covers were ripped and stained with black mould. The walls bore the graffiti of former residents – Shayne from Walsall, Lee on tour from Manchester, Spud doing easy bird, and Foster ov Tipton.

David dropped his bag and stepped to the low window, stooping to peer out between the bars. Immediately outside the window was a small courtyard surrounded by a high wire fence which was topped with rolls of razor wire. Beyond the fence was a lawned area and then another, similar fence. Behind that, he could see a gravel strip and then the high wall that had greeted his arrival. Above the wall, but some twenty yards further back, the tops of a row of trees swayed in the light breeze, their leaves glinting as the last rays of the sun caught them at right angles. Rooks floated in and out of the topmost branches. David looked longingly at the trees, and then turned back to face the reality of his tiny cell.

Using the toilet paper he had been given he carefully brushed up all the rubbish and wiped clean one of the mattresses, turning its best side face up, before making his bed. He stripped off and washed thoroughly at the tiny sink which was suspended from the wall next to the toilet, and then sat on the side of his bed.

Nothing to eat or drink, he thought. No books. No paper or pen. Nothing to do. So this was prison. Punishment by enforced boredom. Nine months. That would mean serving four-and-a-half, he'd been told. That would take until the end of October. He'd miss the whole of Freddy's summer holiday.

Suddenly, there was a noise at the door and it swung open. Another man walked in, carrying his bag of bedding.

"Watcha, mate, y'all right?" said the young man. He was tall and very thin, with a shaven head. His arms and face were covered in tattoos. David guessed he was in his early twenties.

"Hello," said David. "You live here too, do you?" David's heart sank. He had hoped to be alone on his first night, at least. Now he would have to make conversation. Then again, it might stop him having time to feel sorry for himself.

The young man grunted. "Bloody judge. Wouldn't gi' me fuckin' bail. Least 'e coulda sent me to Winson Green where me mates are. Cunt! I didn't wanna come back to this 'ole."

"Been here before, have you?" asked David.

"Seven times. Been to 'em all. 'S all right 'ere really, but I wanted to be wiv me mates."

The man went into the toilet and David could hear him grunting. He returned minutes later with three rolls of a brown substance covered in cling film. He placed the objects on the small table and began to remove the cling film. David could see that the brown substance was tobacco.

"How did you manage to bring that in? Weren't you searched?"

" 'ow d'yuh think, mate? Up me arse of course! Been holding up there all fuckin' day. I was desperate for a shit when I was in court, but I just 'ad to 'old it, didn't I?"

"But don't they check that when they search you?"

"They can't, mate. They're not allowed to go up yuh bum. Can't do it to women neither. Me girlfriend's inside too, and she carries it in front and back. No probs. Your first time is it?"

"Yes."

"It fuckin' shows, mate!" he said, grinning, as he pulled apart the tobacco to reveal small wraps of silver foil hidden inside the rolls. "Gotta strike?"

"Sorry?"

"A strike! A match."

"Oh, no, sorry, I don't smoke."

"Stop sayin' sorry all the time, mate. No sweat."

The young man placed his mouth close to the wall above his bed and called out. "Yo! Next door! Next door!"

David heard a muffled reply. His cellmate called again. "Gotta strike?"

The reply was negative, so he stepped over and stood on David's bed, repeating his call to the other side. David glanced down and noticed what looked like excrement on his boots being wiped onto the blanket, but said nothing. He wondered what the good was of asking neighbours for a match. They were in a locked cell after all, at least two locked doors away, and behind walls which were probably a foot thick. Again, there was a negative response, so the man went to the window, pushed his hands between the bars and forced open the perspex shutters.

"Down below! Down below! Gotta strike?"

He continued shouting for some minutes until he eventually received an answer. David hadn't understood it.

"Did they say yes?" he asked.

"Down below ain't got one, but next to them 'as, so we done a deal."

"What deal?"

"Down below and next to them gets a draw each an' I gets two strikes."

"But how? How are you going to do the exchange?"

" 'ere, I"ll show yuh. There look, see that thick pipe runnin' under the window?"

"Yes."

"Thass the central 'eatin". That pipe runs through all the cells on every floor. Thass the only 'eatin' the cell 'as in the winter. An' now it's summer, so that pipe's cold, right?"

"Yes, so?"

"So, when the pipe's cold it shrinks a bit and there's a little gap all round it, just enough to pass somethin' through to the next cell with a piece o' wire, right? So them below is gonna get me a strike from their next door."

"But how do they get it up here? There aren't any vertical pipes."

"Oh, thass the easy bit. Watch."

He ripped a long thread from his blanket, tied a small package of tobacco to one end, and then dangled it out of the window, swinging it backwards and forwards. After a few minutes of shouting and receiving instructions, he retrieved the thread. David was amazed to see that the tobacco had been replaced with two matches, tied securely onto the thread. The man rolled a cigarette, and lit it, sitting back on his bed, and inhaling deeply. Within less than half an hour of arriving in the cell, having been previously searched and apparently stripped of all possessions, David's cellmate was now smoking his first cigarette.

* * * * * *

A few hours later, with the light turned off, David lay back on his narrow, hard bed and looked up into the darkness. Was this a dream? Would he wake up and see his own familiar bedroom ceiling? No, he was in prison. David Bates, in prison! The reality was slow to sink in. This was never meant to be. He had always been a law-abiding citizen. Prison had never even been thought about. That was where criminals went. What had gone wrong? How on earth had he got himself into a position where he could be convicted for committing a crime? It was just ridiculous, the whole thing. And how had his legal team got it so wrong? Damien had said that it would be a failure if David went to prison. But now it had happened. Had the judge been unduly harsh? Well, the appeal would decide that, if they went for an appeal, but how long would that take? He could still have to serve weeks or even months before he was released. How could he possibly survive that? But he knew he must. For the children's sake. He mustn't weaken . . .

* * * * * *

At seven in the morning he heard a metallic clanking noise which grew closer and closer, and realised that the doors were being unlocked. He was already dressed and sitting on the side of his bed. His cellmate slept on. When the door swung open he jumped to attention, but the guard

263

simply looked at him, and walked away, leaving the door ajar. Was he supposed to go out, or wait for further instructions? Tentatively, he approached the door and peered out into the landing. Men sauntered along the metal walkways, and up and down the iron staircase. Presumably they were going to and from breakfast, but where was it? He stepped out of the door and asked a passer-by. The man pointed down the staircase, so David followed the others going that way and soon found himself in a large dining room with rows of grey tables, where several hundred men noisily ate breakfast. As he walked in, David felt all eyes on him, a newcomer, but he chose not to meet any of the stares head-on. He joined the queue at the servery, and took a tray which already contained a portion of cornflakes, two pieces of toast, and a small carton of milk. He looked around for cutlery but could find none. Not wishing to draw more attention to himself as the new boy, he went to sit at an empty table, ate the dry toast and drank the milk. Others seemed to have found butter and jam, and were eating cereal with spoons, but David decided that he would simply have to start using his eyes and ears to find out how things were done. He watched other men taking their empty trays to a large dustbin into which they scraped leftovers before returning trays to the servery. David did the same, and then followed others back to the spur. On his landing, men stood on the balcony leaning against the rail which overlooked the suicide net. David did the same.

"Gotta roll-up, mate?" asked the man standing next to him.

"Sorry, no, I don't smoke."

"Bastards won't give us no canteen 'til tomorrow. 'ow yuh s'posed to last 'til then without a burn? Can't even make a phone call."

"Not right, is it?" said David, not quite sure what the man was talking about, but anxious to find out more.

"Fuckin' ain't. You can't do nothin' without your canteen. They should at least gi' yuh some baccy an' a phone card when yuh comes in to tide yuh over 'til the first canteen."

"They should. That's right," nodded David. "So canteen is tomorrow, is it?"

"Yeah. You need to get your form in today though, by twelve. If you don't, you won't get none."

"Right! So where d'you get the form from then?" asked David.

"On the spur gate, down there," said the man, pointing. "Oh, 'ang, on, I picked up two. 'ere, you can 'ave one o' mine."

"Oh, thanks!" said David.

He glanced at the form. It contained lists of sweets, drinks, tobacco, writing paper, stamps and phone cards, with tick boxes for ordering.

"So I just tick what I need and hand it in, do I?" asked David.

"Only if you got cash. You got any private cash, 'ave yuh?"

"No, they took it off me yesterday."

"Thass what I mean, mate. If you 'ad money on yuh when you come in, thass yuh private cash. They writes it down in a book. You can spend ten pounds a week. Canteen comes twice. An' when you gets a job, you gets wages, and that goes with yuh private cash too."

"Oh, right. So I can spend ten pounds on phone cards and get them tomorrow then, can I."

"Well, you can, but I shouldn't spend it all in one go if I was you. There's another canteen on Wednesday. Keep a bit for then. You never knows what you might need."

"OK. Thanks for your help."

"Thass all right, mate. This your first time, is it?"

"Yes."

"How long you got?"

"Nine months."

"What you in for?"

"Um, fraud."

"Fraud? What d'yuh do then?"

"Uh, well, I persuaded some building societies to part with rather a lot of money to finance non-existent property deals."

"Crafty sod! Thass good, that is. Well, they can afford it, can't they? So, 'ow'd they catch yuh then?"

"Computers."

"Oh, bloody computers. Well, thass all right then."

"What is?"

"You – in for fraud. Must say, I 'ad yuh down as a nonce. Most posh blokes of your age what comes in for the first time are nonces. I 'ate fuckin' nonces. Everyone does."

David remained silent, and nodded in agreement.

"So, what are you in for?" he asked the man.

"Cut me girlfriend. Well, she 'ad it comin', know what I mean? Been puttin' it about she 'ad, the slag. Only thing is, she didn't make it to the 'ospital. Fuckin' died on me, she did."

"Oh," said David, looking sideways at the little man, whom he now realised was a murderer.

"Bled like a pig, she did," continued the man. "So I'm up for murder, but me brief says 'e can swing to manslaughter."

"So how long have you got to serve then?" asked David.

"Still on remand. Lookin' at fifteen, I expect. I got form, see."

"Fifteen years?" repeated David.

He had only been in prison for twelve hours and already felt as though his four-and-a-half months would go on forever. But fifteen years! How could anyone come to terms with that? Fifteen years! It was an eternity! A whole generation would grow up or grow old in that time. So much would have changed.

Suddenly, a distorted tannoy announcement rang out. David couldn't understand what had been said.

"Come on," said the man. "Fuckin' induction."

* * * * * *

An hour later, David followed others out of the room where they had been watching a video about electronic tagging. It seemed odd to David to be told about a scheme for early release on the first day of their incarceration, especially for those expecting to serve fifteen years, but of the prison officers he had met so far, sensitivity didn't appear to be a quality in great supply.

He stood in a corridor at the end of another queue, waiting for his name to be called. Two hours later, he entered a small office.

"Sit down, Bates, I'm the allocation officer."

David nodded, not knowing what that meant, but sat down.

"Right," continued the officer, "what're you in for?"

David hesitated. "Fraud," he said, dutifully.

The officer glanced down at his notes. "That's for them, not me, understand? I'm an officer, not a con. Right, peddling child pornography and indecent assault, is it?"

David sat up straight. "No! Unlawful sexual intercourse and taking photographs!" he corrected.

"Well, we don't get full details from the courts for several weeks. I'm just going by what I've been given here," he said, looking again at his notes. "Indecent photographs, was it?"

"Yes."

"Of children?"

"Um, yes. Well, a fifteen-year-old, actually."

"Children then," insisted the officer. "Right, well," he continued, "your earliest release date is in four-and-a-half months, and your tagging date is in two-and-a-half months."

David was suddenly elated. "So I get out in two-and-a-half months then?" he said, leaning forwards.

"No. Not in your case. Forget it. You won't get tagging because you're a schedule one sex offender. They don't let sex offenders out early. Too much of a risk."

"But I'm not a risk. If you look at the details of my case, I . . ."

"And schedule one," interrupted the officer. "No chance."

"What is schedule one?"

"Offences against children. So yours is not just sexual offences, but sexual offences against children. That's the worst you can get."

"But hang on, my so-called sexual offences wouldn't have been offences against an adult at all. It's only the fact that the girl wasn't sixteen . . ."

"Can't go into the details of your case. That's for your brief to do. I'm just the allocation officer. I'm just telling you that you won't get tagging. That's the rule. And you're cat C."

"Cat C? What's that?"

"Category C. All prisoners are divided into four categories. A is for terrorists and mass murderers, B is for your ordinary murderers, and hardened cons, C is for people on short sentences, and D is for low-risk prisoners or those about to be released. This is a cat B prison. You could ask to be transferred to a cat C prison if you want, but there's not much point 'cos your sentence is short. You'll probably stay here. You won't get an open prison."

"Oh," said David, trying to take it all in.

"And will you be getting any visitors under eighteen?"

"Um, yes, my son."

"Write his name and address down here."

David wrote it down. "What's that for?" he asked.

"Social Services. They'll check him out."

"What d'you mean?" said David, alarmed.

"They might not let you see him."

"What? Why not?"

" 'cos, like I said, you're schedule one. They have to decide whether you're a risk to children. That means every child who visits you here, and when you've been released, every child who comes to your house, if you have any more children of your own, or marry someone who's already got children – they check it all out. For the rest of your life. "Cos you committed sexual offences against children."

"For the rest of my life?" spluttered David with indignation. "What d'you mean, the rest of my life? What's this all about? No one told me about this. Why am I considered to be a risk to my son? My offence was against a teenage girl!"

"Listen, like I said, I'm not your brief. See your solicitor if you want anything explained to you. You're in prison now, and you just do as you're told. No fuss, no bother. It's not like the outside world. You don't have normal rights. You make waves, and you'll get noticed. Just keep your head down, and do your bird."

David remained silent, and nodded. Why hadn't George or Damien told him about this? If he'd known this, perhaps he wouldn't have pleaded guilty. It made a big difference. He was stigmatised for life.

"And I need to tell you one or two other things," continued the allocation officer. "As a section one offender, all your outgoing mail will be read. Like the other prisoners, you don't seal the envelopes of outgoing mail, but in your case, it will all be read. If the officer reading it suspects that you are trying to contact a child for illegal purposes, the letter will be copied and sent to the police, understand?"

David nodded.

"And all your phone calls will be recorded for the same purpose. Every time you want to use the phone you must inform your spur officer so that your tape can be put in and the recorder turned on. And then you go back and tell the officer when you've finished."

"But what if another prisoner overhears me telling the officer? They might guess why I'm in here."

"Then you'll have to be discreet, won't you? That's your problem. Unless you want to be transferred to D wing?"

"What's that?"

"It"s where all the nonces go. And the other vulnerable prisoners. Those who would be attacked. I wouldn't recommend it. You can't work if you go there. You spend all your time banged up. Time drags. And you might be sharing your cell with someone who has raped or tortured babies."

"Oh, nonces like me, you mean?" said David, cynically.

"You said it, Bates. I didn't."

"OK, well, thanks for your advice. I'll stay where I am, if that's all right. I'm sure I'm better suited to being with ordinary murderers and robbers. They're obviously the good guys around here."

David joined another queue in the corridor.

"Bates! Job interview!" called a guard standing at the opposite end of the line of men. David went into another room and sat down. A woman wrote down his name.

"This is a working prison," she explained. "Everyone has to work or do education. No work or education, means no canteen, understand?"

"Yes," said David.

"Can you read and write?"

"Yes."

"Any qualifications?"

"Yes. BSc Hons, MSc, MBA, and Fellow of the Institute of Town Planners."

The woman's pen remained motionless. She looked at him over her glasses.

"So I take it you've got GCSE's then? My form only goes up to GCSE."

"Yes," replied David.

She ticked the boxes on her form.

"So you won't be doing education then. No point."

"Well, perhaps I could do some research. Does the prison have a library?"

The woman ignored him. "Do you like indoor or outdoor work?"

"Well, as it's summer, perhaps outdoor. Gardening would be nice. Is that available?"

"No."

"Well, I don't mind. Anything. I just want to be busy."

"Right. Well, for the rest of this week you will remain locked in your cell for twenty-one hours a day, but perhaps next week you will be assigned to work. That will reduce your cell time to fourteen hours."

Back in his cell David sat at the table with several forms to fill in. The key to learning the ropes, he had discovered, was to fill in and submit the right form at the right time, and to be early for whichever queue he was supposed to join. Without a canteen form he couldn't get a phone card. Without a phone card, he couldn't ring his family to arrange a visit. Without a visit form, sent to them and then brought with them on the day of the visit, they wouldn't be allowed in. Without a property form, they wouldn't be allowed to bring him books and other essentials which would make bearable his long hours in the cell. But before he could even fill in the forms, he needed to obtain a pen. He soon realised that bartering, though against the rules, was the key to survival. He had swapped his meagre ration of sugar for a half-used biro. Now he could fill in his forms. Tomorrow, he would be able to get writing paper and stamps. On Sunday, he might get a visit.

The next afternoon, he stood by the window. His cellmate was still sleeping, having risen only for meals and the toilet in the previous two days. He looked at his watch. Three-thirty. What would he be doing now if he was still at home? What was Sophie doing? Freddy would be just coming out of school, rushing home, clutching his homework for the weekend, looking forward to going to scouts.

David looked out of the window and watched the rooks bobbing over the trees, and then taking it in turn to glide down into the courtyard in long sweeping arcs. Two were squabbling over a morsel thrown from a cell window. He watched one rook take her booty back over the first fence onto the lawned area, where two smaller, scruffy-looking fledglings waited with their mouths open and wings outstretched for their mother to feed them. What the rooks didn't take from below the windows, an army of pied wagtails cleaned up, diving head-first towards the tarmac surface like kamikaze pilots, only swooping up into the horizontal a few centimetres above the ground, and landing in a two-footed hop, their tails wagging furiously from the vibration of impact.

Previously, David had never really liked rooks: big black noisy birds, malevolent and greedy, but now he admired their resourcefulness, their aerobatic skills, and he longed to join them as they swirled upwards and over the high wall into the freedom of their trees. The claustrophobia of his cell made him feel nauseous. How could he cope with being in this tiny cell for so long? He looked at his watch again. Three thirty-seven. He walked up to the door, and then back to the window again. Three-and-a-half paces. The man asleep farted, and turned over. David sat down on his bed. Nothing to read. Think about something nice. Freddy. Freddy playing his trumpet. Freddy playing on his computer game. Freddy laughing. Wrestling with Freddy. Four-and-a-half months. The whole summer and most of the autumn. Freddy would be so different in four-and-a-half months. Three fifty-one. Nothing to drink. At home he'd just put the kettle on, go for a walk, fetch a newspaper, turn on the radio. So many things just taken for granted.

* * * * * *

It was Sunday, and Sophie and Jeremy were coming. In the afternoon, he was allowed out of the cell for 'association', a time when prisoners played table tennis, pool or, more likely, plotted wrongdoing with new-found friends. Some chose not to associate. David spent most of the two hours hovering near the loud speaker waiting for his name to be called, worried about not hearing it, and then missing his visit.

"Bates! Visit!" twanged the tannoy.

David jumped, and went straight to the spur gate, waiting for it to be unlocked. From where he stood, he could see the guards in their office, talking and laughing. Come on, come on, he thought. They were ignoring him. Eventually, one of them got up, came out of the office, and slowly walked over. He raised one eyebrow as if to ask David why he was standing at the gate.

"Did you call 'Bates'? Visit?" asked David, politely.

The guard slowly opened the gate and pointed towards the office. David went to the office door and knocked. Again, the guards inside ignored him. He waited, patiently. The door opened.

"Bates. Visit?" asked David again.

He was given a slip of paper and told to wait by another door. Four doors and two gates later, he waited outside the visitors' block. Having presented his slip of paper, he was told to remove his shoes and socks, was searched, and then told to go into another waiting room. Twenty-five minutes after that, he was called, searched again, and given a large red football-type bib to put on. After passing through two more barriers he at last found himself in the visitors' hall. Tables were set out in straight rows with three chairs on one side of each table, and a single chair for the prisoner on the other. The prisoner's chair was fixed to the floor and set back at an awkward distance from the table. Some tables were occupied with huddles of families, grasping prisoners hands, all leaning as closely as possible in a communion of tears and smiles and hugs. David was sent to table forty-nine, and waited. He could see the entrance where visitors arrived, and he sat with his eyes fixed firmly on the door, watching. And there was Sophie, her face beaming broadly as soon as she spotted him, and Jeremy, looking flushed, embarrassed, awkward, confused, following Sophie as she strode across the hall, oblivious to her surroundings. David stood up.

"Dad!" Sophie threw her arms around him, and David burst into tears. He turned to Jeremy, and saw that he was crying too.

"Sit down, Dad. Sit down, Jeremy," said Sophie, taking control. "I'll get some coffee, OK?"

"I'm sorry," said David, recovering. "It's just so good to see you both. It's just the tension, that's all. I've been bottling it up, I suppose."

Jeremy smiled, and wiped away his own tears.

"It's OK, Dad," he said. "It's OK."

They held hands, the three of them, clinging on, and not wanting to let go. Sophie updated David on all the family news, how everyone sent their best wishes, how they were all shocked and horrified, what an injustice it all was, no one could believe it, it wasn't fair, wasn't right, everyone would be sending him letters, what did he need, did he need stamps, and did he want visits?

"And you must appeal," said Sophie. "George said so."

"He would," said David. "And how much will it cost?"

"He said about four-and-a-half thousand."

"That's what I thought. That will bring the total bill to nearly twenty thousand. All my savings. And more."

"But I still don't understand why you didn't get legal aid," said Jeremy. "Your income isn't that high, surely?"

"But it's not just income," replied David. "It's because I own land and property. They'd expect me to sell that before giving me legal aid."

"But that's not fair. That's your main source of income. They can't expect you to sell that."

"But that's the system, Jeremy. But anyway, is it worth appealing? I mean, it might shorten the sentence by a couple of months. Is that worth four-and-a-half grand?"

"Yes, said Sophie. "Of course it is. It's only money. Your freedom is much more important."

"But what if the appeal fails?" said David.

"Sophie's right, Dad. It's still worth trying."

"OK. Tell George to visit me as soon as he can, and we'll set it rolling."

"By the way, Dad, we brought your cassette radio for you but they said you have to fill in a form before they'll give it to you. And they wouldn't let us leave the lead and plug."

"No. They wouldn't. I have to fill in a second form to borrow a prison one. It's all to do with security. Everything here is about filling in a form!"

"What's it like. Dad? What the food like? How are you being treated?"

"Oh, everything's fine. Really. The food lacks variety but it's plentiful. I'm being treated well. What's it like? Well, in one word, boring! For me, that's a worse torture than being put on the rack!"

"Poor Dad!"

"Only joking. Now that I've got writing implements, and I"ll soon have my books and a radio, I'll be fine. And I start work next week. That'll help time go."

* * * * * *

Two hours later, David felt infused with a new strength, a warmth, his head was full of love for Sophie and Jeremy, full of gratitude for all the messages of support, and equipped to go back through all those locked doors again to face the confinement and the boredom. He would survive. Whatever the discomfort, it was all worth all the love his predicament had enabled his family and friends to show him. For the first time in years, he felt loved and wanted. Good had come from this bad thing. It had given people the chance to show they really cared.

* * * * * *

The next morning David was mopping the floor of his cell when a guard pushed open the door.

"Bates? You're moving. Pack your things. Two minutes."

David stood holding the mop as the guard walked away. Moving? Where? He turned to his cellmate. "Did you hear that? I'm moving."

"They keep movin" yuh, mate. Until you gets a job, they'll move yuh every few days. They might ship you out to another prison. You never knows where yuh goin'. Bastards don't like cons settlin' down too much."

David started packing his things into a plastic bag.

"Careful what yuh take, mate. That extra bog roll you got. Don't take that. If they check yuh bag you'll go on report for that. Just take what you should 'ave. No more."

"OK. Thanks. You'd better have this extra sugar I was saving then."

"OK, mate. Ta. You got the idea. Yeah, they shipped a load off to Wandsworth this mornin'. Two minutes' notice. Poor buggers were all shittin' themselves 'cos all their family an' friends an' that're in the Midlands. "Ow the fuck're they gonna get visitors down in Wandsworth? But the screws, they don't fuckin' care."

The guard reappeared. "Follow me, Bates," he said.

When David saw his new cell, his heart slumped. It was much smaller than the first one, being barely five by nine feet.

277

The second bed was accommodated by one being on top of the other – a pair of bunk beds bolted to the wall – and the toilet was at the end of the bunk beds without screen around it, affording no privacy to the user. The window faced north onto an exercise yard, and there was nothing green in view. He was pleased, however, to see the ubiquitous rooks hopping around under the window.

On the top bunk, a young man slept, wrapped tightly in a dirty, brown blanket.

"Don't mind him," said the guard. "He won't bother you. He got life last week, so he'll be moving in a few days."

The guard left, and locked the door. David unpacked his things and made up the bottom bunk. He noticed the young man had one eye open, and was looking at him.

"Gotta burn, mate?" said the man.

"Sorry, no. Don't smoke," replied David.

The man rolled over and faced the wall. David noticed that he was fully dressed.

* * * * * *

After tea, David was standing outside the cell waiting for lock-up at seven o'clock. The man from the neighbouring cell stood next to him.

"You in with Roy the Tramp then, mate?"

"Uh, yes."

"Been in bed for a week, 'e 'as. Never takes 'is clothes off. Never washes. Never gets visitors. Given up, 'e 'as."

"Given up what?"

"Life, mate. Life. Jus' given up."

"But he's young. What about his parents? Won't they visit?"

" 'specially not 'is parents, mate. That's why 'e's inside. Did 'em in, 'e did." He nodded, when he saw David's surprised expression. "What you in for then?" he asked.

"Fraud," said David.

"Cat D then, you are. You'll be off to an open prison soon."

"No, I'm cat C."

"You can"t be, mate, not if you've done fraud. Unless you shagged the judge's daughter!" laughed the man.

David thought quickly. This was the first serious test of his story.

"Uh, no, I didn't fancy her! No, um, it was 'cos I missed a magistrate's hearing. They changed the date and my solicitor didn't tell me. I was on holiday. So now they think I'm a security risk 'cos I missed a court hearing. Gave me a cat C."

"Oh," said the man. "Bastards, ain't they?"

"Bastards," agreed David, relieved that his story was accepted. "So how long have you got?"

"Me? Three weeks to taggin'. Just finishin' a twenty-seven month stretch. Bit off a bloke's ear in a pub."

"Twenty-seven months?" sighed David. "Well, nearly over now, eh?"

"Yeah, but I'll be back soon."

"Why?"

"'cos when I get out, I'm gonna find the same geezer an' do a proper job this time."

"Why? What did he do?"

"I just 'ate the cunt. Slimy little toe rag."

"But if you get him again, won't they give you a longer sentence?"

"Nine years, I reckon, for what I'm gonna do to 'im. No sweat. I"ll be out before I'm thirty-five. I can start a new life then."

"Is it worth it?"

"Oh yeah. I can't rest while that cunt's still walkin"
around. 'e won't walk no more when I've finished. I'll 'ave
'im."

"Bates! Spur gate!" screamed the tannoy.

David jumped."That's me, I think. Wonder what they
want? See you later."

"OK, mate."

David walked down the iron stairs and up to the gate.
As before, he could see guards in the office, but they ignored
him. He watched the office door open and a guard stood in
the doorway. David nodded at him, and called out.

"Excuse me? Did you want me?"

The guard strolled over.

"Why would I want you? What's your name?"

"Bates. Someone called out Bates."

"Bains, not Bates, you fuckin' turd. Fuck off back to your
cell where you belong, and don't waste my fuckin' time."

David turned, and walked back.

Fifteen minutes later he thought he heard his name
called again. This time, he was more reticent. He walked
slowly towards the gate and waited, patiently. Two other men
were also waiting. After another ten minutes and guard with a
clipboard walked over and asked their names.

"Bates," answered David.

"You start work tomorrow. Eight o'clock. Bin run. Be
ready."

"Bin run?" David asked. "What's that?"

"Picking up litter, cleaning the walkways, emptying the
bins into the skips, sweeping and polishing. You're joining the
prison dustman team."

"Right," said David. He was pleased. He'd been told
about the bin run. It was a coveted job. It meant being outside

and roaming the site for two or three hours each morning and afternoon. The bin run men and the gardeners were the only prisoners ever to walk on grass. That small thing meant a lot to David. The fresh air would be marvellous, and he didn't mind hard work.

* * * * * *

"Don't work too hard," advised one of the other prisoners on the bin run, as they put on the Wellington boots, overalls, and gloves the next morning. "Just take it easy. There's eight of us doing what two could do. It suits the boss, and it suits us. If they think there isn't enough work, they'll cut the team down. Watch out, here comes the boss."

A young prison guard was walking towards them. He noticed David immediately.

"Name?"

"Bates."

"First name?"

"David."

"Right, David. I'm Mr Jenkins. You're David. Right?"

"Right!" said David. So some were human, after all, he thought.

"OK, David, this is how it works. Always look busy, right? Don't fuck me about. You fuck me about and you're off the bin run, right? You nick anything, and you're shipped out, right? Toe the line and you can stay on the team. This is one of the best jobs in the prison. You get twelve pounds a week, and you work twelve half-day shifts out of fourteen. You get two shifts off if you want it. OK?"

"OK," said David

"Right, and when you're picking up the litter under the cells windows, watch out for sharps."

281

"OK," said David.

* * * * * *

"What sharps?" he later asked another prisoner.

"Needles, mate. They chuck 'em out the windows."

"What, from drug use?"

"Course."

"But how do they get them into the prison?"

"All sorts o' ways, mate. In books an' radios and that. And at visitin" time."

"But they always seem to search so well."

"Not well enough. Three quarters of the blokes in the prison are on drugs. Yesterday a bloke was caught gettin' speed off his girlfriend in visitin'. She had the tablets in cling film in 'er mouth. When they kissed goodbye, she pushed them into 'is with her tongue. But the screw on the camera spotted it, so she was arrested and she'll get six months. He'll lose 'is remission. You ain't on no drugs, then?"

"No. I don't even smoke."

"Me neither, mate. Reckon we're the only ones. But you should buy some baccy with your canteen though."

"Why?"

" 'cos some blokes'll give anythin' for a bit of extra baccy. It's like money. You gotta trade, see. An' always 'old out for a good deal."

"Yes, I've already found that out."

"Yeah, you 'ave to look after yourself. No one else will. Never show weakness, thass 'ow to survive. You show weakness an' they'll gobble you up straight off. You won't get no respect. You always gotta be one step ahead of the next bloke."

"Most of the blokes I've met seem OK."

"Most are, mate. Course, you get some slap 'eads and nutcases. You're bound to. Some like to push their weight around a bit, but you just 'ave to stand yer ground and then they won't bother you much. No, the ones you need to worry about are the screws. Some of 'em can be really nasty. You need to keep right away from the nasty ones. Don't let 'em provoke you. Especially the women. Some o' the women screws are fuckin' psychopaths. No, you'll do all right, mate. You gotta a good job now. This boss is all right. Keep "im sweet an' you"ll do fine. Just take it easy and watch the days go by."

* * * * * *

Twenty-one days gone, one hundred and sixteen left. David was looking at the handmade calendar he had fixed on the noticeboard above his bed. Three weeks. Eighty-five percent still to go. He hoped it might be a lot less if the appeal came through.

The daily routine was well established. He was always awake before the cell was unlocked at seven, and made a quick dash to the bathroom to be first in the shower. Then back to dress and tidy up in case of an unannounced inspection or cell search. Searches usually happened twice a week and sometimes involved a dog sniffing through belongings for drugs. Whilst any form of contraband found would have serious consequences, there could also be trouble if any prisoner was found with extra comfort items like additional pillows or towels or blankets. All of these were subject to a strict quota and, whilst some guards would turn a blind eye, others would use the discovery to have the inmate transferred to the punishment block, or be hauled before a disciplinary hearing, which could result in weeks being added to a sentence. David decided to forego his extra comforts.

Breakfast was usually at seven-thirty and work started at eight, finishing at four, but occasionally there were security alerts which meant that work was cancelled and everyone was locked in their cells instead. David rarely got to find out what these security alerts were about. Some were called when there was a suicide or a medical emergency, and others when the strains of incarceration caused an inmate to flip, and he started smashing up his cell or harming himself. He was usually never seen again.

Weekends were the worst times. Work and exercise periods were often cancelled due to staff shortages, and lockup periods in the day were a common occurrence. Time dragged. Worst of all for David was that there was no mail at weekends, and he had come to depend heavily on letters from his family to sustain him through the bad moments. He loved writing back, and had rediscovered the art of letterwriting, producing six or seven long letters every day.

The days were punctuated by queuing for the issue of clothes, for clean sheets and blankets, for medication, for visits, for work, for the bathroom, for the exercise yard, for tabletennis or pool, for the telephone, for the library, for church and, three times a day, for food. He was now on his sixth cellmate. The latest was a young man from Hereford who was serving twelve months for selling Ecstasy. He played loud music incessantly. David struggled to listen to his favourite Classic FM, even with a headphone.

"Why you lookin" at them blackbirds all the time, mate?" shouted his cellmate above the noise of his music.

"They're rooks actually."

"Wass the difference? Ugly bloody things. Can you eat 'em?"

"Yes, I suppose so. I think people used to eat them, years ago. They'd eat you too, if you were already dead."

"Ugh, thass fuckin' 'orrible. I'd shoot the fuckers if I 'ad a gun."

"I was thinking," said David, ignoring the last comment, "that these rooks seem to live entirely on what the prisoners throw out of the windows. They've set up home in those trees because they know there's a good and constant supply of food here."

"I like canaries, meself," said the cell mate, ignoring David's comment. "Birds're better in cages."

"Oh, like us, you mean?" laughed David.

"Fair point," said his cellmate, lighting another cigarette.

All of his cellmates to date had smoked heavily, and David had asked one of the more sympathetic guards whether he could share with a non-smoker.

"If we can find one," came the reply.

* * * * * *

"Nuh, I'm a fuckin' smoker, mate."

David's next cellmate unpacked his bedding and placed a large ghetto blaster by the window. "An' I don't like sharin' with a fuckin' 'onky, neither." Jerome opened the front of his trousers and urinated in the general direction of the toilet, splashing carelessly on the floor. "So jus' watch yuh fuckin' back!"

David sat on the side of his bed and sighed, quietly. As if confinement itself weren't bad enough, he was now banged up in his shoebox of a cell with six feet six inches of raw, anti-white aggression. Until then, David had been surpised how little trouble he had seen, especially considering the cramped conditions in which everyone lived. But fights, when they did break out, were brutal affairs, always ending in spilt blood. He had discovered that being helpful and friendly went a long way to diverting any potential animosity, but he bore in mind the advice of his workmate, taking care never to allow his kindness to be confused with weakness. The weak became victims of the bullies, and spent most of their days hiding in corners.

Jerome took a mobile phone out of his pocket and put it on his bed.

"How the hell did you get that in here?" asked David, in amazement.

"Bent screw. I can get anythin' I want. Geezer's on heroine. I can supply 'im from the outside. Listen 'onky," said Jerome, squaring up to David, "I run this place, right? I'm King. Got it?"

David got it. Trading might be difficult with Jerome. A few hours later David sat reading. His eyes streamed from the thick, noxious smoke Jerome was producing.

" 'ere, 'onky," said Jerome, 'you any good with forms?"

David put down his book. "What forms?"

"I dunno. Fuckin' forms. This lot," he said, putting them in front of David.

David leafed through them. Income tax, council tax application for housing benefit, resettlement grant . . .

"You need to fill these in?" asked David.

"Yeah, man. I ain't no fuckin' good with forms. You do it, 'onky."

"Why are you filling in this one?" asked David, holding up a maternity grant application for Jerome to look at.

" 'ow the fuck should I know? Just fill it in, OK?"

David suddenly realised that Jerome couldn't read and write. He put the papers down and turned to Jerome.

"Right, Jerome. I'll fill all these forms in for you, but it's a trade, all right?"

"Fuck off, 'onky. You ain't got nothin' I want."

"Yes I have," said David. "I can do all your forms, letters anything like that."

Jerome looked David up and down and narrowed his eyes.

"All right, 'onky. Whadya want?"

"Number one. You don't call me honky. It's David, or mate, OK?"

Jerome grinned.

"Two, you only smoke next to the open window."

"Fuck off!"

"Next to the window!" insisted David.

Jerome shrugged his shoulders. "All right. What else?"

"And you only play your music with an earphone. Right?"

Jerome stared at David again. David stared back.

Jerome's face suddenly split into a broad, toothy smile.

"All right, mate," he said.

Two hours later, all the forms were completed and three letters written.

"Thass fuckin' great!" said Jerome, peering at what David had done. "You're all right, you are. Tell yuh what, mate, you go on doin' that an' I"ll put the word 'round that you're with me. Anyone give you any bother, and you jus' tell 'em that you're with Jerome. Any fuckin' trouble, an' they"ll end up like that fuckin' Wayne Richards did last week."

"Wayne Richards?" asked David. Where had he heard that name? Of course! Wasn't that the name of Mandy's brother? "Did you say Wayne Richards?"

"Yeah. Little cunt. Tried to operate a racket on my patch, 'e did, 'im an' that little squirt of a brother, wass 'is name? -

Kevin, yeah, thass it. The two of 'em thought they could do a bit of poachin', and then they grassed me up, the cunts. But that Wayne didn't know 'e'd end up in The Green, where I was. I jus' been shipped out for doin' 'im in, I 'ave. Fucker nearly passed out when 'e saw me in the exercise yard. Went runnin' to a screw to go in isolation, but the screw ignored 'im. 'e's in 'ospital now. Prob'ly took 'em two hours to get the snooker cue out of 'is arse!"

Jerome rocked with laughter.

"Sweet justice," muttered David. "And what about the brother?"

"Kevin? 'e's next on my list. I"ll make sure them two never grass again. Right pair o' little shits them two are. I feel sorry for their sister with them for brothers. She's all right, she is. Little Mandy. Yeah, Mandy. Ain't seen 'er for years. Used to work for me, she did."

"Worked for you?" asked David.

"Yeah. She was one o' my girls. Nice earner."

"Doing what?"

"On the streets, of course. Don't think I ran a fuckin" 'airdressers, do yuh? Thass all they're good for, women. Just fuck 'em and put 'em to work. Slap 'em about from time to time so they knows who's boss. They love it. Honest! Just love it. Can't get enough of it. Always come back for more, they do."

David frowned. "And what if they don't come back?"

"They always do, 'specially when I've got 'em 'ooked on crack. Slip it in their fuckin' alcopop, I do. After a few o' them they're mine. I can do what I fuckin' like with 'em. They'd eat my shit if I told 'em to. Anythin' for a fix."

"So, you don't like women much then, Jerome?"

"Me? Love 'em. I do! Mind you, if I 'ad my way, I'd 'ave all women all put down once they turned twenny-one. I'd have gas chambers for 'em. Wass the good of a woman after that? Go on, you tell me! They just eats yuh grub and spends yuh money, don't they? Nah, women are only good fuh one thing, and when they can't do that, there's no point wasting any time on 'em, is there?"

David was much relieved when Jerome was shipped out five days later and was replaced with a political asylum-seeker from Pakistan, who actually enjoyed David's music. Bashir was a devout Muslim and observed his prayer routine by laying out a towel and kneeling on the hard floor several times a day. Now David had peace and quiet, and he hoped that Bashir would stay.

* * * * * *

"You're looking thin, Dad," said Sophie, as she sat opposite David in the visitor's room five weeks into his sentence. As usual, it had taken her nearly an hour to get through the various search procedures and queues before she was able to see her father, but what was worse, she said, was the rudeness of the prison officers who seemed to regard families with the same contempt as they often showed towards prisoners. David squeezed her hand.

"Oh, I don't think I've lost any weight. Well, maybe a little, but I'm feeling very healthy actually. I'm not drinking any beer, which can't be a bad thing, and I'm trying to keep fit."

"How? Is there a gym?"

"Well, there is, but the only options are very macho weight training with some of the most undesirable prisoners, or endless queuing for five minutes of badminton. So I've given that a miss. Instead, I always make sure I get out for the hour in the exercise yard, and I walk round and round doing

289

laps as fast as possible, a few miles each day. Also, I'm doing pressups and situps in my cell. It's important to look after yourself in a place like this."

"I'll bet. How on earth do you manage, being cooped up in a tiny cell for so many hours each day?"

"I make sure that I take every opportunity to get out when I can. I work morning and afternoon, go to the exercise yard, go to the library when I can, and I even go to chapel on Sundays!"

"Chapel? You?"

"I'll have you know, young lady, I was a chorister when I was a lad! No, it's not for praying, just a chance to go somewhere on a Sunday morning. It's nice and peaceful and the chairs have upholstered seats! You've no idea what a luxury that is!"

"Oh, Dad, that's so sad. I can't bear it." Sophie looked tearful.

"Look, Sophie, I'm fine, really. There are many people here who aren't fine. Since I've been here there have been four suicides."

"What? In five weeks?"

"Yes. And besides that, many others go in for self-harm of one sort or another. In my case, I've got the system sorted out. I have a routine, I know how to get what I need, I keep my head down and avoid confrontation with the guards. I'll survive, no problem. Mind you, if I was here for a lot longer, it might be a different story."

"But what about the other prisoners? Do you avoid confrontation with them?"

"You might find it difficult to believe, but almost all the men I've got to know here are really quite decent guys underneath, and if you met them in the street you really wouldn't know they were convicts. It's really opened my eyes.

Most of them shouldn't be here at all. It's not doing them any good and it's causing untold misery to their families. But the Government and the courts seem to use prison as a first rather than a last resort far too often simply to appease the right-wing politicians, and the baying tabloid press. There's so much hatred, intolerance and hypocrisy in this country."

"Yes, that applies to your case in particular."

"Maybe."

"And none of the other prisoners have guessed what you're in for?"

"No. In fact, the bin run team think I"m Keyser Soze!"

"Who?"

"From the film 'The Usual Suspects'. He was the quiet guy with the limp, who turned out to be the criminal mastermind whose exploits had reached mythical proportions."

"But why do they think you're like him?"

"Well, one day a guy in the team got a bit stroppy with me. He was just having an off day, I suppose. You have to bear in mind that when you're threatened in this place, you must never back down or you'll lose face. So I turned and squared up to him and told him that I needed men like him in my team, and would he like a job when he got out. It did the trick. Now, he can't do enough for me! So the rumour started that I was some sort of Mr Big. They'd been wondering for some time what a middle-aged well-spoken guy was doing amongst them, and this was all I needed. The rumours spread and grew. Trouble is, I've now got a lot to live up to, but it's already opening doors."

"You be careful, Dad. Not sure I like the sound of that."

"Oh, don't worry, it's just a game. Anyway, enough of that. How's Freddy? I ring him every week but he's never very forthcoming on the phone, and I can't speak for long."

"Oh, he's absolutely fine, Dad. He misses you, of course, but he's always into something or other. He's coming down to stay in two weeks and I'll bring him to see you."

"Oh, that would be marvellous. And will Rachael come?"

"Doubt it. She moaning that you should have made arrangements to pay her an allowance for Freddy while you're in here."

"But I did. I told her simply to ask you for anything she needs, no questions asked."

"But she doesn't like asking me. She thinks you should have set up a standing order or something. I tried to explain that you had other things on your mind at the time and that she just had to tell me what she needs and I'd send her a cheque, but, well, you know what she's like. Empathy was never her strong point."

"Ok, I"ll write to her."

* * * * * *

"Hello David, yes, it's George here."

It was the day of the appeal and David had been given a number in London to call George.

"So, what's the result?" asked David. His heart was beating. If he had won the appeal, he could be going home the next day. If not, he had to serve out the remaining eleven weeks of his sentence.

"Sorry David, we lost."

David screwed up his eyes and cursed under his breath.

"We gave it damn good go," continued George. "Damien was marvellous. It all hinged on whether they thought the sentence was right given the powerful mitigation. But they thought the judge had been fair. They couldn't find any fault in what he'd said and done. They expressed a lot of sympathy for you actually, and agreed what a difficult case it was, but the issue wasn't what they would have done if they'd been the judge, but whether the judge had missed anything, or misinterpreted and been unfair, and they just couldn't fault him. I'm really sorry David. I'll send you a full copy of their judgement."

"OK. Thanks anyway," said David, quietly. "Thanks for trying."

He went back to his cell and looked again at the calendar on his wall. Seventy-six days still to go. Forty-seven percent done. It should be easier once the halfway mark was passed, he supposed. He had recently been moved to another wing and was waiting for enhanced status, the top rung of the privilege system for prisoners who had managed to avoid trouble, and receive good work reports. Providing he was able to satisfy the officers on his new wing, it would only be a matter of days before he was moved onto the enhanced wing. The only obstacle to that might be Miss Flavour.

Miss Flavour was a female guard who hated men, all men, but male convicts in particular. The degree of her hatred spread over a spectrum which ranged from mere seething to screaming hysteria. If the prisoner was a simple, ineffectual, bumbling idiot, Miss Flavour seethed. If he was typical card-carrying football fan with pictures of scantily-clad girls above his bed, she frothed. If he was a too-clever-by-half older man, like David, who dared to ask her questions, or even had the temerity to query some of her methods, she exploded. But if she found out that he was also a sex offender, which she often did, the hysteria that followed surpassed force eight on the Richter Scale.

It was Saturday morning and rumours were rife that Miss Flavour was doing the weekly cell inspection. Even the hardest inmates, the lifers, the muggers, the murderers and the wife-beaters, were all up in the cells before seven with mops and polishers and dusters.

At eight-thirty David was sitting at his table writing a letter, having cleaned every inch of his cell, when the door swung open, and there stood Miss Flavour, clipboard in hand, her broad frame filling the doorway, and her peroxide blonde hair standing in spikes on the top of her head.

"Bates!" she shrieked.

David stood up.

"D'you work Bates?"

"Yes," said David.

"Yes what?"

"Yes, um, Miss Flavour. I work on the bin run."

"That's no excuse not to clean your cell. Don't expect your cellmate to do it."

"I don't," said David, trying not to sound argumentative.

"Are you arguing with me, Bates?"

"No, Miss Flavour."

"Look at that!" she said, pointing to a microscopic spot on the wall behind the door. "That's shit! Shit, Bates! That's your shit! This place is a shit'ole."

David stared at the wall, unable to see the mark, but said nothing.

"I know what you're in for, Bates. They may not know. But I know. D'you think I know?"

"I'm sure you do, Miss Flavour."

"I do! And you know what you are, Bates?"

"No, Miss Flavour."

"Pond Life! Aren't you, Bates?"

"Yes, Miss Flavour."

"Right. Now you get this shit off the wall by next week, or you'll be down the block, you understand?"

"Yes, Miss Flavour."

David knew he'd got off lightly. He turned to his cellmate.

"She was in a good mood today, wasn't she?"

His cellmate laughed.

"I"ve seen worse. She only does it 'cos she can get away with it. That's why she's in the prison service, so's she can get at men. She wouldn't be able to do it on the outside. One of these days some geezer's gonna find out where she lives. An' she's married too. Pity 'er fuckin' 'usband! Can you imagine 'avin' to shag that every Saturday night?"

"No," smiled David. "I'd rather not."

* * * * * *

With only eight weeks to go David was moved onto the enhanced wing where life was a lot easier. Time locked in the cells was reduced to ten hours a day and the other prisoners tended to be more mature, and quieter. David felt like an old lag. He had seen many hundreds of prisoners come and go, some on their way to longer sentences elsewhere, and some only in prison briefly before being released into the tagging scheme.

Sophie had been to see him every week, and Freddy had come twice. A stream of letters had sustained David throughout, particularly those from his first wife, Sue. Sue had known him since he was nineteen, after all, and wrote immediately after his conviction to say that the whole thing was nonsense, there was no way he was a sex offender, and that she would write to him as often as possible. She'd kept her promise, and had written nearly three times a week. It was strange, thought David, that a few years earlier they hadn't really been on talking terms but now, since the conviction, they'd become very close again. Adversity did that sometimes: it brought people together.

Rachael, on the other hand, had written only twice, both times, asking for money. He wondered how someone who had once loved him, and who had lived with him for twelve years, could be so unconcerned with what he was going through, or be unable to express that concern.

* * * * * *

On the day before his release the senior officer called David in for a routine interview.

"So," said Mr Cannon, smiling, "will we be seeing you again?"

"Not on your life! Nothing personal, you understand," joked David.

"You've done well. You've even survived our Miss Flavour, I understand, and managed to establish yourself a bit of a reputation with the hardened cons."

"Well, it was better than them finding out why I was here. I've seen the way they catcall the D Wing prisoners when they're on their way to the exercise yard. It was better for them to believe I was head of the Mafia than a nonce."

Cannon smiled again. "So, have you got somewhere to go tomorrow?"

"Oh yes. My eldest son is collecting me. I've got a home and a business. I don't know how some of these guys manage when they are released. So many seem to have nothing to go to."

"Well, that's why a lot of them end up back here. But in your case, it's not the end of the story."

"No?"

"Well, you don't have to report to any probation officers or anything like that . . ."

"So I don't have to go on their course then?"

"No. Your sentence was less than twelve months, so there are no conditions attached, but you realise you are on the Sex Offenders Register for ten years?"

"Yes, but what does that mean, exactly?"

"It means that the police will come to visit you from time to time to check that you haven't moved. When you do move, and every time you go abroad, you have to go to the police station, and fill in a form."

"Oh, I didn't realise that. What, for ten years?"

" 'fraid so."

"I was hoping to turn away from it all, to rebuild my life. It will be difficult, with all that hanging over me."

"Well, in your case, they probably won't bother you too much. Their work is cut out looking after the predatory paedophiles, but you need to be aware of problems you may have with the general public."

"Yes, I'd thought about that."

"Some newspapers want to out all those convicted of offences against children so that would include you. Not only does that mean you might have to keep moving home, but you need to guard against vigilante action against you. It might be a good idea to move to a completely new area as soon as you can."

"But my business is well-established. It would be difficult to move."

"Well, even if you aren't outed or victimised, you need to bear in mind that people who knew you before might not want to do business with you."

"That's already happened. It started before I was sentenced."

"Well, there you are. It's up to you."

"I know. Thanks for your advice, but I think I'm going to stand and fight it. I've managed to survive in prison, so I reckon I can survive out there too. Time's a good healer. Eventually, there'll be more people who'll have met me since my release than knew me before, and I think I can deal with the odd rumour still flying."

"OK. Well, good luck."

David stood and shook hands. Unaccountably, he almost felt sad to be leaving. He had enjoyed the camaraderie and had learnt a lot. Now he faced the challenge of life on the outside.

* * * * * *

The Post Script

David was unpacking the last of his boxes after moving house when he suddenly realised that four-and-a-half months had gone by since he had been released from prison. That was the same amount of time that he had served inside. How could it have passed so quickly? In prison he had counted every day and, for the last few weeks, every hour, to the moment he would be free, and now that it was over, time had resumed its normal pattern of passing ever more quickly the older he became.

It helped that he had been busy. The business was still ticking over but there had been a big backlog of things to do which kept him fully occupied. An offer for his house had come through only a few weeks after his release, and he had then spent time with Sophie looking for a new home on the other side of the city. He had also made it a priority to visit all the people who had given him support while he was away, while the momentum of their support could be used to secure long-lasting friendships.

Now he wanted to rebuild his life and fill his time so that he could move right away from the causes of his troubles, and from the memory of police, courts and prison. But he knew that some people were not prepared to let him move on. He often dreaded going to the city centre for fear of bumping into an old acquaintance. It wasn't so much his own discomfort as their obvious embarrassment on seeing him, which he feared. Some would look away or even cross the street if they saw him. Others managed to say hello but bore a pained expression throughout the brief conversation, and were clearly relieved when it was over. Despite having moved and changed his phone number, some more determined individuals managed to find him and sent threatening mail, or made abusive telephone calls, all of which he decided to ignore in the hope that they would soon tire of the game. Which they did. One joker at the leisure centre took great delight in deleting David's name from the squash leagues when they went up each month, but David simply painstakingly wrote it back in again each time and this, too, ceased eventually. He applied to join a private squash club nearer to his new home but received a polite rejection letter. He phoned to find out why, and was told that reasons for refusal were never given. Obviously, he thought, someone on the committee thinks I would be a danger to children using the club.

Going to the police station to fulfil his obligations as a registered sex offender filled David with horror, bringing back so many bad memories of his arrest and interrogation, and he often had nightmares in which he was going through the whole thing again.

But, despite all this, he was determined to ride it all out. He had survived prison, where there was a constant danger of exposure and violence, and now he would find the strength to survive living in a society where men convicted of sex offences, no matter what their nature, were reviled and loathed.

His resolve was tested to its limits one evening when the doorbell rang and two men stood in the doorway asking if they could speak to him about what they called 'a very serious and confidential matter'. They seemed unwilling to show any form of identity, and would not discuss the matter on the doorstep. But from concern that this might be about a member of his family, and also out of sheer curiosity, David let them in.

"This is a very delicate matter," said the first man, sitting down on the opposite side of the table while the other remained standing by the door. "We have obtained a very large file containing information on you and we want to know whether your neighbours are aware of your background."

David suddenly realised he should not have let them in.

"What information?" he asked.

"About your criminal conviction."

"Look, who are you, and what do you want?"

"As I said before we came in, Mr Bates, we work for an investigation bureau, and we have been employed to investigate you."

"Employed by whom? For what purpose?"

"You were sent to prison for . . . let me see . . ." he opened his folder and glanced at some papers, 'for taken indecent photographs of children, and for unlawful sexual intercourse'. Is that right?"

"Look, I don't know who you are or what you want, and so I certainly don't intend to confirm or deny anything you think you have found out about me."

"But we've been to your previous address, and your former neighbours had you petitioned out, didn't they?"

"No, they most certainly did not."

"But have you told your new neighbours about your past?"

"Why should I? What is there for them to know?"

"Well, there are two schools near here. I'm sure your neighbours would be very unhappy to know that they have a child sex offender living here."

"Look, whether or not there is a sex offender living here, the neighbours do not have a right to know that. That information, where it exists, is guarded closely by the police and other relevant agencies."

"Oh really, then how do we know? How come we have all this information?"

"Well, since you won't tell me who you are, I can't comment. All I am saying is that the general public do not have access to that sort of information, and they have no right to know. Whatever you may think may be in my past, I am under no obligation to discuss it with neighbours if I choose not to do so."

"But we think they should know."

"What are you, some sort of vigilante group?"

The man laughed.

"Oh no, as I said, we are private investigators."

"Well, if that's the case, you would have shown me you identity when asked to do so."

David glanced across at his desk and saw that he had left out his digital camera. He stood up, walked over and picked it up, pointing it at the man opposite. The man suddenly looked very alarmed.

"I wouldn't do that if I were you," he said.

His reaction told David everything he wanted to know. Suddenly, he was in control. He began clicking the button. The man grabbed a tablemat and tried to cover his face. David turned and took photos of the other man, who was already heading out of the door.

"I want you to leave now," said David. "Tomorrow, I will be showing these to the police."

The man at the table stood and followed his colleague.

"That doesn't scare us," he said, still covering his face. "We're far more powerful than the police."

"Really?" said David, following them out into the driveway, still clicking the camera in their direction. "Well, we'll see what they say."

The men reached the gate, and stopped.

"We'll make sure all your neighbours know about you by tomorrow."

"Fine!" said David, still clicking, as they turned and walked quickly up the road.

David went inside and bolted the door. He was shaking. He felt triumphant, yet very uneasy. Who they hell were they? Who had sent them? After several minutes of thought he decided that they must be blackmailers. Perhaps they were simply cashing in on the fear many convicted sex offenders were feeling since one of the Sunday papers had committed itself to public exposure of all on the register. Perhaps they had decided there was money to be made from doing their own research of local newspaper archives and finding people they could blackmail. This would account of their having been to his previous address first, which had been printed in the local paper.

He looked at the camera and discovered that the battery was flat. Only one picture was held in the memory and, in it, the man was covering his face. Nevertheless, David decided to report the incident to the police, and the next day the officer monitoring him called for a chat. Although he listened carefully and expressed sympathy, David was surprised that he intended to take no action, even though there was a photograph and good fingerprints on the tablemat. He praised David for having the composure to take the photographs.

"They'll be thinking that you've got several pictures of them so they won't be back," he said, "but if they do return, just call me immediately. Here's my mobile number. You can get me on that any time."

David was now left feeling even more unsure about who the men were, and even wondered whether they might be connected to the police, given the underhand tactics that had been used against him during the investigation. Or perhaps they were ex-police officers who still had good connections. More likely, they were reporters, hoping to feed more scandal

into the ever-yawning mouth of the tabloid press. He felt he
might never know.

More weeks and months passed, and the incident
receded into memory. Business was now going well, despite
little co-operation from the local council, and David had
joined an opera group out of town, and was playing more
squash. He still lacked the special relationship he craved, but
decided to be patient and simply keep busy. One day he was
in the shopping precinct in the city centre, and he sat down on
the edge of the water fountain to tie his shoe.

"I used to sit there when I came 'ere shop-lifting," said a
voice.

David looked up. In front of him was a young woman
standing behind a baby buggy. She was smiling.

"Mandy!"

" 'ello, David. 'ow're you keeping?"

David looked into the smiling face, and down at the
infant in the pushchair.

"Is this yours?" he said.

"Yeah. Rebecca. She's four months. D'you think she
looks like me?

David smiled. Mandy looked happy. Rather thin, and
with dark shadows under her eyes, but still beautiful.

"She's a gorgeous baby, Mandy. Yes, just like you! It's so
good to see you, Mandy!" he said. "I often wondered if we
would ever meet again."

"Oh, I knew we would. You're not embarrassed then?"

"Embarrassed? No, of course not. I feel I let you down."

"You let me down? After what my family did to you?
You must be joking! Listen, David, I'm really sorry about what
happened. And you should never've gone to prison. It was
wrong. I blame myself."

"Oh come on, Mandy. You were just a kid. You can't be blamed for anything. I always knew you never had anything to do with the robbery, and as for lying about your age, well, I can't blame you for that"

"You know, when you never turned up for that last date, it broke my fuckin' 'eart, it really did. I think I was in love with you, you know."

"No you weren't. You were just in love with the glimpse of the life I showed you. The probation officers said I used my supposed luxurious lifestyle to dazzle you."

"What the fuck do they know about anythin'? Course I was dazzled, but I was ready to drop me knickers for you before I'd even met you, so it didn't make any difference. Well, it did in a way."

"What way?"

"Well, I'd never met anyone like you, or ever been in a nice 'ome like that, an' so on, and it wasn't like a job. I really enjoyed it. That's why I didn't want any money off you. I really wanted to be your mistress."

"Yes, I'm sorry about that. But I suppose it wouldn't have worked out, in the end. But listen, thanks for not making a statement against me. You must've been under a lot of pressure to do that. It made a big difference that you didn't."

"Why should I? I must admit that I was upset when they told me that you'd sold my pictures, but then later, I knew they were lying – me mam, the police, everyone. They all wanted me to go against you. But I knew you were decent. And then, when Wayne and Kevin robbed you, well, that did it for me. I walked out. Never been back. My mam can stew for all I care. She was a crap mother anyway. I won't make the same mistake with Rebecca. I'm gonna be the best mam in the world to 'er."

"I'm really pleased to hear that, Mandy. I think you'll be a wonderful mother – well, I'm sure you already are. So, are you with Rebecca's dad? You're not married are you? You're still only . . . what – seventeen?"

"Seventeen and three quarters! But I started early, remember? An' you did say I was mature! But no, I'm not married yet. Yeah, I'm with Rebecca's dad. He's a good bloke. He's thirty. I like older men, remember? He's a plumber. Earns good money. He knows what I did, an' 'e's OK about it."

"He's a very lucky man, Mandy. So you're not working now? And given up the idea of modelling?"

"Nah, stopped workin' soon after I met you. I'm not saying I'll never do it again, but I don't need to for now. As for modelling, well, my boobs 'aven't survived breast-feeding too well, but I'd rather 'ave Rebecca than nice tits!"

"You still look pretty damned good to me, Mandy."

"An' I'm going to college two days a week. Takin' five GCSE's next summer, then A levels. A bit late, but I missed out on a lot of school. The teachers say I should get good grades."

"I bet you will. You're obviously very intelligent. I always thought that, Mandy."

"Yeah, I know. I really liked that. It was important to me. So, you all right, are you? You still gettin' bother from the police?"

"Not too bad really. I have to keep reporting to them. There's lots of things I can't do now because of the criminal record, and being on the Sex Offenders Register. I went to Ireland last summer with a friend and her seventeen-year-old daughter, and they took me into a room at the ferry port and wanted to know what I was doing. It was all very embarrassing. I wanted to go to the USA next month for a break, but decided against it because they don't like admitting people with criminal records, let alone people who have committed sex offences against children. It's a terrible stigma to carry for the rest of my life. It gets me down sometimes."

"It's all fuckin' crap if you ask me. No way was I a child and no way was it a sex offence. Anyone would think you were a fuckin' paedophile."

"Well, the judge said I wasn't that, but the media and general public seem to disagree."

"Not everyone, David. Look, just hang in there. It'll blow over eventually. Anyway, they got that Phil Watson, did you know?"

"The policeman?"

"Yeah, the one who arrested you."

"What d'you mean 'got' him?"

"It was in all the papers. Probably while you were still inside. His oppo shopped 'im. The bastard was turning a blind eye to some woman's drug racket in exchange for shagging 'er daughters. His oppo caught 'im with 'em. The youngest was only twelve."

"You're joking!"

"No. Straight up. He got eight years."

"My god! I don't believe it!"

"I do. I knew 'im from years back. 'e was always bent. He raped me once."

"What? No! When? Did you report it?"

"Oh, no, it's all a long time ago. Doesn't matter now. They'll get him in prison. They hate ex-police officers as much as they hate nonces. More, even."

"I think I've been pretty naïve about all this. I hadn't given much thought to your past, Mandy. You've obviously had a hard time, and then I came along and dangled my lifestyle in front you. Maybe they're right when they say I manipulated you, that you were my victim too."

"Bollocks! Look, David, you may have been a bit daft not to guess I was fifteen, but there's no way I was your victim. No, you were the victim. Me mam an' me planned that first date down to the last detail – what she'd say, what I'd wear, 'ow I'd speak, an' bringin' along Avril in 'er 'orrible 'ot pants! It was all a plan to make sure you'd pick me, and the idea was to get as much money off you as possible. That's exactly 'ow girls are with all the punters. It's the punters that're the victims most times. Anyway, look, I must be goin'. This one wants feeding and I ain't doing it in the street! An' I've got to pack! You'll never guess where we're goin' tomorrow – the seaside!"

David smiled broadly. "Oh, that's great, Mandy! Well, have a really good time, won't you! I hope we can meet again some day."

Mandy turned and started to push the buggy up the slope. David watched her bottom sticking out as she leaned forwards, and he remembered the touch of her. Suddenly, she stopped and turned around. She stepped back towards him.

"Just one thing, David. Somethin' I've always wondered. On that first date, when you were 'oldin' me in your arms, and we were kissin' and cuddlin' an' that, an' both of us gaggin' for it, if I'd suddenly said to you I wasn't quite sixteen, would you still've shagged the arse off me?"

David burst into laughter. Mandy stood looking at him, her eyes twinkling, as she waited for an answer.

"Mandy," he said, looking serious for a moment, "wouldn't most men?"

* * * * * *

THE END

In 2003, it became illegal to take 'indecent'   photographs
of anyone under the age of
eighteen, or to pay them for sex, even if they
were over sixteen, the age of consent.